C000173413

Hidden Heroines

THE FORGOTTEN SUFFRAGETTES

Hidden Heroines

THE FORGOTTEN SUFFRAGETTES

Maggie Andrews and Janis Lomas

ROBERT HALE

First published in 2018 by
Robert Hale, an imprint of
The Crowood Press Ltd,
Ramsbury, Marlborough
Wiltshire SN8 2HR

www.crowood.com

© Maggie Andrews and Janis Lomas 2018

All rights reserved. No part of this publication may be
reproduced or transmitted in any form or by any means,
electronic or mechanical, including photocopy, recording
or any information storage and retrieval system, without
permission in writing from the publishers.

British Library Cataloguing-in-Publication Data
A catalogue record for this book is available from the
British Library.

ISBN 978 0 7198 2761 7

The right of Maggie Andrews and Janis Lomas to be
identified as authors of this work has been asserted by
them in accordance with the Copyright, Designs and
Patents Act 1988.

Typeset by Chapter One Book Production, Knebworth

Printed and bound in India by Parksons Graphics

CONTENTS

The Movement Takes Off

A Groundswell of Support

Campaigners from All Walks of Life

The Next Generation

To Neil, Clare, Laura, Emily, Tom, David and Gregg, Lynton, Oli and Sophie, Dom and Sonya, Annie and Peter, Lucia, Erin, Edu, Florence and Stanley.

May your lives live up to the dreams and hopes that the hidden heroines of this book have struggled to realize.

ACKNOWLEDGEMENTS

This book is the product of numerous scholars of women's suffrage history. We owe a huge debt and thanks to the writers and experts such as Elizabeth Crawford, Leah Leneman, Jill Liddington, Angela John, June Purvis[1] and many others whom we have encountered, particularly through the Women's History Network, and drawn upon here.

Friends and colleagues Paula Bartley, Carol Frankish, Lesley Spiers and Jenni Waugh have provided support, discussion and the biographies of women. University of Worcester students have also contributed to writing the histories of individual women for this book: undergraduates studying History or Law – Holly Fletcher, Mollie Sheehy and Leah Susans – as well as postgraduates – Amy Dale, Lisa Davies, Elspeth King, Rose Miller, Anna Muggeridge and Linda Pike. Thank you all. We hope that you never lose your interest and enthusiasm for women's history.

Our families have, as ever, lived with our enthusiasm, exhaustion and pre-occupation as we have struggled our way through completing this text. A huge thank you, as always, goes to Neil and John for all their love, support and shopping undertaken while we were writing. Thank you also to the good-natured forbearance of the next generations: Neil, Clare, Laura, Emily, Tom, and to David and Gregg, Lynton, Oli and Sophie, Dom and Sonya, Annie and Peter, Lucia, Erin, Edu, Florence and Stanley.

ABBREVIATIONS

AFL	Actresses' Franchise League
BWSS	Birmingham Women's Suffrage Societies
BWTA	British Women's Temperance Association
CUWFA	Conservative and Unionist Women's Franchise Association
ELFS	East London Federation of Suffragettes
ILP	Independent Labour Party
IWFL	Irish Women's Franchise League
LNS	London National Society
LWLL	Leeds Women's Labour League
MLOWS	Men's League for Opposing Women's Suffrage
MNSWS	Manchester National Society for Women's Suffrage
NCSWS	New Constitutional Society for Women's Suffrage
NFWW	National Federation of Women Workers
NLOWS	The National League for Opposing Women's Suffrage
NUSEC	National Union of Societies for Equal Citizenship
NUWSS	National Union of Women's Suffrage Societies
SWH	Scottish Women's Hospital
SWRI	Scottish Women's Rural Institutes
TRL	Tax Resistance League
WEC	Women's Emergency Corps
WEU	Women's Emancipation Union
WFL	Women's Franchise League
WFL	Women's Freedom League
WNASL	Women's National Anti-Suffrage League
WSPU	Women's Social and Political Union
WTUL	Women's Trade Union League
WVR	Women's Volunteer Reserve

TIMELINE

1832 The Great Reform Act is passed, extending the electorate to about 12 per cent of men. The first women's suffrage petition is presented to Parliament by Henry Hunt MP.

1867 Second Reform Bill goes before Parliament. A women's suffrage petition with nearly 1,500 signatures is presented to the House of Commons. Manchester National Society for Women's Suffrage formed. London National Society formed.

1881 Women are enfranchised on the Isle of Man.

1884 Third Reform Bill is passed, extending the franchise to approximately 60 per cent of men. An amendment to include women is rejected.

1894 The Local Government Act is passed, enabling some married and single women to vote in elections for county and borough councils.

1897 Twenty suffrage societies amalgamate to form the National Union of Women's Suffrage Societies (NUWSS).

1902 Women textile workers from the north of England present a petition with 37,000 signatures to Parliament asking for votes for women.

1903 Women's Social and Political Union (WSPU) is formed by Emmeline Pankhurst.

1905 First militant act: Christabel Pankhurst and Annie Kenney are arrested and imprisoned in Manchester.

1906 WSPU moves its headquarters from Manchester to London.

1907 Qualification of Women Act allows women to be elected onto borough and county councils and become a mayor. There is a split in the ranks of the WSPU. The Women's Freedom League (WFL) is formed by the breakaway group of suffragettes.

1908 H.H. Asquith, who is implacably opposed to women's suffrage, becomes prime minister. Women's National Anti-Suffrage League (WNASL) is formed. WSPU organizes the Women's Sunday demonstration in Hyde Park. 250,000 people attend from across the country; it is the largest ever political rally in London.

1909 The first forcible feeding of suffragette hunger strikers in prison takes place.

The Tax Resistance League is formed, adhering to the principle of no taxation without representation.

1910   The National League for Opposing Women's Suffrage (NLOWS) is formed from an amalgamation of the Men's League for Opposing Women's Suffrage and the Women's National Anti-Suffrage League. The First Conciliation Bill, which would have enfranchised one million women, fails to become law, resulting in an escalation of suffragette violence.

1911   The Liberal Government is re-elected. The Second Conciliation Bill, which would have given a limited number of women the vote, passes its second reading with a large majority. Suffrage activists are optimistic. In November, the bill is 'torpedoed' by the Prime Minister, Herbert Asquith. The WFL organizes a boycott of the 1911 Census.

1912   Window-smashing campaigns start in earnest and Christabel Pankhurst flees to Paris. The WSPU splits again. The NUWSS forms an alliance with the Labour Party, which agrees to campaign for women's suffrage and to include this in its manifesto.

1913   There are widespread bomb and arson campaigns. Prisoners' Temporary Discharge for Ill-Health ('Cat and Mouse') Act is passed, enabling women on hunger strike to be released from prison and then re-arrested a few days later, once their health has improved. Suffragette Emily Wilding Davison dies from injuries received on Derby Day. The NUWSS organizes a pilgrimage of law-abiding suffragists from across the country, which culminates in a rally of 50,000 people in Hyde Park.

1914   The violence continues until Tuesday 4 August, when war is declared. Suffragette prisoners are released. The WSPU declares a cessation of violence.

1917   House of Commons begins the process of passing the Representation of the People Act, granting the vote to women aged 30 or above with the necessary property qualifications.

1918   The enfranchisement of some women finally becomes law on Wednesday 6 February. The Parliamentary Qualification of Women Act is passed in November. Women vote for the first time on Saturday 14 December. Of the seventeen women who are parliamentary candidates, only Constance Markievicz wins her seat, but, as a member of Sinn Féin, she never sits in the House of Commons.

1919   NUWSS re-named National Union of Societies for Equal Citizenship (NUSEC).

Nancy Astor becomes the first woman to take a seat as an MP.

1928   Women entitled to vote on same terms as men. Emmeline Pankhurst dies.

1929   The first general election where women can vote on the same terms as men produces fourteen women MPs. Margaret Bondfield becomes the first female member of the British Cabinet. Millicent Garrett Fawcett dies.

INTRODUCTION

ON SATURDAY 14 December 1918, some women voted in a parliamentary election for the very first time in Britain. Earlier that year, the Representation of the People Act had passed into law and given the franchise to those women who were both aged thirty or over and also met the property qualifications. According to the *Leeds Mercury*, an experienced poll clerk had reported that the December poll was one of the 'jolliest of all elections' he had experienced. The paper went on to explain:

> At this particular booth it had been a day of smiles. Nine out of ten of the women voters had a smile for the policeman at the door of the room of secrets, and he, gallant man, returned the glad look unfailingly.
>
> Inside the room the poll clerks, men and women dispersed smiles with the ballot papers, and the Presiding Officer, a grave man usually, and fully aware of the dignity of his office, could not help himself. He smiled with the rest....
>
> In all five divisions of the city the women displayed an unexpected keenness and enthusiasm in exercising their vote. At one booth a number of women turned up a few minutes before eight o'clock in the morning and they waited in a queue until the hour struck.[1]

This election was the culmination of years of struggle and campaigning by thousands of women from all walks of life and in all parts of the country. Many have heard of the role played by the Pankhurst family in the struggle to win the vote 100 years ago. History books often tell of the windows that were smashed, the post boxes that were set on fire, and the marches that took place in London and Manchester. Some of the leaders of the women's suffrage movement are publicly celebrated: Emmeline Pankhurst's statue can be found in Victoria Gardens, in the shadow of the House of Commons, a visual reminder of one of the heroines of this infamous struggle that disrupted the capital in the Edwardian era. The centenary of women's suffrage is being marked by the erection, in Parliament Square, of a statue of Mrs Fawcett, the leader of the National Women's Suffrage Societies, recognizing another heroine of the women's suffrage movement. There were, however, many other women in other parts of Britain and Ireland, including Cardiff and Cumbria, Edinburgh and Glasgow, Leeds and Leicester, County Sligo and Dublin, Preston and Plymouth, Warwickshire and Wolverhampton, who also marched and campaigned, gathered signatures for petitions, organized pilgrimages, burned down football stands, boycotted the census, scored graffiti on churches, refused to pay their taxes, chaired meetings, and risked both ridicule and their freedom fighting to obtain for women the right to vote.

This book is about the lives of forty-eight of these hidden heroines and the part they played in the campaign for women to become full citizens of the United Kingdom, able to cast a vote in parliamentary elections. They are a sample of the thousands and thousands of women involved in years of campaigning. Their stories, their struggles and sacrifices demonstrate that support for the suffrage come from all classes and all walks of life: Catherine Blair and Mrs Arthur Webb were brought up on rural farms in Scotland and Wales, respectively; Lady Henry Somerset and Princess Sophia Duleep Singh lived in palatial surroundings, but many more came from much more modest backgrounds – Alice Hawkins and Jennie Baines lived in working-class terraced houses in Britain's industrial towns and cities.

The exploration of these women's lives before, during and after their involvement in the suffrage campaigns demonstrates the multiplicity of political persuasions, interests, inclinations and social issues that women were involved in. Their lives convey the complex range of responsibilities, social expectations, sacrifices, struggles and priorities that women had to navigate to undertake suffrage activities. Some were wives and mothers; for them, there were issues about who would look after their home and children if they were imprisoned after a run-in with the police. Some had the benefit of an independent income; others were struggling to earn a living and had to consider carefully the consequences of any action they might take on their employment prospects. Some were confident public speakers, easily able to cope with heckling and abuse; others had to conquer their fear of speaking in public. Many paid a high price in terms of damage to their mental and physical health for their part in suffrage campaigns, which was frequently accompanied by antagonism not only from strangers, but also often from within their own families. It is no coincidence that many of these women were outsiders, loners, marginalized in many ways and for many reasons from society.

When, in 1912, at a suffrage meeting at the Royal Albert Hall in London, Emmeline Pankhurst encouraged women to 'Be militant each in your own way', and incited the meeting to rebellion[2] she was giving voice to an already existing situation: women were already rebelling against a political system that treated them as second-class citizens, and they had been doing so in numerous different ways for many years. The struggle for women's suffrage was long and slow and, overall, painstakingly polite and peaceful in its methods. It was an example of the exasperating powerlessness of political campaigning for the disenfranchised. It was the misnamed Great Reform Act of 1832 that specifically restricted the right to vote in parliamentary elections to 'male persons'. The inequality of this was not lost on women, and the first petition for women's suffrage appeared soon after. Over the next sixty-five years, further petitions were put together to try to persuade Parliament to introduce a women's suffrage bill, or to amend parliamentary reform acts to include women's suffrage – all to no avail. In 1866, John Stuart Mill presented the first mass petition of women to Parliament. It contained nearly 1,500 signatures, gathered in just two weeks by a group of determined women, from across the country, including Scottish mathematician and scientist Mary Somerville, Priscilla Bright McLaren, who had been involved in the anti-slavery campaigns and became president of the Edinburgh Women's Suffrage Society. Frances Buss, a pioneer of women's education and Josephine Butler, who campaigned against the sexual exploitation of women were also signatories.[3]

The petition, although unsuccessful, galvanized many women and, in the last quarter of the nineteenth century, pro-women's suffrage events, activities, campaigns and societies blossomed and caused some alarm. In July 1875, the *Edinburgh Evening News* announced:

> The opponents of female suffrage felt that the movement for the extension of the franchise to women is becoming so serious that it must be met by a rival organisation. An Anti-suffrage Suffrage Society has accordingly been started under influential political direction.[4]

In March 1880, over three thousand people gathered to hear a speech on Women's Suffrage by Lydia Becker of the National Society for Women's Suffrage; an event probably organized by the Norwich Committee for Women's Suffrage.[5] In discussions about which women should have the vote and why, a meeting held in Bangor, North Wales, in November 1883 heard one proponent of women's suffrage suggest that only women who were householders should be able to vote, while another suggested women tea drinkers should have the vote to counteract the influence of male beer drinkers. The meeting also heard anxiety expressed about what the effect women's enfranchisement might have on the two main political parties.[6] For the next thirty years, concern over the possible influence of women voters on the fortunes of the Liberals and the Conservatives and the determination of the leaders of parties to oppose any change to the suffrage that might disadvantage them, played a major role in denying women the right to vote.

In 1889, an 'Appeal Against Female Suffrage' was launched, which a number of women enthusiastically signed. Party allegiance and political self-interest were not the only reasons for the antipathy to enfranchising women. It was argued that most women were not interested in politics; that their natural sphere of influence was the home and motherhood; and that involving them in politics would upset the natural order of both society and the home. Undeterred, a Private Members' Bill was introduced into Parliament in 1892, only to be defeated by twenty-three votes.

Another petition was launched and displayed in Westminster Hall in 1896 to coincide with Mr Faithfull Begg's Parliamentary Franchise (Extension to Women) Bill. This petition had 257,796 names on it, with signatures from every constituency in the country.[7]

In 1897, numerous suffrage groups were brought together beneath one umbrella organization – the National Union of Women's Suffrage Societies (NUWSS), under the leadership of Mrs Millicent Fawcett. This was by far the largest suffrage organization, which, by 1909, had over 50,000 members.[8] In 1903, frustrated by the slow progress of the genteel campaigning of many women's suffrage societies, Emmeline Pankhurst and her daughters formed the Women's Social and Political Union (WSPU) in Manchester. It was this new organization, particularly after it moved to London, that developed many inventive methods of gaining publicity for their cause – methods that included creating disturbances at political meetings, attempts to storm the House of Commons, mass window-smashing, arson and the destruction of property. In 1906, a *Daily Mail* headline writer coined the word 'Suffragette' to refer to those campaigners who used these more militant tactics, but the term was often used interchangeably with the term commonly used to describe law-abiding campaigners – 'suffragists'.

Among women's suffrage campaigners there were differences of opinion about both tactics and priorities. The publicity that the militant tactics received and the bravery of the women involved initially gained admiration from across the suffrage organizations. At the Savoy Hotel on Tuesday 11 December 1906, a banquet was held for released prisoners, chaired by Mrs Fawcett of the NUWSS.

However, in time many of the law-abiding suffragists in the NUWSS became very uneasy about the more extreme activities of the WSPU supporters who damaged property such as pillar boxes, large houses, paintings in galleries, the tea house at Kew gardens and sporting venues and, consequently, inconvenienced ordinary people. These actions caused a backlash against suffrage campaigners from some of the general public. Furthermore, operating a militant group that broke the law was in many ways incompatible with running a democratic organization and, in 1907, a number of the members complaining about Mrs Pankhurst's autocratic leadership left the WSPU and formed the Women's Freedom League (WFL). Charlotte Despard became the leader of this organization, which undertook a form of militancy that involved passive resistance. They were the main instigators of the Census Boycott in 1911.[9] The lives of the forty-eight women discussed in this book suggest that the antagonism and splits between the militant and non-militant groups within the suffrage movement should not be exaggerated. For example, Isabel Margesson worked with the NUWSS, the WSPU, the WFL and the Tax Resistance League (TRL) simultaneously, and there are numerous instances of the different factions and groups within the suffrage movement sharing platforms at meetings, organizing joint processions and events.

One of the strategic differences of opinion amongst women's suffrage campaigners was how much emphasis to place on the symbolic significance of granting the vote to any one group of women. Initial campaigners sought to enfranchise single women or women householders only; the main suffrage groups requested the vote for women on the same terms as men, but the majority of men could not vote in the nineteenth century. Indeed, even in 1914, at the eve of the First World War, fewer than 60 per cent of men were enfranchised. The right to vote was based on either owning or renting property of a sufficient value, and in some of the poorer districts of the country, such as Glasgow, half of men were also excluded from the franchise. Enfranchising women on the same terms as men would have left many working-class men and women without the vote. A number of Conservative politicians were inclined towards enfranchising wealthier women who they considered most likely to vote Conservative; while Liberals were concerned that enfranchising women on the same terms as men would favour the Conservatives. The Labour party favoured adult suffrage, and Margaret Bondfield, who was chairperson of the Adult Suffrage Society, became the first female cabinet minister in Labour's 1929 administration, just one year after universal franchise was finally introduced throughout Britain.

A multitude of suffrage groups appeared in the Edwardian era; some, like the Barmaids' Political Defence League and the Gymnastic Teachers' Suffrage Society, were quite niche. The TRL was formed as an offshoot of the WFL in 1909, based upon the idea of no taxation without representation, with members refusing to pay a variety of taxes. Clemence Housman did not pay inhabited house duty whilst Emma Sproson resisted paying her dog licence, one of the only taxes working-class women paid. Women's suffrage supporters often had multiple allegiances to a number of organizations. As Hilary Frances points out, whilst some of the WFL members belonged to no other organization, the women who joined the TRL:

> belonged to a number of other societies, including the National Union of Suffrage Societies (NUWSS), the New Constitutional Society, the Conservative and Unionist Women's Franchise League, the Church League for Women's Suffrage, the Actresses' Franchise League, the Artists' Franchise League, the Women Writers' Suffrage League'.[10]

In 1909, the Liberal government introduced a Suffrage Bill, which would have enabled approximately one million women, and virtually all men, to vote, giving many suffrage campaigners the hope they were at last making progress. But when an election was called and the new government prioritized other issues, the WSPU responded by stepping up their militancy and there was a matching increase in violence by the police attempting to suppress the women's efforts to win the vote. On Friday 18 November 1910, the WSPU sent a delegation to the House of Commons. Some of these delegates were assaulted in ensuing clashes with the police, and

Letter to one of the hidden heroines of the suffrage movement from Millicent Fawcett, leader of the NUWSS.

the day became known as 'Black Friday'. Emmeline Pankhurst's sister, Mary Jane Clarke, a paid organizer of the WSPU in Brighton, was amongst 156 women arrested and sent to Holloway Prison, where she was forcibly fed. Although she spoke at a WSPU 'welcome' luncheon after her release on the 23 December, two days later she was dead, the first martyr of the suffrage movement.

In selecting the forty-eight women to be included in this book, we have avoided any of the families of well-known women's suffrage leaders. A few of the women we have chosen you may have heard of; you have seen the names of one or two inscribed on the statue of Millicent Fawcett in Parliament Square.[11] Others will be totally unknown outside the particular geographical region, political or interest group to which they belonged. We have found traces and mentions of numerous other women about whom very little is known or able to be known. For example, Elizabeth Crawford has tried to track down Susan Cunnington, a Brighton teacher who donated five shillings to the WSPU in 1911. She was the principal of a private girls' day school in Brighton who from a modest background went to Girton College, Cambridge, and wrote a mathematics textbook, but little else is known about her.[12] Similarly, we have not been able to trace what Miss Laura E. Price did as a secretary for the NUWSS that led to her receiving praise for her role in the movement from Mrs Fawcett in 1924. Her letter remains a tantalizing reminder of how many suffrage campaigners remain hidden from history.

Contemporary understanding of the women, and some men, who sought to drum up support for women's enfranchisement, is shaped by the historical sources that have survived, and this makes it particularly difficult to trace the lives and work of the law-abiding suffrage societies. Newspapers in the early twentieth century tended to focus their coverage on the more spectacular events of the WSPU and the activities of celebrity campaigners. There is, for example, a multitude of newspaper coverage of the exploits of Mrs Pankhurst, but only occasional mentions of the foot soldiers of women's suffrage movement. Public meetings receive perfunctory attention, arrests and court appearances are described while the speeches that ordinary women made in court are rarely reported.[13] Those women who, perhaps because of other responsibilities, were only able to make donations to suffrage societies or sell suffrage newspapers on street corners, left little record of their activities.

A few women, like Hannah Mitchell, wrote their autobiographies; others, like Kate Parry Frye, kept a diary. Even so, such insights into the lives of women in this era are rare, particularly if they are working class. Some records have survived from the suffrage organizations, but they contain little of what life was like for the ordinary suffrage campaigner who traipsed door to door trying to drum up support for the movement, or who organized bazaars and fêtes to raise money, sewed banners, and tried to encourage women to attend meetings. Their stories were no more newsworthy then than they would be today. Yet, without the efforts of the women who did these things and who chaired meetings and sat in audiences and were quietly heroic, the movement for women's suffrage would not have been successful.

Popular mythology has often suggested that the suffrage campaigns came to a halt on the outbreak of the First World War as women threw themselves into the war effort and were rewarded with the franchise in 1918. The life stories of these forty-eight women suggest a far more complex story. Some women, like Chrystal Macmillan, opposed the war and campaigned for a negotiated peace throughout the conflict. Many women with a strong background in philanthropy undertook welfare work. Some found the conflict offered them new career opportunities; for example, Mrs Arthur Webb became something of a domestic guru. When the wartime coalition government granted the vote to some women in 1918, seventeen women put themselves forward as candidates for Parliament in the 1918 election. Many are included in our chosen forty-eight. Like Nora Dacre Fox, they were unsuccessful and are largely forgotten. Only one woman, Countess Markievicz, won her seat, but as a member of Sinn Féin did not sit in the House of Commons; and, although well known in Ireland, she receives little attention across the water and so we have included her here, along with Margaret Wintringham, the first English-born woman to become an MP.

The biographies of these forty-eight hidden heroines demonstrate the multiplicity of political persuasions, interests, views, hopes, dreams and ideals that women had, which they found either combined with or collided with their campaigning for women's suffrage. Many belonged to other women's groups, temperance societies, the Women's Co-operative Guild, the women's sections of political parties, or women's trades unions. Some, like Grace Hadow and Edith Rigby, went on to take a very active role in the Women's Institute movement, which formed in 1915, and campaigned to improve rural women's lives. The vote, for many women was but one part of a re-working and re-imagining of women's role in the public sphere. A number of the women campaigning for the suffrage were pioneers in their fields of work: they were doctors, writers or became radio broadcasters, barristers and magistrates in the inter-war years, once the Sex Disqualification Removal Act was passed in 1919. For many women in the suffrage era, teaching provided an acceptable and attainable job. It was through education, it was hoped, that women would gain entry to employment and be able to interact with men as equals. In many ways, teaching was seen as an extension of women's domestic role of nurturing children, an area in which women, by virtue of their gender, could be acknowledged as experts. It is no coincidence that the first professor in Britain, Millicent MacKenzie, was a professor of education. She and a number of other women whom we have included championed new innovative experimental approaches to learning – the ideas of Rudolph Steiner, Montessori or Froebel.

Many of the women featured in this book were politically motivated and public-spirited before, during and after the suffrage campaigns. Householder women could vote and stand in local elections, for school boards, prison boards and as Poor Law guardians, from as early as the 1870s. Women like Annie Barnes and Ada Croft Baker took an active role in local politics in the inter-war era, whilst Ellen Wilkinson moved from the suffrage campaigns into national politics and became a government minister during the Second World War. But for a significant number of women, their utopian dreams of a better, brighter future when women took part in the political process gravitated towards Eastern religions. Many suffrage campaigners were vegetarian years before it was popular or fashionable, and campaigned against cruelty to animals. Margaret Cousins and Elsie Howey were not alone in their enthusiasm for Theosophy, a movement founded in 1875 by Helena Blavatsky, which seeks understanding of the mysteries of life and nature through the unity of religion, science and nature to bring about the happiness of humanity.[14]

The forty-eight women discussed here are but a tip of the iceberg of the thousands of women who have in the past and continue now to campaign to improve women's lives in society in Britain and elsewhere. They deserve to be remembered and recognized as heroines of the Women's Movement. But behind them are the many millions of women they fight for: women for whom carrying on with the daily grind of everyday life is in itself heroic.

Pioneering Victorian Women

1

BARBARA LEIGH SMITH BODICHON (1827–91)

Victorian suffrage campaigner

Janis Lomas

In 1857, Barbara Leigh Smith Bodichon wrote:

> I am one of the cracked people of the world, and I like to herd with the cracked
> … queer Americans, democrats, Socialists, artists, poor devils or angels; and
> am never happy in an English genteel family life. I try to do it like other people,
> but I long always to be off on some wild adventure, or long to lecture on a tub
> in St. Giles, or go to see the Mormons, or ride off into the interior on horseback
> alone and leave the world for a month…. I want to see what sort of world this
> God's world is.[1]

Barbara Leigh Smith was the eldest of Benjamin Leigh-Smith and Anne Longden's
five children. Her mother was a milliner and her father a radical MP, a Dissenter,
a Unitarian, and a benefactor to those less fortu-
nate than himself. Anne Longden met him when
he visited his sister in Derbyshire, and when
she became pregnant Benjamin moved her to
Sussex and rented a lodge for her where Barbara
was born in April 1827. Benjamin lived at his
own house nearby, Brown's Farm, but visited
his family daily and eight weeks after Barbara
was born her brother was conceived. After his
birth, the family went to America for two years.
On their return, they lived openly together, but
after her fifth pregnancy Annie became ill with
tuberculosis, and when Barbara was just seven
years old her mother died. Barbara's biographer
Pam Hirsch suggests that it could have been

THE WOMEN'S LIBRARY COLLECTION, LSE LIBRARY

Barbara Leigh Smith Bodichon.

25

Benjamin's objection to the marriage laws, which would have made a wife and children his property, that prevented her parents marrying.[2] Whatever the reason, Barbara felt the stigma of her illegitimacy for the rest of her life. Her cousin Florence Nightingale and the rest of the Nightingale family refused to acknowledge the existence of Barbara or any of her siblings. Barbara's father played a large part in her childhood, which she spent in Hastings, and, like all her siblings, when she was twenty-one she received investments, which provided an income of £300 a year. Barbara as a financially independent woman gave generously to help people less fortunate and supported her many friends her whole life. Importantly, her money also allowed her to take up the cause of women's rights and fight for change.

Perhaps due to her unusual upbringing, Barbara's views in relation to women's work and education were ahead of her time. Her brother Ben studied at Jesus College, Cambridge, but, as universities were not then open to women, she attended Bedford College and studied art, becoming a skilful artist. Years later she wrote:

> … ever since my brother went to Cambridge I have always intended to aim at the establishment of a college where women could have the same education as men if they wished it.[3]

She was unconventional and, in her early twenties, she embarked on an extensive, un-chaperoned walking tour of Belgium, Germany, Switzerland and Austria with her friend Bessie Parkes. While abroad, they decided to stop wearing corsets and to shorten their skirts to four inches above their ankles as they were so uncomfortable. Barbara celebrated her freedom in a little verse she wrote:

> Oh! Isn't it jolly/To cast away folly/And cut all one's clothes a peg shorter/And rejoice in one's legs/ Like a free-minded Albion's daughter.[4]

Barbara may not have been a great poetess, but her ditty celebrated their jollity and freedom, three decades before the Rational Dress Society advocated the abandonment of restrictive corsets. By the age of twenty-five, Barbara had established her own progressive school in London with Bessie Parkes's help. It was an experimental school, non-religious, co-educational, and admitted children of differing class backgrounds; other experimental ideas followed. In the 1850s, 1860s and 1870s, Barbara was a leading figure in four major campaigns: for married women to be given independent status under the law; for women's right to work; for women to have an equal education to men; and for women to be allowed to vote.

In 1854, Barbara wrote an influential pamphlet titled *A Brief Summary, in Plain Language, of the Most Important Laws concerning Women*. In her opening remarks, she acknowledged the importance of the vote for women:

... a single woman has the same rights to property, to protection from the law, and has to pay the same taxes to the State as a man. Yet a woman of the age twenty-one, having the requisite property qualifications, cannot vote in elections for Members of Parliament.[5]

She saw clearly that if married women had the right to their own property and earnings, it would make it harder for politicians to refuse to give women the vote. She was asked to give evidence to the Law Amendment Society, which was looking into the legal position of married women. Its deliberations led to the 1857 Matrimonial Causes Act being passed, allowing divorce for the first time outside the ecclesiastical courts and the Houses of Parliament, making divorce possible for more couples through a separate civil divorce court. Although the law was by no means equal, it did protect the property rights of divorced and separated women, something that Barbara had campaigned for.

However, for married women the position remained unchanged: when a woman married, her husband controlled her possessions, earnings and property and she could not dispose of any belongings without his consent. Barbara formed a committee, the Langham Place Group, to try to change the law. Within a year, Barbara's committee had become a nationwide campaign group, and she drafted a petition, which, when presented to the House of Lords in March 1856, had 26,000 signatures on it and was the first petition organized by a woman in the UK. Unsurprisingly, it was rejected; it took until 1870 for the first Married Women's Property Act to be passed, and a further twelve years until a more comprehensive act finally gave women the rights to both their own property and their earnings. Barbara campaigned for these changes throughout that period.

In 1857, Barbara published *Women and Work*, arguing that a married women's dependence on her husband was degrading. Her views on the legal position of married women led her to say she would not marry, as she was fearful of losing her independence. Yet, in 1857, she met Eugene Bodichon, and compromised her principles by marrying this French doctor. She hoped to have children and did not want her children to be illegitimate, as she had been. Eugene lived in Algeria, North Africa, for much of his life. He dressed in Arab robes, spoke little English and was seventeen years older than Barbara, but he shared Barbara's radical political views and loyally supported Barbara in her many campaigns for women's rights. Unsurprisingly, their marriage was unconventional. He continued to live in Algeria, and Barbara travelled to and fro, between winters in Algeria and her campaigning in London. Her family was shocked by her marriage, and her father set up a trust to safeguard her money. As a result, she had less freedom as she now had to ask the trustees before spending money. Eugene treated poor patients for free and had no money of his own. Although at first they were happy, in time their differences became more marked and Barbara spent more time in England where

Eugene refused to live. She remained loyal to him; they wrote to each other when separated; and she paid all his bills, even when he began to drink heavily and had dementia. Barbara even sold her London home to pay for live-in help for him.

Alongside marriage and a honeymoon in America, Barbara founded the *English Women's Journal* (EWM) in 1858. This monthly publication was owned and run by women; even the press machinery was operated by women. The *EWM* discussed education, female employment, equality issues and the reform of the laws regarding women. She also founded the Society of Female Artists. In 1859, Barbara, with Jessie Boucherett and Adelaide Proctor, also set up the Association for Promoting the Employment of Women, one of the earliest women's organizations, and the *EWM* became the society's mouthpiece. As Elizabeth Crawford recognized, the groups Barbara assembled were extremely important in establishing a feminist network to promote later campaigns.[6]

In 1865, Barbara, as one of the founding members of the Kensington Ladies' Discussion Society, helped to organize a petition calling for women's suffrage, and persuaded John Stuart Mill MP to present this to Parliament. He asked for 100 women's names: in fourteen days, Barbara and her friends used a chain-letter technique to secure almost 1,500 signatures.[7] Mill attempted to amend the proposed 1867 Representation of the People Act to replace the word 'men' with the word 'person'. The amendment secured seventy-nine votes, but was lost by a majority of 123. At a meeting of the Kensington Ladies' Discussion Society, Barbara gave a talk on women's suffrage that led to the formation of a Women's Suffrage Committee. This talk became an article in 1866, *Reasons for the Enfranchisement of Women*, and was read at the Social Science Association in Manchester. One of the women who heard it was Lydia Becker, who was immediately converted to the women's suffrage cause and who, the following year, went on to become the secretary of the newly formed Manchester Women's Suffrage Committee. Lydia asked for 3,000 copies of Barbara's article, which were distributed to all women householders in Manchester. Lydia Becker became an important early leader of the suffrage movement, founding and editing the *Women's Suffrage Journal* in 1870.

In 1869, Barbara finally realized her long-awaited dream of a college where women could be educated to the same standard, and in the same subjects, as men, when she co-founded Girton College, Cambridge, with Emily Davies. Emily was incensed when friends suggested that Barbara was a co-founder, insisting that the idea for the college was hers alone, and the two women often clashed. Emily was more autocratic and a strict disciplinarian, who wanted her students to concentrate on the Classics and mathematics, while Barbara, putting the women students' needs first, wanted a more radical, wide-ranging course of study. Barbara raised much of the money to found Girton, giving £6,000 of her own money over her lifetime. The college was the achievement of which she was most proud, and she left £10,000 to the college in her will.[8]

Barbara was under no illusions that the struggle for the vote was going to be anything other than difficult and protracted. Apparently, she remarked to Emily Davies: 'You will go up and vote upon crutches and I shall come out of my grave and vote in my winding-sheet.'[9] These were prophetic words, as Emily Davies was aged eighty-eight when she was able to vote and Barbara had been dead almost thirty years before the vote was finally achieved for some women in 1918. Throughout Barbara's adult life, she wrote an average of fifteen letters a day,[10] but, tragically in 1877, when only fifty years old, she suffered a stroke that left her weak, partially paralysed and dependent on others to write the letters she dictated. She had great difficulty in walking and was only able to paint for short periods. Her condition also largely curtailed her political activities, although she built a room onto her house in Hastings and set up a school for working men to study in the evenings. In 1884, she had another small stroke and, with her husband Eugene (with whom she had an unconventional relationship) becoming more and more mentally unstable in Algiers, they were not able to see each other before his death in 1885, aged seventy-four. Barbara herself died in Hastings in 1891. Her obituary in the *Hastings and St Leonards Observer* was in no doubt about her achievements:

> While she was still Miss Leigh Smith a movement started by her culminated in the Married Women's Property Act … [and] with a little help from Miss Davies she founded Girton College … Her aim through life was to do as much good as she could and no matter who they were, the poor always found a friend in Madame Bodichon.[11]

2

ROSE CRAWSHAY (1828–1907)

Philanthropist and Welsh iron-master's wife

Maggie Andrews

When, in 1870, Mrs Crawshay addressed one of the first public meetings to discuss women's suffrage in Wales, she was criticized by local newspapers for disturbing the peace of South Wales and requested to 'reconsider before she sows the seeds of politics amongst the female population of her part of the country'.[1]

Rose Mary Yeates was born in Horton Grove, Berkshire and, at the age of eighteen, married Robert Thompson Crawshay, whom she had met at the Reading County Ball. Robert, who was then aged twenty-nine, had a home in Berkshire, but his family's main residence was Cyfarthfa Castle in Wales, a mansion with seventy-two rooms and fifteen towers, which was built in the 1820s and stood in 154 acres of parkland. Robert Crawshay came from one of the larger iron-making dynasties, who owned Cyfarthfa Ironworks near Merthyr Tydfil, and it was in Wales that the couple lived and brought up their five children and where Rose focused the majority of her philanthropic and suffrage activities.

According to Angela John, Robert Crawshay was 'an autocratic showy man … who not only lived in a castle but practices [sic] droit du seigneur – it was widely believed he employed a procurer to supply him with daughters of workmen.'[2] Rose Crawshay was, however, committed to women's rights and the early feminist movement, and by the 1860s very active in these areas. She became the vice-president of Bristol and West of England National Society for Women's Suffrage, witnessed twenty-six signatures by women with Welsh addresses for the first women's Suffrage Petition of 1866 (including three from Merthyr),[3] and joined the London National Society for Women's Suffrage. She became friends with Elizabeth Garrett Anderson and Mrs Millicent Fawcett, who became the leader of the NUWSS. Indeed, Millicent Fawcett came and spoke on women's rights in Merthyr at Rose's request.[4]

Rose was one of what Ursula Masson has referred to as 'a small number of unusually active women … whose connections and social position enabled them to ignore pious conventions'.[5] These early suffrage speakers seem to have been well received by religious leaders, councillors and professional men and helped to drum up support for the nearly seventy suffrage petitions that originated in Wales between 1869 and 1874.[6] As well as giving public speeches, organizing meetings in her home and further afield, Rose penned a number of engaging letters to newspapers articulating the case for women's suffrage and refuting the arguments of those who opposed it. In a letter to *The Examiner*, she countered the suggestion that many women did not want to be enfranchised by asking:

> Why has no one proposed disenfranchising all men because a great many think it a bore to vote? This would be the proper corollary to denying the franchise to women who wish to vote because some don't wish to do so.

Her ironic tone continued when she dealt with the suggestion that only single women should be enfranchised:

> I see no objection to denying the vote to married women. If it should happen that hereafter some women on counting this up among marriages disadvantages, men who may find it less easy to get young and pretty wives would only have themselves to thank.[7]

Her feminism was not restricted to political rights for women, but also embraced the needs for women's employment, a commitment to education and philanthropy and to alleviating the distress of those who lived in poverty.

She set up soup kitchens and ensured that any surplus from the castle went to those in need in local towns and villages. Her cantankerous, industrialist husband seems not to have been altogether supportive of her actions and apparently complained that the castle had become a refuge for the destitute. Nevertheless, her paternalism and commitment to those less fortunate meant that she visited the families of everyone killed in a colliery explosion in February 1862, and sought to alleviate some of the worst excesses of Victorian industrialization. Rose was a particular proponent of finding work for what was often described as 'superfluous' women, i.e. middle-class women who had not married, but financially found that they needed to work. She contributed £200 to the Society for Promoting the Employment of Women, set up by Jessie Boucherett in 1859, and was an advocate of the idea of middle-class women becoming 'lady's helps'. The concept seems to have been something of a re-working and expansion of middle-class women's traditional option of employment as a governess. 'Lady's helps' had a similar betwixt and between situation in households, neither treated like other servants nor accepted as equals by the middle- and upper-class householders. She brought five into Cyfarthfa Castle and gave them spruced-up rooms once inhabited by the servants.

Like many women in the Victorian women's movement, Rose Crawshay was passionate about education, arguing that improved education was one of the ways that women could give a 'helping hand' to 'their poorer sisters'.[8] Rose was one of only 200 who attended a conference where Emily Davies put forward plans for what became Girton College, Cambridge. She also set up classes for local women to learn to make their own clothes and was also one of the first women to be elected to local school boards. She served on the Merthyr Tydfil board and also chaired the Vaynor school board. In education, as in other areas, she was in many ways ahead of her time, advocating alternative methods of discipline to corporal punishment, asking:

> Might it not be possible, it is asked to banish the stick from our schools by a system of rewards? Considering the underfed condition of many of the Board's school pupils, some kind of extra food suggests itself as the most desirable shape of the reward.[9]

Other very twentieth-century causes she espoused were decimal coinage and cremation. She was one of the first members of the Cremation Society of England, a founder member of their council and, alongside the writer Anthony Trollope, was one of the original signatories of the formative Declaration in 1874. This identified the organization's disapproval of the custom of burying the dead (which was becoming a problem in the rapidly growing cities of the Victorian era) and instead sought a better solution 'to render remains perfectly innocuous. Until such better method is devised we desire to adopt what is usually known as cremation'.[10] Rose, who died in 1907, did not live to see women's enfranchisement, but one of her granddaughters, Mildred Mansell, was a suffragette, an organizer in Bath who was imprisoned in Holloway for breaking windows at the War Office.[11] Rose's memory also lives on in The Rose Mary Crawshay Prize, a literary prize for women scholars set up in 1888.

THE LATE MRS CRAWSHAY.   Rose Crawshay, newspaper report of her death.

3

HARRIET McILQUHAM (1837–1910)

Petitioner and local politician

Linda Pike

Suffrage workers organized 'Grand Demonstrations' hoping to impress upon Parliament the seriousness and popularity of women's emancipation campaigns. From being a delegate in 1890 at St James Hall, London, Harriet McIlquham, together with Maria Colbey, co-organized the Birmingham 'Grand Demonstration', which took place on 22 February 1881. The city's central position made it a popular and convenient destination.

Harriet was born Harriet Medley on 8 August 1837 in Brick Lane, London, but moved to Staverton House, Boddington, near Tewkesbury, when she married James McIlquham in 1858; the couple subsequently had four children.[1] Her Unitarian family upbringing encouraged political discussions, whilst her wealth from property in her own name enabled her to buy a large estate in Staverton where she managed a farm for forty years. Here she became interested in political issues, especially that of women's suffrage.[2]

Gloucester suffrage groups first petitioned Parliament on 4 May 1869 and nearby Cheltenham followed on 12 May. Such activities laid the foundation for the Municipal Franchise Act (1869), which enabled single and widowed female ratepayers to vote in local municipal elections. On 14 November 1876, a meeting was held at Tewkesbury's Music Hall, Barton Street, in support of women's parliamentary enfranchisement, and Mrs Harriet McIlquham attended a further meeting at Tewkesbury's Philharmonic Hall on 9 December 1881. As a property owner and a ratepayer, Harriet could vote in local elections after 1869 – an opportunity she seized with great enthusiasm.

Her own electoral success was at Boddington in April 1881, as the first married women to become a Poor Law Guardian. She argued that as a property owner and ratepayer, she was entitled to stand, and went on to beat her male opponent, Mr Henry Arkell, by forty-eight votes. However, despite receiving enthusiastic support for this historic occasion, several people, according to the *Tewkesbury Weekly*

Register, 'worked themselves into a feverish state' in protest at the result. Mr Arkell was determined to have the result annulled and requested a re-election, which Harriet duly won again. Her success was viewed as creating political awareness within rural areas not known for political progress.[3]

Harriet served as a Poor Law Guardian for thirteen years, during which she criticized the behaviour of staff towards the inmates of the local asylum on the basis of information from an inmate. During this period, many women also believed that single mothers and their illegitimate children were a drain on society and Harriet supported the Local Government Board's decision to compulsorily detain illegitimate children in the workhouse. Although progressive in her campaign for female enfranchisement, she opposed children's compulsory smallpox vaccination. It had been recommended by the government in the 1850s, but the anti-vaccine campaign reached a peak in the 1890s. After serving as a guardian, she urged other women to stand for local government roles. Her letter in the *Tewkesbury Weekly Record and General Advertiser* said she had been treated courteously and seriously and aimed to dispel the belief that women, if elected, may face male hostility.[4]

Her initial experience in local government, therefore, encouraged her to stand as a Liberal candidate for Gloucestershire County Council in January 1889. She was one of four candidates selected to test women's eligibility in the newly formed Cheltenham Central Ward. The *Cheltenham Chronicle* noted that she was 'admired for her pluck' although she received only thirty votes, just under 3 per cent of those cast.[5] Even if she had won, she would have been unable to take up her seat because of her gender, as occurred when Lady Sandhurst won Brixton for the Liberals, but had to stand down when the defeated candidate, Conservative Beresford Hope, petitioned against her. With the Court of Appeal ruling against her, Sandhurst was fined £5 for every vote she had been given during her tenure.

By 1899, Harriet had become a member of Boddington School Board and, despite being the only woman, was unafraid of voicing her opinions. Her concern for children manifested in 1901 when she requested a farm to close all barriers to prevent further cases of diphtheria when a child died after passing the farm on the way to school. She also became an overseer for the Parish of Staverton (another unique position for a woman), a rural district councillor in Boddington, and a board member of the Education Management Committee following the 1902 Education Act. She was also the first chairman of Staverton Parish Council and acted as their returning officer in their parish council elections.[6]

Harriet's experience at local government level led to her taking a prominent role in the women's suffrage movement. Besides caring for four children, managing a farm and her local government business, Harriet promoted women's rights through regular correspondence to local newspapers. She was a founding member of Cheltenham's Suffrage Society in 1871, the Bristol and West of England Society for Women's Suffrage, and the Manchester National Society for Women's Suffrage.

She spoke at meetings, including one in Tewkesbury on 12 January 1884 to discuss the 1884 Reform Act. Harriet eventually became a member of the Cheltenham National Union of Women's Suffrage Societies and its affiliated branch in Tewkesbury.

Harriet concurred with her close friend Elizabeth Wolstenholme Elmy that demanding a limited suffrage perpetuated the inequalities of enfranchisement, especially the exclusion of married women from voting, which re-enforced the idea that woman's legal rights and obligations were subsumed by those of her husband upon marriage. Together with Alice Scratcherd, Elizabeth and Harriet founded the Women's Franchise League (WFL) in London in 1889, with Harriet as its president. This was the first women's suffrage organization to expressly include a married women's franchise. After a disagreement with Ursula Bright in the WFL, in 1891, Elizabeth and Harriet helped form the radical Women's Emancipation Union (WEU), and Harriet was a member of its council.[7]

Letter from Mrs Alice Cliff Scatcherd to Mrs McIlquham.

As a fervent promoter of female enfranchisement, Harriet published her first pamphlet in 1892, *The Enfranchisement of Women: An Ancient Right*. Further articles ensued in the *Westminster Review* including *Early writers on the Woman Question* (1902) and *Woman's Suffrage in the Early Nineteenth Century* (1903). She also published two articles entitled *Mary Astell: a Seventeenth-Century Advocate for Women* (1891) and *Lady Mary Wortley Montagu and Mary Astell* (1899). Her 1902 critique of marriage, *Marriage: A Just and Honourable Partnership*, echoed Astell's views that when men marry they believe a wife is subservient; Harriet declared that Astell should be regarded as a pioneer of the 'Women's Rights Movement'.[8]

It is unclear if Harriet actually joined the WSPU, but on 21 February 1905 she lobbied MPs in the House of Commons alongside Sylvia Pankhurst, the only example of her militant behaviour, and attended the first meeting of the WSPU's Cheltenham Branch on 28 September 1906. She was also at the WSPU meetings on 20 January 1907 at Glevum Hall, Gloucester, where Emmeline Pankhurst's daughter Christabel, spoke, with the *Gloucester Journal* reporting in January 1907 that 'Mrs. McIlquham Joins The Insurgents'. Furthermore, Harriet donated money to both the WSPU and Women's Franchise League in 1908 and 1909.[9]

Harriet died from heart failure, after a bout of influenza and bronchitis, on 22 January 1910, before women's campaigns for suffrage came to fruition. She is buried in Tewkesbury Abbey. Her obituary in *The Times* read that she was a 'tireless worker for the rights of her sex' through her career in local government work, whilst the *Cheltenham Chronicle* described her as a 'pioneer' and an 'advocate of women's suffrage and of women's share in all the functions of citizenship'.[10]

Whilst Harriet's achievements were in small rural communities, away from London and the major industrial conurbations so frequently thought of as being central to women's political suffrage movements, she should rightly be viewed as a hidden figure in the campaigns for women's suffrage and a pioneer of women's work in local government.

4

CHARLOTTE CARMICHAEL STOPES (1840–1929)

Shakespearean scholar and proponent of the Rational Dress Society

Maggie Andrews

In 1894, Charlotte Stopes suggested that:

> It would be better for men too if women were represented. They would then understand the meaning of Justice and enjoy the return blessing of fairplay. They would discover that in the very difference of women lies one great argument for their being consulted. If public spirited women continue to be denied the power of offering their judgment in the consensus of public opinion on political matters, the nation will be the poorer.[1]

Charlotte Stopes was born in Edinburgh, where her extended family lived and her father, James Ferrier Carmichael, was a landscape painter who taught art and exhibited at the Royal Scottish Academy. As a child, she was enthusiastic about literature, writing and the outdoors; she went climbing with her uncle and learnt to swim.[2] She excelled at school and in another era would undoubtedly have gone to university and had an academic career. At this time these were not options open to her. However, in 1865, Edinburgh University opened up a series of courses and lectures to women to gain tertiary education (though not degrees) and 'by 1872 she had completed several of the women's certificate courses, winning first and second prizes in English literature, geology and botany'.[3] After further courses and teaching posts, Charlotte accepted a post at Cheltenham Ladies College in 1877. This school, despite being founded only twenty years previously, was a leading provider of girls' academic education.

MARY STOPES-ROE

Charlotte Carmichael Stopes.

37

Having embarked on a successful career, which she seemed to enjoy, and by the age of thirty-nine, become something of a 'bluestocking', she maintained her efforts to improve women's access to higher education and attended meetings of the British Association of Science, which helped her to broaden and shape her thinking through contact with more members of academia.[4] Even so, in 1879 Charlotte married Henry Stopes. Her new husband was several years her junior, an engineer, brewers' architect, and a geologist. The newly-weds initially went to live near Colchester where Henry's family had a business that he and his brother briefly ran together. The nature of Charlotte and Henry's marriage has been a subject of much conjecture: Ruth Hall suggests that Charlotte's frigidity caused problems and Henry withdrew from the relationship,[5] while Stephanie Green points to more complex interactions between them.[6] Either way, they were compatible enough to produce two daughters: Marie and Winifred. Fear of further pregnancies, Henry's repeated difficulties with business ventures, and some money problems could have put a strain on their relationship. Furthermore, they both had very separate interests: Charlotte's lay in literary scholarship, feminism and writing, while Henry was increasingly pre-occupied with collecting rocks and flints. When he died there were over 200 crates of them, which Charlotte sold to the National Museum of Wales.

Over the following years, the couple had various homes in London, initially taking a house in Norwood. There, Charlotte founded a discussion society for ladies and a Shakespeare reading society, and began to write. In 1888, she published an article titled 'The Bacon Shakespeare Question in relation to Wine, Spirits and Beer', and went on to write more extensively about women's issues. She embraced the Rational Dress Society, which opposed tight corsets, high heels and unwieldy skirts that restrained women's movement, were injurious to their health, and less than ideal for the workplace. In 1889, Charlotte gave a paper supporting the Society at the British Association in Newcastle, later turning this into an article for *Woman's World*.[7] She also wrote for the *Rational Dress Society Gazette*.

In 1894, Charlotte's book, which was perhaps her most significant contribution to the suffrage movement, was published: *British Freewomen: Their historical privilege*. The historical accuracy of the book, which suggested a previous golden age of greater freedom for women, was very questionable. It was, however, enthusiastically received in newspapers, which suggested it:

Ought to be in the hands of every woman who thinks fairly on great subjects. It is a cheap little volume written with the greatest moderation, in fact, offering only accurate historical information to those who seek for it. The quotations from the statutes of 800 years afford evidence of the curtailment by men, century after century of the liberty once allowed to and enjoyed by women.[8]

Mayhall argues that to Charlotte: 'British women constituted a racial group with ancient rights and privileges continually worn away by successive invaders – Roman and then Norman.'[9] In Charlotte's argument – that women's suffrage was an ancient racial right – lie the foundations of some of the Far Right and Fascist ideas that a few suffragettes adopted in the 1930s; and perhaps also the eugenicist ideas of her daughter, the birth control campaigner, Marie Stopes.

According to *Freewomen*, a further significant moment in the curtailment of women's liberty was the use of the word *man* in the 1832 Reform Act, which formally disenfranchised women. She argued that the political and economic position of women in the nineteenth century was inherently 'unbritish'. In the years that followed its publication, Charlotte took an active role in the suffrage movement, making speeches, and writing articles for magazines and journals. She worked with campaigners from across the spectrum of suffrage campaigners. She was, however, wary of the effectiveness of militant tactics; she considered that, in the long run, they would be counter-productive and that persuasion might more effectively bring about change.[10]

Charlotte's writing, which was extensive, was financially important as she struggled to make ends meet when her husband's earnings were erratic after he suffered from ill health, and then died, in 1902. Her books included *Shakespeare's Family* (1901), *Shakespeare's Warwickshire Contemporaries* (1907) and *Burbage and Shakespeare's Stage* (1913). Although she had her critics, and certainly fuelled the status and interest in Stratford-upon-Avon, these publications contributed to her being awarded the Rose Mary Crawshay Prize for female scholars by the British Academy in 1916. That same year, she enthused about the tercentennial of Shakespeare's birth in the *Graphic*. In the year that Charlotte was allowed to vote in a parliamentary election for the first time (1918), her daughter Marie published *Married Love*. This book, which promoted sexual understanding for women (albeit wrapped up in very flowery language), received enormous media attention and popular sales. It turned Marie Stopes into a celebrity, an inter-war phenomenon, so that when Charlotte died in 1929, in many newspapers she was described only as Marie Stopes' mother.

5

ELIZABETH AMY DILLWYN (1845–1935)

Industrialist and novelist

Maggie Andrews

Amy Dillwyn (as she was commonly known)'s feminism, which came through in her politics and her literary output, can be summed up by her words:

> All I say is give women a chance. Don't despise them without knowing what they can do. A woman's duty like a man's is to serve her generation in the way she can do it best.[1]

Elizabeth Amy Dillwyn was born in Wales in the middle of the nineteenth century, the third child of John Lewis Llewelyn Dillwyn and his wife Elizabeth. She had an elder brother, Harry, and a sister, Mary. Seven years later, in 1892, her younger sister Sarah was born, and her father, who owned the Dillwyn Spelter works at Swansea, became a Liberal MP for Swansea. Amy was brought up in Hendrefolian House, an impressive Tudor-gothic style property on the outskirts of Swansea, and educated by a succession of governesses. Even at an early age she did not really embrace the ideal of Victorian femininity: she enjoyed climbing trees, swimming, fishing, and seems to have been both intelligent and determined.[2]

At the age of eighteen, accompanied by her parents, Amy travelled to London to make her debut in London society, well aware that it was now her responsibility to acquire a suitable husband. She met and became engaged in 1863 to Llewellyn Thomas, the sole heir of a wealthy mid-Wales landowner. Her future father-in-law was also a colliery magnate and chairman of the county magistrates. This was not to be a happy-ever-after story. Llewellyn's father's unexpected death in December delayed the wedding and, only two months later, Llewellyn himself died of small-pox while in Paris. It seems that Amy contemplated

Elizabeth Amy Dillwyn plaque in Swansea.

joining a religious order, but after her mother's death in 1866, she became the mistress of her father's household and responsible for the care of her younger sister, at least until her sister reached an age at which she could come out in society and marry. Amy also undertook philanthropic work in the local community, teaching children at the school her uncle, Reverend Welby, had set up to provide religious education to the young. She also provided assistance during the cholera epidemic in 1867. This work began to give her a new sense of the inequality and the poverty experienced by those who were unemployed, and it informed both her later political work and writing. For example, she joined the Mourning Reform Society in the 1890s, concerned about the growing pressure on working class families to partake in expensive rituals around death they could ill afford.

In the 1870s, as her sister married and her father and brother were pre-occupied with their own interests, Amy began to suffer from ill health, possibly linked to depression. She had, like many women of her class in this era, toyed with writing short stories, but apparently inspired by reading George Elliot's *Middlemarch* she took to writing with more perseverance, and was rewarded when, in 1880, Macmillan published *Rebecca Rioter*. This novel explored the experiences of working-class men who dressed up as women to take part in the Rebecca riots in Wales in the 1830s through the life of a young working-class man, Evan Williams. In just over ten years, she published six novels and established something of a literary reputation. All her novels had elements of autobiography and the theme of social reform. As Kirsti Bohata has pointed, she was also a writer who explored how women could live outside marriage and lesbian romance: *Jill*, which was published in 1887, is the story of Amy's 'long hidden love for another woman'. Olive Talbot was a distant relation with whom Amy had had a close friendship from her teenage years until Olive's death in the 1890s, and to whom Amy refers frequently in her diaries as her 'wife'.[3] Openly lesbian fiction was not part of Victorian literary culture, but Bohata points out that 'Dillwyn encoded lesbian desire through cross-class disguise and masquerade'.[4]

When Amy's father unexpectedly died, after collapsing at a political meeting in Swansea in 1892, her literary career was curtailed. Her brother had died two years previously and the family business, thanks to her father's focus on his political career and her brother's propensity towards drink was not in a strong position. Amy became chief executive of the firm and, supported by a manager, was one of the first women industrialists of the Victorian era. In the years that followed, Amy, through the daily grind at the office and factory, sorted out the firm's debts and secured the financial stability of the Spelter works. In doing so, she saved the 300 jobs of those who worked there, but not her family home, Hendrefolian House.

Her political interests were also growing at this time. As an industrialist, she paid the wages of many men who could vote in parliamentary elections, whilst she, a woman, could not. Women could both vote and take up positions as members of the school boards, something she did very successfully in Swansea until they were abolished in 1902. Although she stood for election to the Swansea Harbour Trust in 1903 and the Swansea County Council in 1907, she was, according to her biographer David Painting, on each occasion 'defeated by entrenched bias against female interlopers into a strictly male preserve'.[5] Her preoccupation with women's politics led her to take an active role in supporting the strike of twenty-five women employees of Ben Evans' Emporium in Swansea in 1911. Amy called for a boycott of the store until the women's demands for a living wage had been tackled by their employers. Furthermore, Painting suggests that:

> When the National Union of Women's Suffrage Societies (NUWSS) was formed at the turn of the century Amy was among its earliest supporters in South Wales, and never wavered in her fight for female emancipation. She could not, however, ally herself with the militant suffrage movement.[6]

This however underplays her role, for she was president of the Swansea branch of the NUWSS.[7] As a woman with a significant family tradition and social presence in the town, her very public affirmation of women's suffrage was very important in building support for the movement.

In the Edwardian era, recognizing the instability of the relatively small family concern in an increasingly global trade market, she sold her major shareholding to a German metallurgical company from Frankfurt, maintaining only a small interest and a seat on the board for herself and her nephew. In the years that followed, she travelled, continued philanthropic work, was a benefactor of Swansea Hospital and was something of an eccentric figure in Swansea:

> fond of good cigars, which she smoked at the many public dinners she attended.... She invariably wore a trilby hat and up to a short time before her death was very active and possessed all her facilities.[8]

She was highly esteemed in Swansea and, in 1923, a new building society set up in the city by John Oliver Watkins was named after her. When she died in 1935, at the age of ninety, she left over £100,000 in her will. Of this, £3,000 went to her maid and £1,000 to her parlour maid and chauffeur, and she was described in newspapers as 'a keen business woman'. There is considerable interest in Amy Dillwyn and her family in Glamorganshire, and she was included in the International Women's Day exhibition at the National Waterfront Museum in 2017. That little is known about Amy Dillwyn beyond Wales says more about the London-centric nature of much of women's history than it does of her pioneering life.

6

LADY HENRY SOMERSET (1851–1921)

Leader of the Women's Temperance Movement

Maggie Andrews

Speaking at the annual meeting of the Central National Society for Women's Suffrage in 1893, Lady Henry Somerset explained that the suffrage movement:

> … had passed through two stages of being ignored and ridiculed and was entering upon the third or triumphant stage. The country was tired of being governed by men for men, and wanted government by the people, of the people, and for the people. Of the 6,000,000 adult women in the country, 3,000,000 earned their own bread, and 2,000,000 were entirely self-dependent. Surely if they could earn their own bread they were entitled to a voice in national councils.[1]

Isabella Somerset Cocks was born in London, the eldest daughter in a wealthy aristocratic family; her father Charles Somers became the third Earl Somers and her mother Virginia was a renowned society beauty. The family owned Reigate Priory in Kent, Eastnor Castle in Herefordshire with estates stretching into Worcestershire, and Somers Town, a district of north-west London near the modern-day King's Cross. She had two sisters, Adeline and Virginia, but after the younger of these had died of diphtheria in childhood, Isabella and Adeline became heiresses to the family fortune. They were both educated at home by a succession of governesses until, at the age of eighteen, Isabella was launched into society.

Isabella's social engagements, dances and parties were intended to ensure that she fulfilled the family expectations and married a suitable husband. She initially developed a close friendship with Lord Lorne, who later became Duke of Argyll. Queen Victoria, however, intervened and he re-directed his attention onto her fourth daughter, Louise, whom he subsequently married.[2] Despite having initially rejected his proposal, in February 1872 Isabella married the second son of the Duke of Beaufort, who was also an MP and justice of the peace in Monmouth.

As an impoverished second son, Henry Somerset no doubt saw her as an attractive match. Unfortunately, Henry's sexual preferences lay in another direction entirely and although the couple did manage to produce a son and heir, their relationship was soon somewhat strained and sexual intimacy became non-existent.

The couple's separation led to a court battle for the custody of their son; Lady Isabella's deposition to court accused her husband of both cruelty and homosexuality (which was then illegal). To support her case, she provided intimate details of their relationship and of Henry's letters and behaviour with his male friends. Her disclosures scandalized Victorian society. The court did not consider her accusations proven, but Isabella was awarded custody of her son. As the daughter-in-law of a duke, Isabella had mixed with the social elite; as a separated woman who had accused her husband of homosexuality in court, Isabella's social circle was significantly curtailed. Henry Somerset went to live in Italy, with a generous allowance from Isabella's father, while Isabella withdrew to Reigate Priory. However, within a year the Earl of Somers had died and Isabella became responsible for managing the family finances and estates.

While spending time managing the Eastnor Castle estate, she engaged in philanthropic work in nearby towns and villages and encountered at close hand Victorian poverty and deprivation. In doing so, she came to identify alcohol (as opposed to low wages and the unequal distribution of wealth) as the cause of poverty and embraced the temperance movement. She undertook a range of philanthropic work during her life to alleviate distress and carried out work to improve working-class housing in the family estates in Somers Town. She closed pubs on her estates as the leases came to an end. After attending a local temperance society in Ledbury, she set up a temperance group at Eastnor and became increasingly involved in the British Women's Temperance Association (BWTA).

Isabella became president of the BWTA in 1890. By 1892, it had 570 branches and 50,000 members.[3] In this new role, she travelled thousands of miles around the country, giving temperance lectures, encountering working-class communities, including Welsh mining areas. She was initially nervous about the many public speaking engagements that her role in BWTA required, but with the assistance of a maid who stood at the back of the hall and waved a white handkerchief if unable to hear her, she learned to project her voice and tame her audiences. A Victorian woman making speeches was inevitably judged according to her femininity and she, like many of the suffragettes who came in her wake, was careful to avoid being criticized as unladylike. Indeed, newspaper reports enthused about how she was:

> ... feminine looking to a degree with soft, dark hair, massed in simple coils around a nobly outlined head' or 'has a charming personality, and frank winning manner ...
>
> Her abundant hair is parted in the centre and loosely curled at the back.

Her fine dark eyes are full of animation and her voice is singularly clear and musical.[4]

Isabella's support for women's suffrage and women's rights grew, and she promoted both temperance and suffrage in her lectures and through the *Woman's Signal*, a weekly British feminist magazine, which she edited from 1894 until 1899.[5] She also sought to broaden the scope of the British Women's Temperance Association so that it would address not merely intemperance but also the causes of drinking, involving them in philanthropic work, social purity campaigns and women's suffrage – views re-enforced when Isabella visited the USA and met Frances Willard, the president of the World's Women Christian

THE WOMAN MILITANT: LEADERS OF THE SUFFRAGIST PROCESSION
AND THEIR SYMBOLIC BANNERS COMMEMORATING GREAT WOMEN OF ALL AGES.

Portraits of various women's rights' campaigners, including Lady Henry Somerset, who took part in the Suffragist Procession on 13 June 1908 from Embankment to the Albert Hall.

Temperance Union. The two women became close friends. Despite speculation, it is hard to assess the nature of this friendship; it may have been a lesbian affair or an intimate romantic friendship. Either way, Isabella was soon elected vice-chair of the World's Woman's Christian Temperance Association.

Isabella's temperance work was rooted in both Christianity and the women's movement, but her politics was grounded in an extension, rather than a rejection, of traditional Victorian ideas of femininity. She argued that, 'women's votes meant home protection.'[6] As she explained to a large gathering of temperance workers in Redruth in Cornwall:

It did not rob a woman of a woman's sweetest attributes that she should go forth to rouse the conscience of the world at large, but in order that the children might be protected.[7]

She saw women's suffrage as leading to welfare reform, including legislation to restrict or ban the sale of alcohol. In the nineteenth century, there were a number of overlaps and links between the temperance movement and the suffrage movements; they shared many members and tactics. Both organizations lobbied, gathered signatures and campaigned for sympathetic MPs to be elected to parliament. When Mrs Fawcett set up and led a Special Appeal Committee for women's suffrage in 1893 bringing together organizations of all political persuasions, the World's Woman's Christian Temperance Association was represented by Mrs Henry Somerset.[8] Yet, for many of the more conservatively minded members of the BWTA, Isabella's views were anathema and, although she was very popular with the members, her presidency was marked by rancour and splits. After Frances Willard's death in 1898, Isabella became president of the World's Woman's Christian Temperance Association, a post she held until 1906 when ill health necessitated her curtailing her commitments. Instead, she focused on the Duxhurst Farm Colony for Inebriate Women, in Kent, which had opened in 1895 and where she lived in a modest cottage. In 1906, she published a novel titled *Under the Arch,* which addresses social divisions and inequality and the role of social reform, suffrage and Christianity in addressing them.[9]

Isabella remained a popular figure in the women's movement. In 1913, readers of the *London Evening News* voted her 'the women they would most like to be Britain's first female prime minister'.[10] She lived long enough to see women's enfranchisement and the curtailment of the opening hours of public houses during the First World War, restrictions that remained in place for over seventy years. When, in 1921, she died of heart failure after an appendectomy, there were numerous tributes to her life and work, but few know about her now; for some, her support for temperance may seem a quaint anachronism, but for many women in the nineteenth century, this went hand in hand with women's suffrage.

7

DAME ETHEL SMYTH (1858–1944)

Composer and campaigner

Janis Lomas

While in Holloway gaol, Ethel Smyth joined other suffragette inmates in a loud rendition of the WSPU's official anthem *The March of the Women*; as the prisoners marched around the prison courtyard, Ethel conducted through her cell window, using her toothbrush as a baton.

Ethel was born in Sidcup, Kent, one of eight children in a military family, her father being a major-general in the Royal Artillery. Although she was born on 22 April, the family always celebrated her birthday the following day, as it was William Shakespeare's birthday, and she liked the connection with him. Her father was very against her taking up a career in music and it took a great deal of defiance to stand up to 'the old General', as she called him; her tactic was to make life so unpleasant at home that he finally gave in and allowed her to study music at the Leipzig Conservatory, Germany.

It was in 1910 that Ethel Smyth, at that time a recognized composer of chamber and orchestral music, operas, piano and vocal music, met Emmeline Pankhurst, after previously being indifferent, even scornful of the suffrage movement. She was immediately attracted to the charismatic leader of the WSPU, writing in her memoirs of the 'devotion a magical personality like hers was able to kindle when she chose'.[1] Within a fortnight of that first meeting, she had decided that once her present musical commitments were over she would devote the next two years of her life to trying to obtain the vote for women, and this she did. Her financial position was secure as Ethel had been given £100 a year for life and a country cottage at Hook Heath, near Woking, by a wealthy American patron.[2] Her neighbours soon discovered that she had a determined approach to her new cause, as the *Daily Herald* reported in 1912:

Ethel Smyth lives in a little house at Woking, with a large board on the front bearing 'Votes for Women' in conspicuous style, an Anti-Suffrage neighbour, in an attempt to annoy her, took this board down, but she promptly put another up, above her bedroom window, that he could not get at it, and there it stays to this day.[3]

When Ethel joined the WSPU she almost immediately became close friends with Emmeline Pankhurst and they often travelled together to meetings and rallies, and Ethel sometimes accompanied Emmeline to see Christabel Pankhurst, who was then living in exile in Paris. Although devoted to Emmeline at the time, Ethel's memoirs portray Mrs Pankhurst in a less flattering light. Apparently, when in their car on their way to a meeting and negotiating crowds of people lining the streets, a woman got caught on the car mudguard and fell to the ground. Emmeline was immediately out of the car, full of pity and solicitude for the woman, and appeared almost in tears. However, once they were back in the car and had resumed their journey, Emmeline apparently turned to Ethel and, in a furious undertone, exclaimed: 'Drunken old beast, I wish we'd run her over'.[4]

Ethel made a major contribution to the movement by writing the music to *The March of the Women*, which was first performed in January 1911 at a social evening for released prisoners. It was pronounced a triumph, and the first major performance was arranged for 23 March in the Royal Albert Hall, London. On this night, in a classic suffragette spectacle, Ethel, dressed in her Doctor of Music robes and accompanied by Mrs Pankhurst, processed up the centre aisle and was

Dame Ethel Smyth speaking at the London Pavilion. Emmeline Pethick-Lawrence and Christabel Pankhurst are also on the platform, with representatives of WSPU branches.

presented with a 'beautiful baton with a golden collar' with which to conduct the choir. The packed auditorium then joined in and the song ended to tremendous applause. The march became the anthem of the suffrage movement; with words by Cicely Hamilton, this stirring song sustained hunger-striking prisoners who sang it from within their cells at night, providing solace and bolstering the courage of those who were feeling lonely or afraid or whose resolve was failing. Supporters from the Actresses' Franchise League gathered outside prison walls and sung the march using a loudspeaker to project the song into the prison. The NUWSS also appreciated and used it; it was played in June 1911 during the Coronation Procession staged by the constitutionalists. Ethel wrote to Mrs Millicent Fawcett, the leader of the NUWSS, expressing her pleasure at hearing her music played.

After the failure of the Conciliation Bill in 1911, the WSPU initiated a window-smashing campaign, and Ethel undertook the task of trying to instruct Emmeline on how to throw a stone with enough force to break a window. She had little success. Nevertheless, on 4 March 1912, both Ethel and Emmeline took part in the stone throwing. Emmeline's stones fell short of their target, but Ethel was more successful and she broke a window at the home of the Colonial Secretary, Lord Harcourt.[5] Windows were broken all over London and 200 women were arrested that night, including both Emmeline and Ethel, who was sentenced to two months' imprisonment. During her imprisonment, the conductor, Sir Thomas Beecham visited her in Holloway and reported:

> I arrived in the main courtyard of the prison to find the noble company of martyrs marching round it and singing lustily their war-chant, *March of the Women* while the composer, beaming approbation from an overlooking upper window, beat time in almost Bacchic frenzy with a toothbrush.[6]

The two friends were given cells next to each other; Ethel was released after three weeks. Shortly after this, she sent four bottles of Château Lafite red wine to the prison 'alleging that wine was necessary to Mrs Pankhurst's health'.[7] The experience of prison certainly did not change Ethel's commitment to the cause of women's suffrage when, in April 1913, Ethel Smyth was asked to comment on an attack on Manchester Art Gallery in which thirteen paintings had their glass broken by three suffragettes. In reply, she drew attention to the treatment of hunger-striking prisoners and the cruelty of the 'Cat and Mouse Act':

> To me there is something hateful, sinister, sickening in the heaping up of art treasures, this sentimentalising over the bodies of the beautiful, while the desecration and ruin of bodies of women ... are looked upon with indifference.[8]

In the middle of 1913, once her two years' commitment to the cause was up, Ethel resumed her musical career while retaining her close friendship with Emmeline Pankhurst. Their friendship floundered during the war when she disagreed with Christabel's extreme patriotism and Emmeline's plan to set up a home for 'war babies'. Finally, an irretrievable rift developed in 1921 after she criticized Christabel in a letter to Emmeline,[9] which was returned with the note from Emmeline saying: 'I return your letter. You may wish to destroy it. I would if I were you'.[10] They did not resume their friendship although, in March 1930, with her Holloway medal on show and wearing her academic robes, in the presence of many of the politicians who had opposed women's suffrage, Ethel conducted the Metropolitan Police Band in the chorale from her opera *The Wreckers* and, of course, *the March of the Women*, when the statue to Emmeline Pankhurst was unveiled in Victoria Tower Gardens.[11]

From 1913 onwards, Ethel Smyth became increasingly deaf and she only produced four more works. Undaunted, she turned to writing and wrote ten successful books. She was made a Dame of the British Empire in 1922, the first female composer to be honoured in this way. Sadly, when her work was performed in a special festival in her honour for her seventy-fifth birthday, she could not hear a word. She died in March 1944, aged eighty-six, in Woking. Even though she received some honours, she always felt that her music had been dismissed and undervalued because she was a woman, which may well have been the case. Her obituary in *The Stage* quotes her as saying 'Oh that I had been born a man'.[12]

The Movement Takes Off

8

MARGARET LLEWELYN DAVIES (1861–1944)

Organizer of the Women's Co-operative Guild

Maggie Andrews

Margaret Llewelyn Davies was a strong advocate of women's suffrage and honorary secretary of the People's Suffrage Federation, in which capacity she wrote:

> Women's Enfranchisement is urgent. They are as much concerned in law and government as men. A large proportion of the wage earners are women and women control the greater part of the people's consumption. Their personal rights need protection as much as men's, and only through full citizenship will justice be done to their claims.[1]

Margaret was born in Marylebone, London. Her father, John Llewelyn Davies, was a Christian Socialist and the rector of Marylebone church and chaplain to the king. Her mother, Mary, was the daughter of Mr Justice Crompton. Margaret's aunt, Emily Davies, was an equal-rights feminist who founded Girton College, Cambridge, which Margaret herself attended. After graduation, Mary began social work in Marylebone, where she encountered the Women's Co-operative Guild, which had been founded in 1883 under the Co-operative Society. She became the honorary secretary in 1889, which coincided with her family's move to Kirby Lonsdale in Westmorland. Margaret held her post until 1921, after which she became president. Under Margaret's influence, the organization shifted from being an adjunct to the male dominated Co-Operative Society to give a voice for working-class housewives in the women's movement. Margaret, an early advocate of women's suffrage, was one of two thousand women who signed a counter-appeal that Mrs Fawcett put together in response to the appeal against

Margaret Llewelyn Davies in 1912.

women's suffrage in 1889.[2] Margaret worked with Sarah Reddish, the organization's first full-time paid organizer to develop the Guild's national conference, regional committees and secure the organization's financial support.[3] In 1904, Margaret wrote a book, *The Women's Co-Operative Guild*, to explain the movement and provide an account of their early history. By 1922, the Guild had 52,000 members.

More than perhaps any other women in her era, Margaret Llewelyn Davies became a vociferous advocate of the needs of working-class married women. She gave evidence to the Royal Commission on Divorce, set up in 1909, arguing that the grounds for divorce should be the same for men and women, in favour of divorce being cheaper and suggesting, where necessary, the state should bear the cost.[4] The Women's Co-operative Society Annual Congress passed a resolution in 1912 demanding the introduction of two years' separation as grounds for divorce – something that was not implemented until the 1969 Divorce Act. The Guild's position was often at odds with many men in the mainstream co-operative movement.[5] In an era of growing state welfare, including the introduction of old age pensions and of national insurance, Margaret Llewelyn Davies articulated the needs and views of working women, when she explained:

> The most serious defect of the bill needing immediate amendment is the total exclusion of all married women who are not wage earners from sickness, medical disablement and sanatorium benefits. They consider that there is no justification for a sick insurance scheme being framed on any basis which should make this arbitrary distinction between women who contribute directly and those who contribute indirectly to the family's spending power. It means that roughly five million women are shut out from what is called a 'National' Insurance Bill.[6]

Margaret can be described as a suffragist, but she was painfully aware that women's petitions, letters and demonstrations did not get the newspaper coverage of the more militant tactics and wrote to the *Daily News* in 1908 to point out that:

> Women alone have no leverage and no 'last resource' and it is the neglect to which our position lays us open which drives women to adopt what are in themselves hateful and often ludicrous methods but which are dignified by the courage and self-sacrifice they entail.[7]

In 1909, she became joint honorary secretary of the People's Suffrage Federation with Mary Macarthur. Emily Hobhouse, who had done so much to advocate the horrors of the concentration camps set up by the British during the Boer War, was the chairman of the Executive Committee. This federation brought together women in the Co-operative Guild and the Women's Labour League who were concerned about the damage class divisions were causing within the wider suffrage movement. In a letter they penned to the *Cambridge Independent Press*, the three women explained that:

> If the House of Commons is to represent the people truly, every man and woman must have the vote independently of property and tenancy…. Property and tenancy qualifications would place women of the working class, whether married or single, at a great disadvantage on account of their low earnings, and because the working housewife though economically self-supporting, is unpaid.[8]

It was this universal suffrage that working-class women in the Women's Co-operative Society supported from 1904. Their congress in 1911 again carried a motion advocating adult suffrage, with only four dissensions amongst 600 delegates. At a related evening debate between Margaret Bondfield, in favour of adult suffrage, and an opponent of women's suffrage, Miss Bondfield won by a majority of one thousand to seven.[9]

Margaret and the Women's Co-operative Guild campaigned strongly for improved maternity care and for maternity benefits, to be paid to mothers, to be included in the amendment to the National Insurance Act of 1913. During their campaigns, letters were gathered from the membership about their experiences of pregnancy, childbirth and motherhood, which, in 1915, were published as *Maternity: Letters from Working Women*. By this time the First World War was underway and with the carnage on the Western Front, there was an increasing focus on maternal and infant welfare. Margaret was one of those who successfully advocated that local authorities should be empowered to make arrangements for securing the health of mothers and infants, pointing out that: 'We have at last begun to grapple with one of the most neglected and serious parts of human life'.[10] Empowering the local authorities to make arrangements was not the same as compelling them to do so and, until the introduction of the National Health Service in 1948, maternal care and maternal mortality rates varied from one region of the country to another.

The outbreak of war brought other challenges for Margaret, who was a committed pacifist. She was a signatory to Emily Hobhouse's 1914 *Open Christmas Letter* to the women of Germany and Austria; she supported the International Women's Peace Congress in The Hague in 1915, the War Resisters' International (WRI), and the General Council of the Union of Democratic Control, which called for negotiated peace.[11] She maintained her commitment to peace in the inter-war years and backed the Peace Pledge Union, War Resisters' International, the No More War movement, and the introduction of the wearing of white poppies on Remembrance Day to signify a commitment not only to remembering the dead, but to preventing further armed conflict and bloodshed.

Her work with the Co-operative movement also continued in the inter-war years, and she became the first woman president of the Co-operative Congress in 1922. Her left-wing political views did not diminish either: she supported the Russian Revolution, and chaired the Society for Cultural Relations with the USSR from 1924 to 1928. In 1931, she again gave working women a voice by putting together a collection of their memories in a book entitled *Life as We Have Known It*. Her close friend, the author Virginia Woolf, a member of both the Women's Co-operative Society and the Women's Institute Movement, wrote the introduction. The volume was published by the Hogarth Press, owned by Virginia and her husband Leonard Woolf, and the book was described in glowing terms by the *Sheffield Independent* under the heading England's 'Heroic Women', noting:

> The brave deeds so simply described in this book are being repeated day by day, year by year in a thousand homes scattered the length and breadth of Britain. They are stories by women who have had little to help them in a lifelong fight against drudgery and poverty.[12]

In her final years, Margaret's health failed and she died in 1944, during the Second World War. She left bequests in her will to both the International Co-operative Women's Guild and to the Peace Pledge Union, two causes close to her heart.

9

MARY HAYDEN (1862–1942)

History don and Irish Nationalist

Maggie Andrews

In 1912, the Irish academic, suffragist and women's rights campaigner, Mary Hayden declared that women's disenfranchisement was 'a flagrant and crying injustice, which should not be tolerated another instant'.[1] She appealed to politicians to take action, pointing out that the suffrage movement had:

> joined on this one issue without sacrificing our individual political opinion, and we ask the members of all parties in the British Parliament to help us obtain this measure of justice to women.[2]

Mary Hayden, the only daughter of Thomas and Mary Ann Hayden, was born into a comfortable middle-class Dublin home. Her father was a physician who became vice-president of the Royal College of Surgeons. She was educated at Catholic convents before obtaining a BA in Modern Languages, and then a Masters. Following two years of travel throughout Greece, India and the USA, where she tutored in women's colleges, she gained a Junior Fellowship in English and History at University College, Dublin in 1895.[3] She obtained this post by competitive examination; she tried unsuccessfully four times to get a Senior Fellowship. She never married, though was engaged for some time to a man who died of tuberculosis. For more than forty years she worked as an academic and educationalist, combining this with a strong commitment to fight for women's equality.

Women's education was one of her key concerns and, in 1902, she was a founder of the Irish Association of Women Graduates, and for many years gave talks or chaired their meetings across Ireland. She was also in demand as a lively public speaker for literary societies and adult education lectures. She became the vice president of the Women's National Health Association in Dublin, an organization set up to eliminate tuberculosis and reduce infant mortality in Ireland. Mary advocated training Irish girls for citizenship and her name frequently appears in the

newspapers as an active participant in numerous suffrage meetings. She contributed to debates, supported motions or gave speeches, and was often in demand as
an able chair of proceedings. In 1911, through her friendship with Anna Haslam,
she joined the Irish Women's Suffrage and Local Government Association; she was
also a member of the Irish Women's Franchise League.

The years from 1912 to 1914 are often regarded as the 'heyday of Irish
Suffragism',[4] but this was also the time when the Third Irish Home Bill was going
through the House of Commons; Irish suffragists felt that it should have included
Irish women's enfranchisement. Diana Hearne has suggested that at this time:
'… there was a distinct divide between suffragists who were primarily nationalists
and those who were primarily feminists.'[5]

Arguably, suffragists did not critique nationalism and home rule so much as the
attitudes to women and suffrage within this culture.[6] Many suffragists, like Mary
Hayden, saw the vote as one of a range of women's issues that needed addressing
and were not convinced that women's issues had a high priority in the culture of
nationalism. Religious and political differences were often obstacles to creating a
broad-based Irish Suffrage movement.[7] The Church Suffrage League was active
in Ireland, but when, during the First World War, the Dublin branch supported
the war effort and members made shirts for the British army, there was a strong
sense that the organization was very pro-British. Hence, in 1915, Mary Hayden (by
now a professor) and Mrs Stephen Gwynn founded the Irish Catholic Women's
Suffrage Association. This Dublin-based group met fortnightly, had a Celtic badge
in green, blue and white, was non-militant, aimed to involve working women and
had seventy members within four months.[8] A Catholic Women's Suffrage Society
had been set up in England in 1911, but in Ireland there was some resistance to
women's suffrage from some of the clergy in the Catholic Church. The organization
was primarily concerned with enfranchisement for women, but also involved in
social issues such as alcohol consumption. The association worked with other suffrage groups on women's issues and, for example, lobbied for the return of Ireland's
only female factory inspector.

Mary Hayden was a member of the Women's International League for Peace

Mary Hayden (far right) at the
Irish Literary Society.

and Freedom, committed to pacifism. Consequently, she did not approve of the violence used by those who sought to declare Irish independence in the Easter Rising of 1916. Although she opposed the rising, she had friendships with some of those involved. For example, in 1903 she and Patrick Pearse had holidayed together. Patrick, an Irish teacher, writer and barrister, was one of sixteen of the leaders of the rising who were executed in the aftermath. Suffragists were also concerned that woman's issues were being sidelined in the attempts to reach a constitutional solution in the months that followed. Mary was at a meeting of Irish Suffrage Societies, which urged that the claims of Irishwomen to the franchise be considered at a forthcoming Commonwealth conference in March 1917. They passed a resolution:

> That in the event of the Irish question being considered, the unanswerable claim of Irishwomen to the franchise shall form an integral part in any settlement to which the Conference gives its support, and in the event of a Government measure being introduced to enfranchise the women of Great Britain, we demand equality of treatment in Ireland.[9]

In 1922, the new Irish Constitution gave the vote to all women over the age of twenty-one, in line with the 1916 proclamation of the Easter Rising. Nevertheless, in the years that followed there were many concerns for feminists like Mary Hayden. In 1925, a motion was passed in the Irish national assembly, the Dáil, prohibiting divorce, and another bill that year attempted to limit women to lower grades of civil service while the criminal code banned artificial means of contraception.[10]

As a professor of modern Irish history, Mary Hayden published articles and reviews on eighteenth-century Ireland; her most famous publication was a textbook jointly authored with G. A. Monan called *A Short History of the Irish People from the Earliest Times*, which was widely used in schools for many years. She retired from her position at University College, Dublin, in 1938, but continued social welfare work with a working-girls' club in one of poorer districts of Dublin.[11] Before her retirement she was involved in one last campaign, against the new constitution introduced in Ireland in 1937. As the British House of Commons passed the 1922 Constitution, there was still some opposition to it, and a desire for a constitution created by the Irish people themselves. Mary, and many other women, opposed the position of women in some clauses of the new constitution. The document placed a very high value on marriage and women's domestic duties in the home while Article 40 provided for the right to life of the unborn child (and thereby prohibited abortion). Mary's involvement in the campaign for women's suffrage was successful in her lifetime; feminist challenges to the constitution have continued long after her death in 1942.

10

CLEMENCE ANNIE HOUSMAN (1861–1955)

Author, illustrator, engraver, tax resister and census evader

Maggie Andrews

In 1911, while in Swanage avoiding the census, Clemence wrote to her brother:

> After the enumerator came the registrar. He came yesterday morning, but was not at all troublesome and did not try to question beyond the necessary or persuade. He said he had to carry out his duty, and I said ditto, ditto.
>
> He would probably be going onto Mrs Smith and would find her flown for I think she was off about 9 and it was after 10.[1]

Clemence Annie Housman was born in Bromsgrove, Worcestershire, the third child of seven children born to Edward Housman, a solicitor, and his wife, Sarah Jane Williams who died before Clemence was ten years old. After her mother's death, the family moved to Valley House in the village of Foxbury, on the outskirts of Bromsgrove. In some respects Clemence's life was lived in the shadow of two of her

THE WOMEN'S LIBRARY COLLECTION, LSE LIBRARY

brothers. Her eldest brother was Alfred, a classical scholar and poet referred to as 'A.E. Housman', who wrote *Shropshire Lad* (1896). Her brother, Laurence, was four years younger than her and, after their mother's death, she looked after him. The two siblings also lived together for most of Clemence's adult life, initially in Lambeth when she studied at the South London School of Technical Art, then in a flat overlooking Battersea Common.

Clemence Housman (right) with her brother (middle).

Clemence worked as engraver for illustrated papers, first for *The Graphic*, then for private presses, claiming that 'masterly translation of beautiful works into black and white is worthy employment of the talent or genius of an artist'.[2]

In the 1890s, Laurence established a career as a dramatist and writer and Clemence published a novella, *The Were-Wolf* (1896), which was followed by two further novels *Unknown Sea* (1898) and, finally, *The Life of Sir Aglovale De Galis* (1905). *The Were-Wolf* is, as the title suggests, a gothic fantasy, which was described as giving voice to *fin de siècle* anxieties about changing roles for women.[3] Melissa Purdue has suggested the *The Were-Wolf* embodies contradictions that:

> plagued women at the end of the century – dutiful wife and mother or single, professional woman – and highlights both the potential and the danger of the New Woman.[4]

The idea of a New Woman encompassed the independent, single, educated, physically fit and free woman that was perceived to be emerging at the end of the nineteenth century. The bohemian London circle of friends that Clemence and her brother began to mix in had many such women, particularly when they settled in 1 Pembroke Cottages, just off Kensington High Street.[5] Their new home had an artist's studio at the back, which was to play a key role in the Edwardian suffrage movement.

Both Clemence and her brother Laurence became firmly committed to women's suffrage; Laurence was on the committee of the Men's League for Women's Suffrage and Clemence subscribed to the Women's Social and Political Union. The siblings formed the Suffrage Atelier, an Arts and Crafts Society that was based in their studio and which created pictorial publications to promote women's suffrage.[6] The Suffrage Atelier encouraged designing and making posters, banners, postcards and cartoons that supported the cause. Indeed, Laurence describes Clemence in his autobiography as the chief banner-maker to the suffrage movement between 1908 and 1914 and how women in numerous different groups, including the Church Suffrage League and Conservative and Unionist Women's Suffrage Association, marched behind banners she had made.

In 1910, Clemence became a member of the committee of the Women's Tax Resistance League.[7] Her brother later recalled in his autobiography how Clemence carefully planned her participation in this particular form of protest.[8] She purchased a holiday cottage, stocked it with furniture, occasionally stayed in it and, in due time, refused to pay the inhabited house duty of 4s 2d. Legal proceedings were begun against her and the costs of this slow procedure were added to her debt. Finally, after a warrant officer came to arrest her, and with her brother in tow, she was escorted to Holloway Prison in a taxi, which cost 4s 2d. The arrest acquired the desired publicity and a newspaper reported that:

Miss Clemence Housman, sister of the well-known dramatist and author, was arrested at her residence in Kensington, and removed to Holloway Gaol. It is understood that the lady, who is a passive resister, will be detained until the Government decides to release her, or until she pays the inhabited house duty – 4s 6d – for non-payment of which she was arrested.[9]

When the prison governor inquired how long she would be in prison for, she replied: 'For life. I am here until I pay and I am never going to pay.' Nor did she pay, but she was released after only a week in response to protests about the treatment of such a polite gentlewoman. In the same year, Clemence also took part in the 1911 census boycott, a campaigning tactic that Laurence and the Women's Freedom League promoted. Clemence went to Swanage during the census count. She filled only the words 'No Vote, No Census, Clemence Housman' on her census form. Her interaction with the census enumerator and registrar was always polite and restrained and the words 'information refused' were added. She returned home to London. On census night other women boycotting the census had hidden in her house. As it happened, there was no attempt to take legal action against any of the women who did not complete their forms, but brave, genteel forty-nine-year-old Clemence could not know this when she decided upon this course of passive resistance.[10]

After the First World War, Clemence and her brother went to live in Hampshire and then, in 1924, moved to Street in Somerset, where their friends, the Clark family, lived and on whose orchard they built a house. It was in Somerset that Clemence died on 6 December 1955.

THE WOMEN'S LIBRARY COLLECTION, LSE LIBRARY

WSPU banner-making.

11

MILLICENT 'HETTY' MACKENZIE (1863–1942)

Professor, educationalist and campaigner

Maggie Andrews

As vice-president of the Cardiff Women's Suffrage Society, the Millicent Mackenzie name appears at the bottom of a letter to *The South Wales Daily News*, critical of the actions of militant suffragettes. The letter ended with the pronouncement that:

> We believe that it is vital for the interests of the nation that the just claims of women to share in the duties and delights of citizenship should no longer be ignored, and we know that the patience, the earnest purpose, and the steady efforts of the constitutional suffragists are gaining the support of public opinion, and that the cause of right and justice will triumph over the forces of reaction.[1]

Hester Millicent Hughes was born in Clifton, a wealthy suburb of Bristol where she initially went to school before completing her education in Switzerland. Her career in education began when she attended Cambridge Teacher Training College. Her father was a prominent figure in the town and her brother Donald Hughes became an artist. By 1891 Hetty (as she was known) was personally involved in training teachers at the University College of South Wales and Monmouthshire, where she also took an active role in setting up the college school. It was while working in Cardiff that she met and married in 1898 John Stuart Mackenzie, a professor of philosophy at the college. Unusually in this era, Hetty, now in

Millicent 'Hetty' Mackenzie.

CARDIFF UNIVERSITY ARCHIVES

her mid-thirties and already established in her career, continued to work after her marriage. She had already co-authored her first book, *Training of Teachers in the United States*, with Amy Blanche Bramwell in 1894 and went on to publish *Moral Education: the Task of the Teacher* in 1909. In 1904 she was appointed the head of the teacher training college for female students in Cardiff and Associate Professor of Education.[2]

Her progressive views on education, which included co-education in teacher training, a greater emphasis on children learning through exploration, and the provision of school meals, were also expressed at public lectures and meetings and reported in local newspapers. She argued that experimental schools should be set up in which:

> meals should be cooked and served and in which mending and making, washing and cleaning should be taught practically. Arithmetic reading and writing ought to take a secondary place in this curriculum.[3]

Hetty's prioritizing of domestic skills over academic learning, for girls to learn only that which directly related to home life or to the development of character, should not be judged too harshly. Hetty was acutely aware of the poverty and poor nutrition experienced by working-class women and girls and sought to improve the material circumstance of their lives immediately. This middle-class, educated and feminist woman's thinking was grounded in her knowledge about working-class women's lives and her realistic understanding of their life chances gained from her and her husband's involvement in the Settlement Movement in Cardiff. Settlement houses were set up in working-class districts of Britain's 'Great Towns' to provide educational activities to underprivileged children and support for their families. Unusually, the settlement house, which Cardiff University college staff and students participated in was intended for girls as well as boys. There was a clothing club, savings bank, and funds for both Christmas dinner and outings for girls. Some forty-five to sixty young women attended the club on Tuesday afternoons where the volunteers sang, read or played games with them.[4]

Both Hetty and her husband joined the Labour Party and she also became strongly involved in the campaigns for women's suffrage. The Women's Social and Political Union set up a branch in Cardiff in 1906, and Hetty Mackenzie is sometimes referred to as their organizer in the area, perhaps because she co-founded the Cardiff and District Women's Suffrage Society in 1908. Whether it was expedient because of her career or, as her letter to the paper in 1909 suggests, because she condemned their tactics – Millicent Mackenzie was not a suffragette, but a suffragist. Although Cardiff had a reputation for anti-suffrage activity and an anti-women's suffrage Liberal MP, the Suffrage Society initially had seventy members and by 1914 was the largest branch outside of London with a membership of 1,200.[5] One of the Cardiff group's first activities was participation in a London demonstration of over 10,000 women who marched from Embankment to the Royal Albert Hall in June 1908 before participating in a meeting. The Cardiff branch, marching behind their banner displaying a red dragon, would have been near the front of the procession, which was organized so that branches marched together in alphabetical order.[6]

Hetty continued both her commitment to suffrage work and the Settlement when she was appointed the first female professor of a fully chartered university in the United Kingdom in 1910. She continued in her role as Professor of Education (Women) until 1915, taking an active role in the university where she was elected to the Senate in 1909. Both Hetty and her husband took early retirement in 1915 in order to write and travel. She had by then become interested in the approaches to education being developed in other European countries and, as she explained in a paper titled 'Ideals from Abroad', she felt that it was the business of teachers:

> to strive much more to understand people than had been the case hitherto. In fitting themselves for the task they might get help from the East, for some of the methods of the East would supplement the methods employed in the West.[7]

Like many others in the suffrage movement, Hetty was becoming interested in the ideas of Theosophy and the methods of educationalist and philosopher Rudolph Steiner. Her association with the university was, however, not yet over. The Cardiff and District Women's Suffrage Society became the Women Citizens' Association when some women achieved the franchise in 1918 and campaigned for equal citizenship, while Hetty was the only female candidate in Wales in the 1918 general election. She attempted to become the Cardiff University MP, a candidate for one of the university seats that existed at the time. Hetty's was one of the first results to be announced – as a Labour candidate she had been firmly beaten by the Rt Hon. H. Lewis, who stood on a Conservative and Liberal coalition ticket and obtained 739 votes to her 176.[8]

In the post-war era, Millicent 'Hetty' Mackenzie became a major proponent of Rudolph Steiner's ideas. In 1921, she organized a visit by a group of teachers to his headquarters in Donarch, Switzerland, and the following year she organized a conference, at Keble College, Oxford, at which Steiner spoke. There were 230 attendees at the conference held under the auspices of the Anthroposophical Society of Great Britain, which served to promote Steiner's philosophies and the importance of studying a spiritual path to freedom. Hetty was the secretary for the society, which had a number of learned and influential members. Hetty continued to write and perhaps her most famous book was *Freedom in Education: An Inquiry into its Meaning, Value, and Condition* (1925), which expressed her spirit of free adventure and her commitment to Eastern philosophies. She suggested:

It is those who accept a spiritual interpretation of the universe and believe in the possibility of human life transcending its present stage of manifestation, that freedom as an end in education makes its strongest appeal….

And linking all to the freedom, which a Steiner approach to education promotes, she indicated that, in her view, it was:

… probable that as time goes on we shall rely more and more upon the children themselves to suggest the kind of education to be given.

Millicent 'Hetty' Mackenzie died on 10 December 1942 in the village of Brockweir, near Chepstow, in Gloucestershire, where she and her husband spent their latter years. She left an estate of £5,572 and bequeathed her cat – Corfu – a sum of £5 a year for its maintenance to her friend Mrs M. C. Williams, who lived nearby in Yew Tree Cottage.[9]

12

LADY ISABEL MARGESSON (1863–1946)

An eclectic supporter of multiple causes

Lesley Spiers

In July 1914, Lady Isabel Margesson took a letter addressed to the king on behalf of Mrs Emmeline Pankhurst, which demanded for the second time that he grant suffragettes an interview. She was not deterred by being refused admission, and she valiantly tried again the following morning, such was the determination of this audacious woman.[1]

Lady Isabel Margesson was born in 1863, the daughter of Frederick John Hobart-Hampden, Lord Hobart, and Catherine Annesley Carr. A descendant of John Hampden, an infamous English politician from the seventeenth century, Isabel Hobart-Hampden had a privileged, country house style upbringing, and fulfilled social expectations when, in 1886, she married Sir Mortimer Margesson. She quickly settled into her marital, and subsequent maternal, role giving birth between 1887 and 1902 to five children: three girls and two boys. However, only the two boys survived her and her youngest daughter died aged just seven years old.

While domesticity and the maternal realm may have been important in Lady Margesson's life, it also appears to have been insufficient to occupy her as numerous endeavours, enterprises and commitment to causes and campaigns testify. She did not confine herself to one or two missions and even found time to invent the 'Lady Isobel' apron fastener, which was reportedly something that was immensely useful to women in '… solving the difficult question of how to hold neatly in place the waistband and shoulder straps of an apron.'[2] In 1894, Isabel became honorary secretary of the Belgravia branch of

Lady Isabel Margesson in 1921.

67

the Parents' National Educational Union. In the same year, she edited a series of articles in a text entitled *A Handbook for Beginners in the Study of Natural Science*.[3] By 1895, Isabel Margesson, with others, founded the Sesame Club and she became a member of its executive committee. The club offered a literary and educational programme to both women and men, but, to attract professional women, it offered a lower subscription to teachers.

Lady Margesson's public engagement intensified when she became involved in the campaign for women's suffrage in 1904 as a member of the National Union of Women's Suffrage Societies (NUWSS) and president of the newly opened branch in Redditch. However, her formal connection with this organization lasted only two years when she resigned and joined the Women's Social and Political Union (WSPU), escalating her involvement so that by February 1909 she was a very active speaker while continuing to be asked by Birmingham NUWSS to appear on its platforms at meetings. Over the next five years Isabel Margesson travelled, initially locally and then nationally, to promote the cause of women's suffrage, and her participation and involvement helped to build her reputation as a public speaker able to use rhetorical flourishes when needed. For example, in April 1909, she presided over the Warwick and Leamington Women's Suffrage Society annual meeting, and, on 11 June in the same year, attended a meeting at the Anerley Town Hall held under the auspices of the Beckenham branch of the London Society for Women's Suffrage, an organization with Mrs Millicent Fawcett as its president. Isabel made an impassioned speech:

> Woman was coming out, not only in England, but all over the world, the spirit of the time was calling her to do something which civilisation knew must be done.[4]

Such rallying cries were well received and Isabel used this platform to raise her profile as a fully committed supporter of women's suffrage, unafraid of putting forward questions linking women's work and wages to their under-representation. By the end of that year, once again, Lady Margesson delivered another rousing speech at a Woman's Suffrage Branch meeting at the Town Hall, Cheltenham. She was reported to have said that, '… this movement was now regarded as one of civilisation'. Furthermore, that '… The Suffrage movement was only a call to woman to take her part in the larger sphere of life.'[5]

Lady Isabel Margesson was a woman who appeared to defy pigeonholing or stereotyping, and her activities moved beyond patronage and 'do-gooding'. This woman symbolizes what Leneman argues is the problem with some accounts of the suffrage campaign and organizations, of tending to present the women involved as either '… law-abiding suffragist or militant suffragette'. For many, their support and allegiance crossed the supposed divide.[6] This position would truly reflect that of Lady Margesson whose activity involved her in a plethora of causes, campaigns and organizations. But she was not the only woman in her family to be involved in the suffrage movement. Her daughter, Catherine, was the WSPU organizer in Reading who later became secretary for industries for the National Federation of Women's Institutes. Like her mother, Catherine also supported militant action and, in October 1909, was arrested for obstructing the footway in The Strand by chalking 'Votes for Women' on the pavement. She could have been imprisoned for seven days, but her fine was paid. Far from being ashamed of this action, Isabel, speaking at a Women's Freedom League meeting the following year, openly talked of never having been involved in any militant action, but having the honour of a daughter who had. Her support of militant action was articulated again in December 1912 when, in response to media reports of damage by suffragettes to pillar boxes, she stated:

> We are making war to provide peace. Recent developments in post offices were an object lesson to people too stupid to appreciate reason.[7]

In November 1913, Lady Isabel Margesson presided at yet another meeting – this time with the Women's Tax Resistance League in the Royal Concert Hall, St Leonards and Hastings. Here she boldly put forward a resolution that if women were denied equality they were:

> ... justified in resisting taxation until women had the same control over national expenditure as male taxpayers possess ... But [she added] there was a bitter opponent to reason ... and that was called prejudice.[8]

All this activity led to the most illustrious moment in Lady Margesson's campaigning when she chaired the much-reported riotous meeting on 9 March 1914 at St Andrews Hall in Glasgow, where Mrs Pankhurst was re-arrested. At a meeting on the following evening in Edinburgh, with Isabel again in the chair, she declared that Mrs Pankhurst's arrest, and absence at this meeting, was a '... disappointment in their hearts ... [but of] no ordinary kind ... [rather it] was coloured by indignation and anger ... because it came from injustice.'[9]

At the outbreak of the First World War, Lady Margesson's focus was diverted from the suffrage campaign, but her drive and commitment did not diminish. In January 1915, she attended a preliminary meeting to consider organizing a Women's Volunteer Reserve in Birmingham. Later that year, she gave the address at the thirteenth annual meeting of the Birmingham and District Lady Clark's Society, where she laid great stress on the significant number of women who were employed in a range of patriotic activities and the significance of the work they were undertaking. She also channelled her energies into food production, both working on her own land and encouraging women to work in agriculture, as a member of the Worcestershire Women's Sub-Committee of the County War and Agricultural Committee. She set up a nursery in Barnt Green, Bromsgrove, and later founded the first Women's Institute in Worcestershire, at her home. She also served on both the Worcestershire and National Federation of Women's Institutes Executive Committees, and went on to set up and speak at the numerous other WIs that sprung up around the country.

Lady Margesson's energies and interests were not confined to the war effort or the suffrage campaigns. In the inter-war years, she continued to be a proponent of vegetarianism, a member of the Eugenics Society, to support the National Council for the Unmarried Mother and her Child, promote Montessori and Froebel education, women police, became president of the Anti-Vivisection League and, in December 1921, was appointed a JP and was added to the Commission of the Peace for Worcestershire.[10] Isabel continued to support a truly eclectic array of causes and organizations that she felt were important until her death on 1 July 1946.

13

ALICE HAWKINS (1863–1947)

Working-class militant and trades union organizer

Janis Lomas

One Sunday evening at Leicester Market Alice was addressing a crowd when a man shouted at her: 'Get back to your family.' Alice replied: 'But here is my family, they are here to support me.' And indeed they were, with Alfred and their children (all teenagers) standing by her side.[1]

Alice's early childhood in Stafford, and then Leicester, was impoverished. Aged thirteen, she found work as a machinist in the Equity shoe factory in Leicester, which was run as a workers' cooperative, with workers encouraged to engage in political activity. But even in this progressive factory, Alice was dismayed to find that a female machinist was paid only half the earnings of a male machinist for the same job. She had joined the Independent Labour Party (ILP) in 1892 and, through this organization, had come into contact with Emmeline and Christabel Pankhurst. Like them, she became disenchanted by the ILP's relative lack of interest in women's enfranchisement. In 1907, Alice Hawkins travelled to London to attend her first rally, followed by a march to the House of Commons to demand that Parliament grant women the vote.

THE WOMEN'S LIBRARY COLLECTION, LSE LIBRARY

Procession for release of suffrage prisoners.

71

A cordon of policemen confronted the marchers and tried to prevent the women from reaching Parliament by breaking up the procession, but the hundreds of women refused to be turned away. Suddenly, the mounted police charged at the women, who scattered to avoid the horses' hooves. Over fifty women were roughly handled and arrested, including Alice Hawkins and Christabel Pankhurst.

At that time, suffrage prisoners were imprisoned in the first division of prisoners, thereby avoiding the harshest aspects of prison conditions. Even so, her fourteen days spent in Holloway Prison affected Alice profoundly and increased her determination to fight for the vote and to better the position of working women in her community. Over 200 suffragettes greeted the prisoners on their release, a band played outside the gates and they were taken to a restaurant in central London for breakfast, attended by supporters including George Bernard Shaw. At the breakfast, Alice read out a letter she had received from her local MP, Ramsay Macdonald. In it, he expressed his regret at her arrest, but was critical of her actions, which, he stated, would seriously damage the cause of women's suffrage. On her return home, Alice invited Sylvia Pankhurst to speak and mobilize women shoe-workers, whereupon she decided to found a local WSPU branch with help from Sylvia and the WSPU organizer, Mary Gawthorpe.

In June 1908, Alice was one of the women speakers at the huge Hyde Park demonstration known as Women's Sunday. Twenty wagons served as platforms and Alice was one of the eighty speakers who braved the hecklers and addressed the crowd, estimated to be between 250,000 and 500,000.[2] The following year, Alice was arrested in Leicester for trying to gain entrance to a meeting held by Winston Churchill, from which women were refused entry. During this term of imprisonment, she went on hunger strike and was released after five days. Her husband, Alfred, with whom she had six children, fully supported Alice's actions and was with her when she was ejected from the meeting. Indeed, he went back into the meeting and spoke on the women's behalf, demanding of Churchill: 'Why don't they [the government] secure the support of women of the country? How dare you stand on a democratic platform?'[3] He too was thrown out of the meeting and arrested. Alice, in line with WSPU policy, refused to pay her fine and was imprisoned. Alfred, a working man with a family to support, could not afford to go to prison, so he paid his fine.

The following year, both Alice and Alfred were in trouble again when Alice was arrested after Black Friday for breaking the windows of Viscount Harcourt, the Secretary of State for the Colonies. She was given fourteen days' imprisonment. At the same time, Alfred was thrown down a flight of stairs by young Liberal party stewards after being ejected from a hall in Bradford for heckling Churchill. He suffered a knee broken in two places and had to spend a month in hospital. When news of his injuries reached the WSPU, Mrs Pankhurst paid Alice's fine to get her released to look after Alfred and their six children. However, Alfred did finally get some recompense as The Men's Political Union raised funds to sue the Liberal Party and Alfred was awarded £100 damages for his injuries.[4] In the 1911 census, Alfred is still listed as an invalid. To add to the couple's troubles, their youngest son, Tom, died suddenly of blood poisoning. Emmeline Pankhurst sent them a heartfelt condolence letter as she had also lost her son the previous year.

Alice continued to work in the Equity shoe factory. However, in 1911 she was again imprisoned in Holloway – this time for three weeks after breaking a Home Office window. In all, Alice was imprisoned five times: twice in Holloway and three times in Leicester. In the midst of all her suffrage activity she also began to campaign to get women equal wages with men doing the same job in the shoe factory and, in 1911, she founded the Independent National Union of Women Boot and Shoe Workers and, by 1913, had already served twice on the executive of the Leicester Trades Council.[5] She frequently travelled to London to take part in WSPU rallies, meetings and marches while working in the factory and spending her Sundays cycling to outlying villages drumming up support amongst women shoe workers for both her trades union and the cause of women's suffrage. In 1913, Alice was one of the working women who met Chancellor of the Exchequer, David Lloyd George, in a meeting organized by Sylvia Pankhurst. Representatives from various trades were chosen to try to persuade the Chancellor to give working women the vote. Apparently, Alice spoke to Lloyd George about her two sons – one in the army, the other in the Royal Navy – who had the vote, pointing out that the woman who had brought them into the world had 'no say and was looked down on'.[6]

The First World War curtailed WSPU activities and from then on Alice focused on trying to improve pay and conditions for working women. Both Alfred and Alice remained committed Socialists and worked for a more equal society for the rest of their lives.

14

CONSTANCE ANTONINA (NINA) BOYLE (1865–1943)

Founder of the Women's Police Service

Lisa Cox-Davies

In July 1913, Constance Antonina (Nina) Boyle used a launch on the River Thames to give a speech to MPs and their guests who had been enjoying tea on the terrace of the House of Commons. It was reported that diners:

> … left their tea tables and crowded to the parapet, where before long there was an audience of from 150 to 200 who listened with good humour to an address from Nina Boyle.[1]

Nina Boyle was born in 1865 in Bexley, Kent, the second daughter and the fifth of six children born to Frances and Robert Boyle, a captain in the Royal Artillery and a descendant of the Clan Boyle and the Earls of Glasgow. When Nina was four years old her father died, leaving her mother to care for six children. Little is known about the first decades of her life, but she eventually went to South Africa where she worked as a journalist for the *Transvaal Leader*, as well as a nurse during the Boer War. Nina never married, but campaigned for those suffering discriminatory treatment, writing to *The Times* highlighting the treatment of both Boer and loyalist refugees. She also founded the Women's Enfranchisement League of Johannesburg.

Upon her return to England, in 1911, Nina became active in the Victoria League and the Colonial Intelligence League for Educated Women, although she later resigned from the latter as she believed they were anti-suffrage.[2] She then joined the Women's Freedom League (WFL), speaking regularly at meetings and was subsequently elected to the executive committee, becoming the political secretary. Nina campaigned diligently on behalf of the WFL; in 1913, she and three other members of the executive committee wrote to every police force urging them not to re-arrest women who had been released from prison under the 'Cat and Mouse Act'. However, she also had a sense that stunts provoked more publicity for the cause and took centre stage in several of these and the subsequent court cases. Nina was arrested on several occasions during the suffrage campaign and was imprisoned on three occasions. In 1913, she and Anna Munro were sentenced to fourteen days' imprisonment for an obstruction offence after attempting to speak in Hyde Park. The two women were transported to Holloway Prison in a prison van, which also contained male prisoners, and they found themselves subjected to lewd gestures. Nina and Anna complained about their treatment and the matter was investigated by the Home Office, which obtained accounts from other suffragists who also alleged that they had been subjected to the same type of treatment.[3] Recommendations were made that

Two early women police officers, Mrs Edith Watson (left) and Miss Nina Boyle (right), both in uniform.

separate transportation be used for women or that vans were altered to convey men and women separately. If any action was taken, it was not to Nina's satisfaction, as she complained about the issue again following another arrest in 1914.

The enfranchisement of women was just one strand of the WFL's campaign: they also focused on the poor treatment women and children received in police stations and at the hands of the judicial system. The WFL highlighted the issue of women and children being forced to give evidence alone about sexual matters; at the time, the practice was for the presiding judge or magistrate to clear the courtroom of all women to protect them from having to hear sexual matters being discussed. The unfortunate consequence of this was victims were left alone in a courtroom full of men, and that children were forced to give evidence without the support of their mother.[4] Nina's fellow suffragette, Edith Watson, monitored as many court cases as she could, but when it became clear that the Home Office was reluctant to tackle the issue, Nina decided upon direct action. On Saturday 11 July 1914, Nina and four other suffragettes chained themselves to the door handle of the waiting room of Marlborough Street Police Station. They were subsequently arrested and charged with obstruction. In court, Nina took delight in ridiculing the prosecution case and drew further attention from the press, advising the magistrate that a question in cross-examination was irrelevant: 'Now, now Mr Campbell, you must not do it. It's naughty', and rebuking a police sergeant: 'I know it is not fashionable in this court to tell the truth but do try'.[5]

After the outbreak of the First World War, Sir Edward Henry, Commissioner of the Metropolitan Police, called for special constables. Nina wrote to him, asking if women may also fulfil this role. Without waiting for a reply, she began recruiting women, advertising in the suffrage newspaper, *The Vote*, for volunteers willing to undertake this role, on a part-time basis. Nina was aware that the recently passed Defence of the Realm Act would impact heavily on women's rights and it was crucial that a female role be established within policing to allow the law to be implemented fairly. Unbeknown to Nina, a wealthy philanthropist, Margaret Damer-Dawson, had also begun to recruit women to address anxieties that unsupervised crowds of Belgian refugees were falling victim to white slavers. Damer-Dawson had the support of Sir Edward Henry, who was not against the idea of women patrols, but was averse to the idea of working with Nina whose suffragist activities had not endeared her to the Metropolitan Police.[6] Nina and Damer-Dawson amalgamated and the Women Police Volunteers (WPV) were duly established, with Damer-Dawson as the head and Boyle, who was still fully committed to the suffrage campaign, as her deputy.

This partnership did not last long, as Nina was concerned about the direction the WPV was taking. Their officers had worked in Grantham enforcing a restriction order and curfew against women and raiding houses in conjunction with the military. Boyle considered such actions against the interests of women while Damer-Dawson believed that by working with the authorities women's place in policing would be cemented.[7] In February 1915, Nina demanded that Margaret Damer-Dawson resign her leadership. However, she called a meeting of the whole corps, which overwhelmingly voted against Boyle. Damer-Dawson resigned and formed her own patrols, the Women's Police Service. Nina's involvement with the WPV continued for a little longer; patrols were mainly in Brighton and the organization pursued a policy of training women to be present in courts within London. By the middle of 1916 the WPV had faded away and Nina had moved onto other projects. She continued to work with the WFL, supporting the Women Suffrage National Aid Corps, and regularly writing articles for *The Vote*. In 1916, Nina travelled to Macedonia and Serbia where she worked in hospitals, later taking charge of one, and was awarded the Samaritan and Allied medals for her work.

Following the success of the 1918 Representation of the People Act, Nina predicted that the next challenge would be to 'test the question whether women have the right to stand for Parliament.'[8] In March 1918, Nina put herself forward as a candidate in the Keighley by-election and declared that if she was refused she would be prepared to contest the issue in court and obtain a judicial ruling. Nina's nomination paper was declared invalid as one signatory was not an elector and the other resided outside the constituency in which she was standing. It is unclear as to why more care was not taken in choosing signatories. Was there a lack of support for Nina and the WFL in the constituency? Was it that Nina did not want to commit to being an MP, and sought to restrict her ability to pursue other causes? Yet she could claim a moral triumph as her actions established the principle that a woman could stand for election as an MP; the returning officer confirmed that if her nomination paper had been in order then the nomination would have been accepted. In November that year this principle was formally enshrined in law with the passing of the Parliament (Qualification of Women) Act.

Throughout the 1920s and 1930s, Nina continued to campaign on behalf of others; she was closely involved with the work of the Save the Children Fund and, in 1921, travelled to Russia to work there for the organization. In addition to working for Save the Children, Nina campaigned for equal pay on behalf of the National Union of Women Teachers and throughout the 1920s she raised awareness of women's rights in Africa, campaigning against the practice of a bride's family paying a dowry to the groom's family, which she equated to a form of slavery. In 1923 and 1929, Nina raised the matter with the League of Nations, urging the organization to take action. She also wrote several articles published in *Women's Leader* criticizing the League of Nations, as well as the Colonial Office and humanitarian organizations for ignoring the issue.[9]

Nina also wrote several novels, which featured strong women characters and which were mainly adventure and mystery based. In later life, she moved towards the right politically; her travels in Russia had led her to become a staunch anti-Communist. In 1921, she spoke at a British Empire Union meeting and, during the Second World War, supported the 'Never Again' Association. In 1943, Nina Boyle died in London at the age of seventy-seven.

15

JENNIE BAINES (1866–1951)

Working-class firebrand

Janis Lomas

The *Nottingham Evening Post* reported Jennie's arrest in 1906 under three headlines: 'A Silly Martyrdom'; 'Rowdyism the High Road to Notoriety'; and 'Suffragists' Xmas in Prison'. The newspaper quoted the commissioner of police as saying in court that he did not wish the women to spend Christmas in jail even if they refused to pay the fine, but the presiding magistrate replied: 'I don't consider when giving sentences whether Xmas Day intervenes or not'. He then fined each woman 20s (£1) and, when they refused to pay, they were remanded in custody for fourteen days, meaning that they would indeed spend Christmas in Holloway Prison.[1]

Jennie, who was also known as Sarah Jane, was born into a working-class family in Birmingham. Her father, James Hunt, was a gun-maker and Jennie herself started work in Joseph Chamberlain's ordnance factory at the age of eleven. Her parents were members of the Salvation Army and, as a young teenager, she helped them in their work. Aged twenty, Jennie was sent to work as an evangelist in Bolton, at a working-men's mission; she was also a member of the Temperance Society. She married George Baines, a shoemaker, when she was twenty-four and had five children, two of whom died in infancy. George's wages of 25s (£1.25) a week were insufficient to keep the family, so Jennie worked as a sewing machinist in Stockport, near Manchester, where they lived. At this time, she joined the Independent Labour Party (ILP).

Jennie was one of the early Women's Social and Political Union (WSPU) supporters who advocated militant action and George Baines, himself a staunch Socialist and trades unionist, supported Jennie's activism. She met Emmeline Pankhurst in 1903 and was present at the Manchester Town Hall when Christabel Pankhurst and Annie Kenney were arrested in October 1905. She later contended that it was the treatment of the two women that spurred her to join the WSPU. Despite her family's lack of means, for two years she worked as a voluntary worker for the WSPU, with her expenses paid, but no fixed salary. In April 1908, she was appointed a paid organizer in the Midlands and North of England at a wage of £2. Her militant activities created havoc in her home life; she even spent Christmas in prison after being arrested for demanding the vote in the lobby of the House of Commons on 18 December 1906. It was the first time that she had been arrested and she had been with other protestors demanding votes for women in the main lobby of the Houses of Parliament. Arrests of suffragettes were still something of a novelty at that time and the women's arrests were widely reported. The *Aberdeen People's Journal* dismissed her arrest and court proceedings in 1906 with the headline 'Another batch of shriekers'.[2] Unlike middle-class suffragettes who had servants, Jennie was reliant on her twenty-year-old daughter keeping things going at home during her imprisonment, although she might have been glad to escape domestic chores, as her granddaughter later said that Jennie 'was a rotten cook and housekeeper'.[3] Whether true or not Jennie was to endure many sentences, in between which she travelled widely, spoke at countless meetings, addressed crowds at factory gates, helped to organize, support and set up new WSPU branches, working closely with Adela Pankhurst, Mary Gawthorpe and others.

In June 1908, Jennie was a main speaker at a large demonstration in Hyde Park and in November that year was charged with taking part in an unlawful assembly and of inciting a crowd to storm the doors of the Leeds Coliseum while Prime Minister Asquith and Herbert Gladstone were inside holding a meeting. This offence was deemed so serious that she was indicted to be tried by jury in

Mass rally in Hyde Park organized by WSPU in 1908.

THE WOMEN'S LIBRARY COLLECTION, LSE LIBRARY

Leeds. Her defence unsuccessfully attempted to subpoena Gladstone and Asquith to appear,[4] and Jennie protested that she had no intention of causing a riot. When she was found guilty, the judge offered her the chance to go free if she agreed to be bound over to keep the peace, but she refused, stating as her reason that: 'I do not recognise the laws of this court administered by men'.[5] Consequently, she served six weeks' imprisonment in Armley Jail, Leeds. She was the first suffragette to stand trial by jury and her release was an opportunity for publicity. She was met by a large crowd, a band playing 'The Cock o' the North' and representatives from the WSPU headquarters in London before being taken by a carriage drawn by mill girls dressed in shawls and clogs to a special breakfast three miles away.[6]

In July 1912, Jennie was arrested along with fellow suffragettes, Mary Leigh and Gladys Evans, for attempting to burn down the Dublin Theatre Royal, the night before Prime Minister Herbert Asquith was due to speak, and was sentenced to seven months' hard labour. But she was released five days later, after she went on a hunger and thirst strike. Jennie was never force-fed as she was considered too frail to endure this gruelling ordeal. However, going on hunger strike was detrimental to her health and she developed St Vitus Dance (now called Sydenham's Chorea) and shook uncontrollably. Despite this debilitating condition, she continued with her militant activities until, in July 1913, she was arrested with her husband and son, Wilfred, and accused of attempting to blow up an empty railway carriage. She always protested her innocence of the charge, stating in court that had she been guilty she would have admitted it as she had always done previously. Before the trial, the WSPU arranged for her and her daughter and youngest son to be spirited away on board a ship bound for Australia. She left her husband and son to stand trial but, as they had clear alibis, the trial collapsed and they joined her in Australia, where they settled in Melbourne, Victoria, in early 1914.

In Australia, Jennie found that she was something of a celebrity: women in Victoria had finally gained the vote in 1908 – some six years after other Australian states, although the women's movement there was one of the largest in Australia. She was in demand as a speaker, albeit somewhat overshadowed when Adela Pankhurst arrived in Melbourne in April 1914, sent into exile by her mother with a £20 note and a couple of letters of introduction. Adela and Jennie both joined the Victorian Socialist Party and the Women's Peace Army, and threw themselves into opposing the First World War. During the conflict, they continued to work together on various causes, in opposition to the war and against conscription. As food shortages became commonplace, they shared a platform and led marches of 2,000–3,000 women to protest at rising prices and food shortages.[7] Their actions led them to be arrested several times during the war.

In 1919, Jennie had her last spell in prison as one of a group who raised the banned Red Flag on Founder's Day (26 January). She was sentenced to one month's imprisonment, but given seven days' grace to think about agreeing to be bound over. During that time, she continued to speak in support of the Russian Revolution and to fly the Red Flag. She was finally sentenced to six months' imprisonment in March 1919. Dragged from the dock, she exclaimed, 'If I do not obtain a speedy release, my death will lie at your door', and then went on hunger strike. She was the first Australian prisoner to do so.[8] In the 1920s, after a dalliance with the Australian Communist Party (founded by Adela Pankhurst), she eventually returned to the Labour Party and concentrated on issues concerning women and children. In 1928, she was appointed a probation officer, and then a special magistrate, to the South Melbourne Children's Court, a position she held for the next twenty years. She still gave speeches up to a few months before her death in 1951. The *Australian Dictionary of Biography* states that Jennie was imprisoned fifteen times in total.[9] Perhaps her grandson summed her up the best when he described her as 'a firebrand, a real firebrand'.[10]

16

EMMA SPROSON (1867–1936)

'Red Emma'

Linda Pike

On 23 May 1911, a newspaper carried the headline 'Suffragette will not pay licence for dog and goes to prison,' elaborating:

> At Wolverhampton to-day Emma Sproson, married, a member of the executive of the Women's Freedom League was sent to prison for seven days in default of paying a fine for keeping a dog without a licence.[1]

Emma Sproson (née Lloyd) was born in Wolverhampton in 1867, one of seven children in a working-class family of a canal boat builder. At the age of nine, she moved to the Daisy Bank area of Bilston, where she began her working life as a half-timer, a child who spent half his or her time in employment. Describing herself as a 'child from the lower depth', Emma had left school entirely by the age of thirteen.[2]

Emma joined the Independent Labour Party in 1895, where she met her future husband, postman and artist Frank Sproson, the secretary for the Wolverhampton branch. Their enlightened political views provided a mutual attraction; Frank believed in sex equality and never denied his wife the freedom of action he also claimed for himself. She joined the WSPU and, in February 1907, joined 700 other suffragettes in a march on the Houses of Parliament. As a result, Emma and six other women were arrested and sent to Holloway Prison for fourteen days. Emma, who had a young baby, had probably not expected to be incarcerated for so long and while in prison apparently suffered from engorged breasts.[3]

Yet, despite the awful food and conditions that were detrimental to her health, Emma continued her campaign for women's enfranchisement after her release. A month later, on 18 March 1907, Emma and another fellow Wolverhampton suffragette, Elizabeth Price, were arrested again, resulting in the mother of three being sentenced to a month in prison where she spent her fortieth birthday. In

THE WOMEN'S LIBRARY COLLECTION, LSE LIBRARY

Edith How-Martyn, Mrs Sproson, Charlotte Despard and Miss Tite
standing outside the Women's Freedom League offices in the Victoria Institute.

1907, Emma was one of a number of women who, concerned about the escalating militancy and autocratic leadership of the WSPU, formed the Women's Freedom League (WFL). This change of organizational allegiance did not prevent Emma clashing with the authorities as she campaigned for women's suffrage. In July 1908, she appeared in a Cheltenham police court for chalking an advertisement for a WFL meeting on the pavement. The local newspaper reported that when:

> asked if she had anything to say, Mrs Sproson said that the court was established on laws made by the will of man and in which women had no say; therefore she did not consider it the proper authority to try her. She would refuse to make any promise, pay any fine or enter into any recognisance.
>
> There was an outburst of applause, and the Chairman exclaimed: We cannot allow that. If it is repeated we must clear the court.[4]

Emma's radical suffragism led her to join the Tax Resistance League when it was formed in 1909. Dog licences were one of the few taxes a working-class woman like Emma could be liable for and so, when she refused to pay it, she was consequently sent to Stafford Jail. She did not, it appears, join the 1911 census boycott that the

WFL strongly advocated. In her memoirs, which are now held in Wolverhampton Archives, she claimed to have removed the females that slept in her house from the census form. However, this may be what she would have *liked* to have done because, apart from her occupation and birthplace, she is compliant with the census, stating on it that she has been married for fifteen years with sons aged eleven and four, and a daughter of fourteen.[5]

Although Emma was a member of the WFL National Executive Committee, she apparently became disenchanted with Charlotte Despard's autocratic style of leadership, and resigned in 1912. It appears that she was not alone in her unease over the direction of the organization. She and six other senior members announced in a number of newspapers that:

> We the undersigned have severed our connections with the Women's Freedom League, as we disagree with the internal administration of the League sanctioned by the recent conference.[6]

Nevertheless, in August 1912 she is reported as leading a campaign to support a Labour candidate in a Manchester election on behalf of the WFL.[7] She fades from suffragette politics at this point, but may have become involved with one of the lesser well-documented or well-known organizations. Alternatively, like so many militant suffragettes, she may have become too mentally and physically exhausted to continue. During the First World War, Emma helped to provide food for the needy in the National Kitchens in Darlington Street, Wolverhampton. It was during this time that she noticed, and attacked, the provision of poor housing conditions in the town and brought this to the attention of the press in the Socialist magazine, the *Wolverhampton Worker*. In a letter to the Wolverhampton *Express & Star*, she commented that emancipation should be a natural evolutionary course, and criticized the opinions of anti-suffragists who accused women in British colonies, like Australia and New Zealand, who had already obtained female suffrage as having little or no morality.[8]

When, in 1918, women were enfranchised, Emma wholeheartedly embraced the opportunities this offered politicized women, and she stood as a candidate in the local council elections in Wolverhampton's Park Ward in 1919 and 1920. Despite losing both times, she was tenacious and her perseverance paid off when she won the Dunstall Ward in 1921, beating her rival 1,765 votes to 1,600, thus giving Wolverhampton its first female councillor. Ironically, the man who committed her to prison for not paying tax as a protest against women's political disability, was appointed to declare her the first woman councillor! On hearing of the milestone victory, she symbolically waved a red flag on the Town Hall balcony, an act that – controversial in the aftermath of the Russian Revolution – gave her the nickname of 'Red Emma'. However, she commented in the local paper that red flags had always been carried through public streets on May Day and that the true meaning of the red flag is international brotherhood, which alone would bring international peace; any inference that the red flag stood for revolution was, according to Emma, 'trifling with fire'.[9]

She was outspoken as a councillor and continued her commitment for women's rights and injustice on committee work, helping the blind, distressed and the mentally ill. However, her somewhat dogged persistence and outspokenness about abuse, malpractice and the corruption that was prevalent in the Borough Fever Hospital at Heath Town led to her being removed from the Council's Health Committee, while those exposed of financial irregularities were exonerated. True to her character, even though she was censured by the Labour Party, she wrote a pamphlet, *Fever Hospital Facts and Fairy Tales*, to prove certain goods were stolen and to give ratepayers an opportunity to form their own opinions. She discovered that the staff were underpaid and badly treated and, by highlighting their plight, laundresses' wages increased by 50 per cent and hours were reduced, while seamstress' wages doubled.[10]

Following rifts in the Labour Party in 1927, Emma stood as an Independent Socialist candidate for the town, but lost. While she continued to campaign on behalf of the disadvantaged and, in October 1936, blamed the rise of juvenile crime on films, her health deteriorated. On her death at her home in 1936, the *Birmingham Daily Gazette* described her as 'an ardent feminist and formerly a militant suffragette and storm-centre of many local controversies'.[11] The achievements of this remarkable working-class, Black Country woman are now recognized by a blue plaque on Wolverhampton's Magistrates Court, in the old Town Hall where she received her soubriquet of 'Red Emma'.

17

COUNTESS CONSTANCE MARKIEVICZ (1868–1927)

Irish Nationalist and first woman elected to the House of Commons

Maggie Andrews

Speaking in public for the first time on Christmas Eve in 1896, Constance argued:

> Now in order to attain to any political reforms, you all know that the first step is to form societies to agitate and force the government to realize that a very large class have a grievance and will never stop making themselves disagreeable until it is righted.[1]

Constance Markievicz was born Constance Gore-Booth in 1868, in London. Her father, Sir Henry William Gore-Booth, was the fifth baronet of Lissadell, an Arctic explorer and adventurer. As one of five children of a wealthy Anglo-Irish land-owning family, her childhood was spent at Lissadell House, County Sligo, where she was educated by a series of governesses, enjoyed a privileged world of parties and social events, and gained a reputation as an expert and daredevil rider. At the age of twenty-five, rather than making a conventional society marriage, Constance arrived in London to train at the Slade School of Art. There she was introduced to a more independent, Bohemian lifestyle and joined the National Union of Women's Suffrage Societies.

In 1896, one of her sisters, Eva, convalescing in Italy after a respiratory illness, met Esther Roper, the daughter of a Manchester factory-worker; the two became partners working for women's suffrage, social welfare and against war. According to Anne Haverty, by the autumn of 1896, the three Gore-Booth sisters – Eva, Constance and Mabel – were 'preoccupied with women's suffrage' and the master of the local Sligo Hunt Club said that 'they discussed little else even in the field between runs in the course of a day's hunt.'[2] In December that year, Eva and Constance set up what was only the third branch of the Irish Women's Suffrage and Local Government Association in Sligo, Constance was president, Eva was honorary secretary.[3]

Constance next went to study at the Académie Julian in Paris and there she met the Polish aristocrat, Count Casimir Dunin de Markievicz, who, when they married in September 1900, was a widower with a son. Their daughter, Maeve, was born the following year and, by 1903, the couple were living in a fashionable house in Dublin and involved in the literary and cultural life of the city, painting, acting and partying. In the years that followed, Constance became increasingly politicized, in the suffrage

Dublin Easter Rising as reported on the front page of *Daily Sketch*, 1 May 1916.

movement, Socialism, trade union politics and Irish nationalism. Her daughter spent much of her time with her grandmother, while Eva often supported and sustained her sister Constance when she was ill or in prison.

Lauren Arrington describes Constance as initially involved in the women's nationalist movement group, Daughters of Ireland, for whom women's suffrage was a thorny and divisive issue. While her sister Eva became embedded in the suffrage campaigns in Manchester, Constance resisted the Irish suffrage movement aping their British counterparts and began to argue that the priority for Irish women should not be the vote but instead an Irish 'Parliament to be represented in'.[4] The political activities in which she engaged suggest a more complex negotiation of priorities as circumstances dictated, and she challenged injustice. When the Liberal government proposed the introduction of a licensing bill (1908) that would restrict both pubs' opening hours and the number of licences issued and, in effect, ban the employment of women, Constance and her sister Eva championed the cause of barmaids, seeing it as a female issue. They worked with Esther Roper in Manchester to oppose the Liberal, Winston Churchill, in a by-election. The two sisters campaigned in a coach, drawn by four white horses, which Constance drove. They made speeches from the roof of the carriage and when a man in the crowd heckled Constance, inquiring 'Can you cook a dinner?', she replied, 'Certainly,' cracking her whip and adding, 'Can you drive a coach-and-four?' Constance later summed up her beliefs as: 'Sinn Féin and the liberty and justice for women and for countries. Fair play for everybody all round is what I want.'[5]

In 1911, it was her nationalist politics and opposition to any celebration of the coronation that led to her appearance in court. In 1912, Constance attended a meeting of various suffrage groups that objected to the 1912 Home Rule Bill not including the enfranchisement of women. During the 1913 industrial unrest in Dublin, which began with a tram-workers' strike and led to lock-outs and riots, she made inspirational speeches and engaged in traditionally female areas of welfare politics. A newspaper later recalled how:

> … she revealed during these riots the human side of her complex nature by labouring indefatigably to provide a soup kitchen for a thousand poor children who were perilously close to starvation.[6]

Her growing involvement in the nationalist movement included her designing the blue flag with a golden sun emerging from the bottom corner, which remains part of the iconography of the Irish Republican movement. She also founded the republican boy scouts, Na Fianna Éireann as a response to the imperialism and pro-English stance of Baden-Powell's Boy Scout movement. As well as engaging in camp-craft and scouting, Constance prepared the boys to fight for their country's independence. She must have come across as an unconventional and exotic figure to these boys. She was tall, a skilled shot, unconventional in her dress, with a cigarette hanging out of her mouth and a little dog at her heels. In time, some of these lads became involved in gun-running and the 1916 Easter Rising.

Constance Markievicz remains the most well known of the 200 women who took part in the Easter Rising against British imperial rule in Dublin on Easter Monday, 1916. The republican revolutionaries sought to occupy strategic buildings within the city and Markievicz was both a sniper and second in command of the group that took over and held St Stephen's Green for several days, despite heavy retaliation from the British army. When the republicans surrendered, the ringleaders, including Constance were court-marshalled and sentenced to death. Some were executed, however, within days the newspapers reported:

> Sir John Maxwell has exercised clemency in commuting the sentences in the other cases to terms of penal servitude. One of these was that of the notorious Countess Constance Markievicz, who as she surrendered to the British officer, kissed her revolver before handing it to him.[7]

Such stories of Markievicz's actions alongside her role in the Dublin lock-out developed Constance's iconic reputation and contributed to her decisive victory in the

December 1918 election, where she became the MP for St Patrick's Division in Dublin. She was the only one of the seventeen female candidates in Britain and Ireland to be successful, and became the first woman to be elected to the British House of Commons. As a prisoner at Holloway, she could not participate in the campaign or any celebrations. As a member of Sinn Féin, she chose not to sit in the House of Commons, but, when released from prison in March 1919, it is said that she visited Parliament to see her name on a peg in the cloakroom, an emblem of her success and that of the struggle for women's suffrage.

The first Dáil, the parliament of the revolutionary Irish Republic, met in Dublin during her absence; she, like many of those elected, was described as 'imprisoned by the foreign enemy'. On her return to a tumultuous welcome in Ireland, she was appointed Minister of Labour, holding the post until January 1922, the first Irish female Cabinet Minister and the first woman to be a government minister in Europe. However, the bitter civil war that surrounded the establishment of Irish Free State in 1922 curtailed her participation in government and it was 1979 before Ireland appointed another women to the cabinet. Constance died in 1927 in Sir Patrick Dun's hospital in Dublin, reconciled with her daughter and stepson, with her by then estranged husband at her side. She has iconic status in Ireland, but in other parts of Europe, the first elected woman British MP is often forgotten.

A Groundswell of Support

18

ADA NEILD CHEW (1870–1945)

Socialist and mail-order entrepreneur

Janis Lomas

Ada Chew campaigned for working women. Under the title of 'All in a Day's Work', she apparently gave an account in the *Englishwoman* magazine:

> of the life of a married factory hand in Lancashire, the most striking feature of which is that the man and his wife do the same work in the factory, but the woman in addition keeps the home clean and comfortable in her 'spare time'.[1]

Ada Neild was born on a small farm in Butts End, near Talke, North Stafford-shire, the eldest daughter in a family of thirteen children. As her only living sister had epilepsy, it was Ada who had to help her mother with the chores and look after her younger brothers. What meagre schooling she had came to an end when, aged eleven, she and her family moved to Worcestershire where they became tenants of a farm near Malvern. Eventually, her father gave up the struggle to make a living from the land and the family moved to Crewe, where he toiled in a brick factory.

Ada worked in a shop, then taught in a school in Lincolnshire for a time, but by the early 1890s she was working in a factory in Crewe making uniforms for soldiers. She noted that when the government inspectors came around, men were put to sewing in the uniform sleeves, but when the inspectors left, women resumed putting in the sleeves, as they usually did. When she asked why, she was told that men received 1s 5d (7p) an hour, while the women were only paid 5d (2p). The contract was based on men's pay enabling the factory owner to pocket the difference. Incensed by the pay and conditions endured by the women factory workers, she took a radical step. In May 1894,

THE WOMEN'S LIBRARY COLLECTION, LSE LIBRARY

NUWSS badge.

Ada Neild wrote the first in what became a series of letters to the *Crewe Chronicle*. Signing herself 'A Crewe Factory Girl', she described the life of women working in factories, explaining in one letter that in busy periods women took work home after a nine-hour day. Their motivation was to make enough money to tide them over in the slack periods when they could not earn even their 8/- (40p) weekly pittance. Her impassioned plea asked readers to put themselves in the position of Crewe factory girls:

> Are you prepared, my reader, to come and work hard with us 9 hours in the factory, and then to come home with us and begin again and sew till you can sew no longer from sheer fatigue – such fatigue as some of you, I hope have not felt – and then to rise early again with some of us and do a little more before it is time to wend our way back for another day of it.[2]

She detailed the anomalies and injustices the women worked under and in the last letter proposed that working girls should organize and join a trades union; in doing this, she jeopardized her job and antagonized her employer. It had become obvious during the course of the letters which factory she was working in and, to turn the workforce against her, her employer closed the tea-room and the sick bay, blaming the letter writer for these actions. One tailor and twelve girls who supported her views were sacked, even though as a last resort, Ada revealed her identity and resigned her own position, hoping that by doing so she could prevent their dismissal. She now joined the Independent Labour Party (ILP), where she met her future husband, George Chew, an ex-weaver and organizer for the ILP. Ada spoke at a meeting organized by the National Union of Gas-workers and General Labourers, alongside Eleanor Marx. Unusually, this trades union made it clear it would welcome women tailoresses as members. The government also promised to examine the contracts placed with manufacturers to see if they were adequate to pay workers a living wage.

Ada's well-publicized stand against sweated labour meant that she had become well known in the Crewe area and, in 1894, she was invited to stand as a Poor Law Guardian in Nantwich, Cheshire. She struggled to improve the conditions the inmates were enduring, but found that most of the other guardians resisted any move in that direction because they were more interested in cutting costs and objected to the idea that those described as 'capables' should support 'incapables'.[3] Ada also travelled around the North of England in a horse-drawn caravan, marshalling support for the ILP and then, from 1900 to 1908, worked with Mary Macarthur as a paid organizer for the Women's Trade Union League (WTUL), undertaking the difficult task of interesting women workers in trades unionism. Mary Macarthur and Ada divided the country between them, with Ada having the North, the Midlands and Scotland. Women were perceived as harder to organize than men, as they had to rush home after a day's work to do housework and cooking for their families and so could not attend meetings. Nevertheless, the two women's efforts helped women's trades union membership to treble in these years. When Ada's daughter was born in 1898, she often accompanied her mother who was travelling from town to town to hold meetings and form union branches. After seeing the drudgery of her own mother's life, Ada had decided she would only have one child.[4] Instead, she continued her political activities, even standing unsuccessfully as a Socialist candidate for the school board in Rochdale in 1900.[5]

Ada was a fervent believer in women's suffrage. However, she took issue with Christabel Pankhurst in a series of letters published in *The Clarion*, in which she argued against any property qualification being used as the basis of women's right to vote. Ada wanted all women and men to have the right to vote equally: '… not because they are more fortunate financially than their fellow men and women'.[6] A lifelong vegetarian and a member of the Fabian Women's Group, Ada began working as an organizer for the National Union of Women's Suffrage Societies (NUWSS) in Rossendale near her home in Rochdale in 1911. When Labour promised to enfranchise women if elected in 1912, the NUWSS supported Labour candidates and Ada took an active role in several local by-elections. None of the Labour candidates was elected, although the suffragist intervention may have helped to prevent the Liberal being elected.

During the First World War, Ada was a pacifist and her political work tailed off, although she worked for the Mayor's Central Relief Committee and the Women's International League for Peace and Freedom, and continued to write articles for *Common Cause*, the periodical of the NUWSS, as well as for other publications or short stories, often with a suffrage theme. As time went on she became increasingly worried and fearful of having an impoverished old age and of being a burden on her daughter, so concentrated on building her own mail-order drapery business and worked fifteen-hour days to ensure her financial security. She never lost her zeal for women's equality. Finally, her long-desired wish came to fruition when, in 1928, women were able to cast their vote on equal terms with men. In the years that followed, as her hard work in her business paid off, she was able to buy her own house and to travel on several foreign holidays, including a four-month, around the world trip on a cruise liner. She drifted apart from her husband in the 1930s as his views became more conservative, although they never completely lost touch. She lived just long enough to see the first majority Labour government elected in July 1945. This event heralded in an era during which some of the worst disadvantages that working women had laboured under were removed and when the welfare state and the NHS were introduced. By the time of her death in December 1945, Ada had also fulfilled her wish to be independent both financially and physically.

19

KITTY MARION (1871–1944)

Actress, hunger striker and birth control campaigner

Janis Lomas

Kitty Marion was arrested after stone throwing in Newcastle in July 1909; she was sentenced to a month's imprisonment. When released from prison, she remained defiant and told the WSPU newspaper, *Votes for Women*, 'I am more than ever convinced of the necessity for militant action'.[1]

Kitty was an only child and her early life was extremely difficult. Born Katherina Schafer in Westphalia, Germany in 1871, she was only six years old when both her mother and stepfather died of tuberculosis, leaving her in the care of a tyrannical father, who appears to have abused her physically and psychologically. When she was just fifteen she left home for good and travelled to England to live with an aunt. Within three years she had changed her name to Kitty Marion, learned English and established herself as a singer, dancer and actress. Starting in a pantomime chorus in Glasgow, she gradually became a named artiste in music halls the length and breadth of Britain. She also appeared on the same bills as big stars such as Vesta Tilley and Marie Lloyd, and performed in musical comedies and pantomimes in provincial theatres up and down the country. However, she refused to succumb to the advances of theatrical agents, some of whom demanded sexual favours in return for bookings. This so outraged Kitty that she became an activist in the Actors' Association and the Variety Artists Federation (VAF). At one VAF meeting held to discuss financial woes and the corruption of agents, she interrupted the meeting by shouting, 'They won't give me work because I won't kiss them', which caused the meeting to burst into laughter amid shouts of 'Bravo!'

In 1908, Kitty Marion joined the Brighton

THE WOMEN'S LIBRARY COLLECTION, LSE LIBRARY

Kitty Marion.

branch of the WSPU, starting as a newspaper seller in Piccadilly Circus, London, but soon moving on to militant activities. She took part in an attempt to present a petition at the Houses of Parliament in June 1909. After being roughly treated by the police, she described the treatment the women received:

> Plain-clothes police who were posing as a 'hostile crowd' broke our ranks by shouldering in and pushing us away in every direction and, as each of us tried to proceed singly towards the House, petition in hand, two and three policemen, one on each side taking us by the arm and shoulder, quite unnecessarily pinching and bruising the soft underarm, with the third often pushing at the back…. Many a small woman, I caught and prevented from falling…. Aching in body and soul, I went home at last to find my arms and shoulders black and blue and painful, as were every woman's who had taken part in this rightful, legal, peaceful petitioning.[2]

Kitty also joined the Actresses' Franchise League (AFL). The AFL did not undertake militant action; its aim was to work for the vote through education, selling suffrage literature and staging propaganda plays. Even so, the AFL often supported the WSPU in various non-violent ways: by fundraising at their plays and events, helping to disguise WSPU activists trying to escape re-arrest under the 'Cat and Mouse Act' and by singing outside Holloway to keep up the spirits of the prisoners undergoing hunger strikes and forced feeding.

Kitty was arrested and went on hunger strikes on several occasions, carrying out activities up and down the country, her previous experiences of working all over the provinces proving to be useful. She knew where good, cheap lodging houses were to be found and, as militant action became ever more desperate, she became an active member of the WSPU's secret arson campaign in 1913. When convicted and imprisoned, she continued her protests. She broke windows, took doors off hinges, ripped pillows and mattresses, broke gas lines, and even set fire to her cell. Additionally, she embarked upon numerous hunger strikes, which were met with violent forcible feedings. On some occasions, feedings were conducted up to three times a day, despite her often begging prison officers to spare her as she was so fearful of damaging her vocal chords and thereby losing her livelihood. In her memoir, she tried to detail the experience of being forcibly fed while acknowledging that 'there are no words to describe the horrible revolting sensations'.[3]

Kitty continued to commit attacks, including an attempt to question Lloyd George at the National Eisteddfod where she was very roughly manhandled, later describing how 'my hair was torn down, handfuls grabbed from every side, and pulled up by the roots. My clothes were ripped back and front, even my very undergarments were torn to shreds'.[4] Her most serious sentence was for setting fire to Hurst Park racecourse grandstand, for which she was sentenced to three years' imprisonment. In all, Kitty Marion was forcibly fed no fewer than 232 times, often being released in a very weak and life-threatening condition, only to be re-arrested under the 'Cat and Mouse Act' as soon as she had recovered. Her suffragette activities ruined her stage career as theatre managers often refused to employ her and she missed performances while in prison, but she refused to give up and only stopped committing serious offences when the outbreak of the First World War brought the cessation of WSPU activity. When Britain declared war with Germany, Kitty, being German by birth, had to register as an enemy alien and was threatened with deportation to Germany. It was only due to the intervention of two influential suffragettes – Lady Constance Lytton and Emmeline Pethick-Lawrence – that she was allowed to leave the country for America, her fare being paid by her suffragette friends.

She arrived in New York in 1915 virtually penniless but hoping to resume her stage career. However, her reputation as a convicted militant activist meant that she was unable to find stage work. Her radicalism also alienated her from American suffragettes, who were much more conservative than Kitty. She eventually found work when she met Margaret Sanger, the American birth control activist who opened the first birth control clinic in America. Kitty became a newspaper seller for the birth control cause for the next thirteen years. Yet, for many older suffragettes, birth control had no place in the suffrage campaign – a fact poignantly illustrated by the treatment she received from Emmeline Pankhurst. When Kitty heard of Emmeline's visit to New York she was excited and imagined a happy reunion with her. She wrote:

> I pictured a joyous meeting, should she come along and see me sell the *Birth Control Review*. I felt sure that with her knowledge of the unspeakable poverty-stricken, overcrowded slum conditions in England she would be delighted with my present activities … One afternoon at Macy's corner she did appear with Miss Pine, dear old 'Piney' who, in her Nursing Home had been such a good, Ministering Angel to me and other hunger strikers. I saw them crossing Broadway and my heart beat high in anticipation of our mutual pleasure of a reunion … when they did see me, their faces hardened, their heads went up and they passed me, staring stonily in front of them. I felt stunned, hurt to the quick.[5]

She was never to see Emmeline again. She had a hard time promoting birth control, being arrested several times for violating obscenity laws and imprisoned for thirty days in 1918. She was granted US citizenship in 1924. She returned to London in 1930 to attend the unveiling of the statue to Mrs Pankhurst and began work in the Birth Control International Centre under Edith How Martyn. However, she finally returned to New York where she worked in Sanger's office once more before retiring to the Margaret Sanger Home in New York State, where she died in 1944.

20

ADA CROFT BAKER (1871–1962)

Magistrate and alderman

Carol Frankish

Ada's adherence to 'the cause' of women's suffrage is recorded in local newspapers, which carry reports of her forthright delivery when speaking in support of women gaining the vote. She became a well-known and sought-after speaker on behalf of women's suffrage in North Lincolnshire.[1]

Ada Croft Baker as pictured in the local newspaper during her time as an Alderman.

Ada Croft Baker, who was born Ada Grant in 1871, was a native of the seaside town of Cleethorpes, where she became one of the town's most esteemed and respected inhabitants. Ada's family was well established in Cleethorpes: her forbears had rights to the Cleethorpes' oyster beds; her grandmother was one of the first caterers for seaside holiday-makers; and, in Ada's childhood, her father had become a wealthy trawler owner. The Grants were well-known trawler and smack owners who, along with others of the fishing fraternity in Grimsby and Cleethorpes, had embraced suffrage ideology from the 1870s. Ada's interest in women's suffrage stemmed from her family and her Methodist upbringing in an area where non-conformism with its associated political agenda was commonplace. However, after 1883 interest in the suffrage movement waned in the area,[2] so the Women's Liberal Association, which was formed in 1900 in Grimsby, became the local focus for women's politics.[3]

It was Ada's involvement as chairman of the local Liberal organization until the outbreak of the First World War[4] that spurred her into action to fight for women's enfranchisement. In 1912, a public meeting on women's suffrage was held in Grimsby, chaired by the daughter of the Bishop of Lincoln. Subsequently, a local women's suffrage society, affiliated to the law-abiding National Union of Women's Suffrage Societies (NUWSS), was re-founded in the town.[5] Although Ada is not recorded as holding an office in this organization, as a committed Christian, a Liberal and a suffrage supporter, this is the group that Ada would have been in sympathy with and where she would have found many others who shared her values. Like so many women, hers was a quiet, determined support for suffrage, which often goes under the radar; she gave speeches to support the cause and no doubt raised funds and attended sales of work and events held across Lincolnshire.

Ada married Harold Croft Baker, a sailing smack skipper who later founded a trawling firm and became a wealthy man. Despite having seven children, Ada continued throughout her marriage and motherhood to carry out both suffrage activities and other public duties. In 1914, in common with other suffragists, her attention was turned to the war effort. With a colleague, she formed a local, successful Women's Emergency Corps (WEC), whose objective was the entertainment and provision of food for troops drafted into the Cleethorpes area. She was made president of the Grimsby Temperance Society during the conflict, so it is safe to assume that the comforts offered to the troops did not include a glass of beer! She was involved in many other war services, including membership of the Food Control Committee, being a member of the Prince of Wales Fund Committee, and also acting as a Ministry of Pensions Representative for the War Pensions Committee.[6] In an interview in 1935 she stated that her adherence to temperance stemmed from her work with the War Pensions Committee, adding that 'Intoxicants are best left alone. It is always the women that suffer.'[7]

Ada's personal values and morality were deeply embedded in her strict Wesleyan Methodist and staunch temperance upbringing, as well as her belief in the rights of women. She had a strong commitment to public service, which was not restricted to wartime. In 1919, she stood for election to the county council and was duly elected as the first woman in Lincolnshire to gain a council seat, where she was later joined by the first English-born female MP, Margaret Wintringham. The following year, in 1920, she was appointed the first woman magistrate in Lincolnshire and remained on the bench until she was seventy-five.[8] Soon after joining the county council, she became a member of the Maternity and Child Welfare Committee; within three years she was its chairman. In 1935, she seemed to be achieving her goal, saying in an interview with *The Grimsby News*:

> The work has grown tremendously and I am very proud of the interest the council is manifesting in child welfare work. I have been loyally supported by the council members.[9]

Partly as a result of her work on this committee, and partly because of her experiences with the War Pensions investigations, her interest in child welfare and maternity services increased. Her husband died in 1928, leaving her a wealthy woman. In 1929, she purchased The Mount, a large house in Cleethorpes, and gifted it to the county council, with instructions that the building was to be used as a maternity hospital, with the proviso that patients only paid according to their means.[10]

Throughout her long life, Ada continued to be prominent in the public services of Grimsby and Cleethorpes and was eventually made an alderman. As well as her positions as county councillor and magistrate, her long list of commitments included being: on the board of Lincolnshire Nursing Association; governor of two Cleethorpes grammar schools; a member of the Child Welfare Association; and governor of Grimsby and District Hospital. In addition to all this public service, she remained, for many years, until her son took the reins, head of the firm of Messrs H. Croft Baker and Sons Ltd, trawler owners.[11] In 1961, Ada turned down an MBE in the Queen's Birthday Honours of that year; a fact that was only made public by the Cabinet Office in 2012.[12]

Ada's long record of public service dated from her involvement with the Women's Liberal Association in 1900 until her retirement as a county councillor in the 1960s. Her commitment to local politics was passed to her son, Jack, who also became an alderman and mayor of Cleethorpes during the Second World War. Ada's legacy to her home town was not just the Croft Baker Maternity Home, which remained open right through her lifetime (only closing in 1984), but also by her own example, her belief in a woman's ability to achieve prominence and satisfaction outside the domestic sphere. 'A great life, nobly lived' was the tribute given to Ada Croft Baker by the minister at her funeral in 1962 – a very justifiable accolade for a women whose work spanned two centuries and included local politics, welfare and campaigning on women's issues, including the suffrage.

21

CATHERINE BLAIR (1872–1946)

Founder of the Scottish Women's Rural Institutes

Maggie Andrews

Catherine Blair's farmhouse was a refuge for suffragettes recovering from hunger strike and hiding from the authorities to avoid re-arrest following the passing of the 'Cat and Mouse Act'.

> She recounted that on one occasion a fugitive suffragette was relaxing in her garden while reading the newspaper report about her disappearance and probable escape to France![1]

Catherine Blair was the third of Susan and James Shields' six children, born and brought up in Bathgate, West Lothian and educated at Bathgate Academy. Apparently, after seeing how hard her father worked, she once vowed that she would never marry a farmer. Nevertheless, in 1894 she married James Blair, a tenant farmer. The couple raised their four children (two girls and two boys) at Hoprig

THE WOMEN'S LIBRARY COLLECTION, LSE LIBRARY

Mains Farm, Gladsmuir, in East Lothian. In her thirties, Catherine Blair joined the militant Women's Social and Political Union (WSPU). As a farmer's wife, with four small children, she somehow managed to fit in a busy schedule: speech-giving, letter-writing, and chairing meetings of the local organization. She did not engage in actions that could lead to imprisonment, but her strong support and

Scottish suffragettes.

defence of those who did, led to her providing both refuge for them and hiding them within her home. Without the safe havens provided by the likes of Catherine Blair and her family, Scottish suffragettes would not have been able to continue their various militant antics. Indeed, her husband's support for her activities led to his resignation from his role as vice-chairmen of the local Liberal party in protest at the Liberal Government's policy on women's suffrage.

Her commitment to improving women's position in society did not cease with the outbreak of the First World War. She was acutely aware of the isolation, poverty and hard work that dominated most women's lives. Catherine, like other members of the farming community, was heavily involved in work to feed the nation; something that became particularly important when submarine warfare increased in 1916 and many of the ships carrying the imported food on which Britain relied were sunk. In her memoir she recalls:

> At a meeting in Glasgow (December 13, 1916) I urged the formation of Women's Institutes to help food production and conservation. My plea was sympathetically received and when, following the Discussion Society meeting, a Scottish Council of Agriculture was formed to deal with the conditions affecting Agricultural Development, I was appointed to represent women's interests and given a remit to report on the conditions affecting the social life in the country.[2]

She was determined that the nearest village to her farmhouse – Macmerry – should have the first women's institute in Scotland. The original plan to meet in the school room in January 1917 was thwarted by an outbreak of measles and so the first meeting was in Longniddry in June 1917 at a meeting chaired by Catherine. The speaker for the occasion was the Canadian Mrs Watt, who was funded by the Board of Agriculture to promote the Women's Institute across Britain. Catherine herself summed up the role of this new organization – popularly referred to in Scotland as 'the Rurals' – as:

> ... centres for social and educational intercourse, and for co-operative effort. They unite women in the effort to lighten the labour of the home and to beautify it; to increase food supply; to use that food to the best advantage; to deal with proper distribution of food; and to consider all questions relating to the welfare of children or otherwise directly affecting the home.[3]

In ensuring the progress of the Women's Institute Movement in Scotland, Catherine Blair was assisted by other suffrage supporters, including Nannie Brown, who walked the whole 400 miles from Edinburgh to London in a march organized by the Women's Freedom League in 1912 to present a petition to the prime minister. A long-standing friend of Catherine, Nannie also worked with her for both the Board of Agriculture and the Scottish Women's Rural Institutes (SWRI).

If in wartime the Rurals prioritized food production, in peacetime they sought to remove the isolation of rural housewives, to allow them to regain their individuality, their creativity and their independence in a new world in which at least some of them were enfranchised. With such ends in mind, in 1919 Catherine Blair set up the Mak'Merry Pottery. Like its English and Welsh counterparts, the SWRI had sought to run co-operative produce and sell food items initially and then craft work, but Catherine believed pottery enabled women to both make money and to express themselves artistically. True to her feminist and suffrage roots, she set up a pottery in a shed on her farm. Women painted and designed pots and taught women in other institutes the craft, which provided much needed extra income. Mak'Merry items became famous the world over and are still highly collectable today.[4]

The role of a farmer's wife, working with the SWRI, and organizing the pottery might have been enough to keep most women busy, but Catherine also became involved in setting up the Lothian Home Arts Guild of Craftswomen and became a magistrate in June 1921. Eleven years later, Catherine and her husband retired and moved to North Berwick; he died four years later, in 1936. She published a history of the SWRI in 1940 and undertook voluntary work for the Red Cross and Polish Relief Fund during the Second World War. Her suffragette independence and social conscience were in no way dampened; she campaigned for housing for the homeless and other social issues.[5] She vehemently opposed the SWRI's decision to take government grants, which she thought would compromise its political independence. She strongly believed that institute members should co-operate and run the movement themselves. In 1941, she addressed the Scottish National Party in Edinburgh to argue for the importance of post-war education, which she suggested should cover:

> not education in the narrow sense of school lessons, nor even in the wider sense of earning a living, but education in how to live, how each individual could discover and develop his own qualities and capacities to the best advantage. The fact that many of our brothers and sisters did not know how to live was brought home to us by the evacuation scheme revelations.[6]

After her death on 18 November 1946, Catherine was cremated at Warriston Crematorium, Edinburgh. She will be remembered for a lifetime spent seeking to improve rural women's lives in many different ways.

22

EDITH RIGBY (1872–1948)

Arsonist, WI activist and bee-keeper

Maggie Andrews

On the night of 6 July 1913, an explosion shook the Liverpool Corn Exchange and surrounding buildings, although it caused little damage. Three days later, Edith Rigby explained to Detective Superintendent Duckworth, 'I am surrendering for an explosion in the Exchange Building'. Edith went on to elaborate:

> … because I bundled the matter on Saturday night. I should have put a label on the package and I am now offering myself as a human label … The reason I have come to surrender today is to draw the attention of the Government to give women the vote.[1]

Edith Rigby was born in Preston, the second of Alexander and Mary Rayner's seven children. Her father was a surgeon, but they lived in a working-class area of the town and she grew up aware of the very great material differences between her home life and that of other families who lived nearby. She was educated at Penrhos College, North Wales, a Methodist, girls-only boarding school with the motto *semper ad lucem* ('always towards the light'). She was apparently the first woman to ride a bicycle in Preston. She was a tall blonde, quietly spoken with a quirky individualistic dress style and short hair. In 1893, when not yet aged twenty-one, Edith married Charles Rigby, a doctor who seems to have been supportive of Edith's forward-thinking, feminist ideas. Unusually, she was always known by her own first name: as Mrs Edith Rigby rather than as Mrs Charles Rigby, which was the more common mode of address for married women at the time. The couple did not have children, but in 1905 adopted a two-year-old boy called Arthur.

Edith was a committed Socialist, involved in the

Edith Rigby.

Independent Labour Party (ILP) and on the executive committee of the Women's Labour League. She entertained the Labour Leader, Keir Hardie, at her home, and a contemporary claimed of her:

> Edith was very critical of her neighbours in Winkley Square where she lived with her doctor husband, Charles. They confined their servants to the attics or basements during non-working hours. Her own maids had the run of the house, eating in the dining room, having the evenings free and did not wear uniforms which Edith considered badges of servitude.[2]

Edith, like many women involved in suffrage campaigns, initially undertook welfare and educational work. She sought to improve the working conditions of young women and set up an 'after-mill club' for girls who worked in the cotton mills, which employed so many women in Preston then. The club provided a mixture of education and entertainment with sport, music, theatre trips and instruction in debating. She was also a prison visitor and secretary to Preston Health Committee.[3] Edith was originally a member of the National Union of Women's Suffrage Societies (NUWSS), but in 1907 became secretary of the newly established Preston branch of the Women's Social and Political Union (WSPU), a post she held until 1914.

Edith led a group of Preston women to take part in the WSPU 'Women's Parliament', held in Caxton Hall in February 1907. She was amongst the fifty-seven women arrested in the disturbances that followed when the women attempted to march to Parliament to petition for suffrage. With gusto, Edith embraced the increasingly militant tactics that the WSPU adopted. She interrupted public meetings – including one where Winston Churchill was speaking – poured acid on the green of a local golf course, and set fire to the stands of Blackburn Rovers Football Club. She even, it is said, threw a black pudding at a Manchester anti-women's suffrage MP in 1913, as 'black pudding is more derogatory than tomatoes or eggs'.[4] These activities resulted in her being a guest at His Majesty's pleasure some seven times, when she went on hunger strike and experienced forced feeding.

When, in July 1913, Edith surrendered to the police for the attack on the Liverpool Cotton Exchange, she also claimed to have set fire to Lord Leverhulme's house at West Pennine Moors in Rivington Pike, where some £20,000 damage had been caused to the building and a number of valuable paintings in the house. She declared from the dock:

> I want to ask Sir William Lever whether he thinks his property on Rivington Pike is more valuable as one of his superfluous houses occasionally opened to people or as a beacon lighted to King and Country to see here are some intolerable grievances for women.[5]

There is some uncertainty about whether she did indeed undertake this arson attack. Suffragettes were often assumed to be the perpetrators of any arson, fires or vandalism that occurred, whether or not they were guilty. Either way, like many suffragette bombers, Edith was sentenced to a harsh sentence, but did not serve much of it. She again went on hunger strike and was released under the 'Cat and Mouse Act', apparently avoiding being returned to prison by escaping to Ireland. Edith Rigby, like many other suffragettes, was a vegetarian and, while in jail, her lifelong friend Mrs Higginson, who ran a local health store, took over her role as secretary of the WSPU branch.[6]

When the First World War began, Mrs Higginson's stocks of food quickly sold out and she and Edith, concerned about the future possibility of a food crisis, set up an impromptu jam factory at the WSPU rooms in Glover's Court:

> … with sweet ripe fruit piled on every shelf, heaped on the floor. Pans, basins and scales were leant by members and friends and many women were employed to clean and weigh fruit and sugar … women were given the work they badly needed.[7]

The operation finally obtained a shop and Edith, who disagreed with Pankhurst's decision to abandon the suffrage campaign, transferred her allegiance from the mainstream WSPU to the breakaway Independent Women's Social and Political Union, and formed a branch in Preston. This organization did not oppose war, but did oppose the increasingly strong patriotic sentiments and rhetoric of the Pankhursts. In 1915, Edith bought a smallholding called Marigold Cottage, near Howick, just outside Preston, and began doing her bit to increase the nation's food supply. She kept animals, including bees, and grew fruit and vegetables. Her food was sold cheaply for the urban poor in Preston. Former suffragettes visited the cottage, as did her husband, at weekends.

By the 1920s, Edith's feminism, ruralism and jam-making came together when she became both a founder member and the president of Hutton and Howith Women's Institute. She took an active role in organizing talks and parties, fundraising, jam-making competitions, and all the other activities of the movement. Her progression from suffrage work to the Women's Institute Movement was by no means unique; many other suffrage campaigners found a home in this radical campaigning women's organization. Edith Rigby also developed a strong interest in the philosophies and the educational methods of Austrian philosopher and social reformer Rudolph Steiner, who sought to mesh together science and spirituality. In 1939, Edith visited the Rudolph Steiner Center in the USA. By this point, Edith was a widow and was living near Llandudno, North Wales, where she died from Parkinson's disease in 1948.

23

HANNAH MITCHELL (1872–1956)

Councillor and Justice of the Peace

Janis Lomas

After a demonstration at the House of Commons in 1906, Hannah Mitchell faced a long journey home on the midnight train. She wrote later that she:

> … wished to get a few hours rest on the journey, as I knew that arrears of work, including the weekly wash, awaited my return. Working housewives, faced with this accumulation of tasks, often resolve never to leave home again. No wonder it is so difficult to interest married women in social reform.[1]

Hannah Mitchell was one of six children born on a small hill farm in the Derbyshire Peak District. She overcame an impoverished, abusive childhood at the mercy of her embittered mother, who treated her as a skivvy and berated her for the slightest misdemeanor. Hannah was almost entirely self-taught, only having attended school for two weeks; she learned to read through the books her brothers borrowed from school, with the support and suggestions from their teacher. In return for her brothers' help, she undertook their chores and, when she ran away from home 'after one of her [Mother's] attacks',[2] she, aged only thirteen, walked to her brother's house seven miles away in Glossop. After trying domestic service, she worked as a dressmaker's assistant, for 8/- (40p) a week, and then moved to Bolton, where she was employed in a dressmaking workroom. She toiled long hours with strict discipline in silence, making evening dresses for the local factory workers. On hearing about attempts to improve seamstresses' working lives, Hannah started to read *The Clarion*, a Socialist newspaper, and met her future husband, Gibbon Mitchell, already a committed Socialist.

Once married, she had to give up her employment and struggled to manage on Gibbon's meagre wages, a task made even harder once their son was born, causing Hannah to vow that she would have no more children. Her husband acquiesed, though exactly how is not clear as she recalled:

I felt it impossible to face again the personal suffering, or the task of bringing up a second child in poverty. Fortunately, my husband had the courage of his socialist convictions on this point and was no more anxious than myself to repeat the experience.[3]

In 1904, Hannah and her family moved to Ashton-under-Lyne, Greater Manchester. Here, Hannah became one of the first women elected as a Poor Law Guardian. She remained a Socialist, but was dismayed by how many male Socialists who, while actively working to get the vote for working men, were not interested in women's suffrage, and so, when she met Emmeline and Christabel Pankhurst, she joined the WSPU. Hannah was soon addressing meetings not just in Manchester but also in nearby towns. In October 1905, when Sir Edward Grey spoke in Manchester Free Trade Hall, Annie Kenney and Christabel Pankhurst were arrested for shouting out 'Will the Liberal government give women the vote' and resisting arrest. Seven days later, Hannah was among the crowd of supporters outside Strangeways Prison awaiting their release. As a working-class woman of very limited means and with a family, supporting a cause as demanding as women's suffrage was not without difficulties, as Hannah herself wrote in her autobiography many years later:

… we badly needed the help of our male relatives, many of whom became 'anti' if we were out too often. No cause can be won between dinner and tea, and most of us who were married had to work with one hand tied behind us, so to speak. Public disapproval could be faced and borne, but domestic unhappiness, the price many of us paid for our activities, was a very bitter thing.[4]

Lancashire and Cheshire Suffrage.

Political meetings in Edwardian Britain were frequently rowdy; the women were often bruised and battered from encounters with young, strong, working men who thought it great sport to disrupt the meetings and shoved the women around. Hannah described being pushed along from man to man like a rugby ball on one occasion, while the police looked on and did nothing to help. As she wrote later, 'Sometimes it seemed the whole world was against us'.[5] Men also accused them of neglecting their domestic duties.

> Such questions as 'Can you darn a stocking?' were so often asked at [our] meetings by men, it seemed that the ability to do such things was regarded as a sufficient qualification for the franchise.[6]

At another meeting, as a 'punishment' she was one of a group of suffragettes kept behind until they missed the last train and were forced to walk seven miles to one of their houses to spend the rest of the night. In 1906, Hannah was arrested after a Liberal Party rally at which John Burns and Winston Churchill were the main speakers; the women took it in turns to stand and demand 'Votes for Women' and were violently evicted. Hannah was brought before a magistrate the following Monday and, after refusing to pay a fine, was sent to Strangeways Prison alongside Adela Pankhurst and Mrs Morrisey, the wife of a local councillor. Hannah was furious when, against her wishes, her husband paid her fine to get her released the next day. Hannah later recalled: 'Most of us who were married found that "Votes for Women" were of less interest to our husbands than their own dinners'.[7]

Hannah was one of six part-time paid organizers for the Women's Social and Political Union (WSPU), appointed at the end of 1906,[8] and her small salary enabled her to feel less guilty about being away from home. She travelled to London to speak at meetings, and worked extremely hard at the Huddersfield by-election with Mrs Pankhurst. The *Sheffield Daily Telegraph* mentions that she was arrested along with seventy-five other suffragettes after a disturbance at the House of Commons in March 1907. She was given the choice of paying a 20/- (£1) fine or being imprisoned for fourteen days. Although Hannah herself does not mention this in her autobiography, it seems likely that on this occasion she took the option of paying the fine and getting back home.[9] Later in 1907, she had a complete breakdown, which her doctor diagnosed as being caused by 'overwork and under-feeding'. She put her recovery down to her women friends who rallied round and helped her through. Some, such as Charlotte Despard and Mrs Coates-Hanson, also sent her money. A year later, she had recovered but she never returned to work for the WSPU, as she was deeply upset that none of the Pankhurst family, with whom she had worked so closely, inquired after her or sent her a letter during the year of her breakdown. Instead, Hannah undertook work in Scotland for the Women's Freedom League (WFL), which she suspected was given to her to help her out financially as she was still very poor. At the time, she had been trying to bring up her son and a niece whom they had taken in on her husband's wage of just 30/- (£1.50) a week. Although her mental health recovered, she contined to suffer from anxiety and was terrified at meetings that disorder would occur, meaning that militant suffragism was no longer possible for her.

She become active in the Independent Labour Party (ILP), after moving to Manchester when her husband secured a better paid job, and she continued to support the suffrage cause. During the First World War she was a pacifist and became involved with the No Conscription Fellowship and the Women's International League for Peace and Freedom. Between 1924 and 1935 she served on Manchester City Council seeking to improve conditions for the poor. She was on a number of committees including the Poor Relief Committee, a role that her own poverty had prepared her for. She recalled:

> I knew just how much food could be bought out of the allowance, knew the cost of children's clothes and footwear; could tell at a glance if the applicant was in ill health.[10]

After being recommended and rejected several times, probably because of her past militancy and imprisonment, she became a justice of the peace in 1926 and served for twenty years.[11] When finally appointed, she wrote:

> This was a far cry from the voteless female who twenty years earlier had been classed with 'infants, imbeciles and criminals'. I should have been more than human if I had not felt a thrill of pride.[12]

She deserved to feel pride in the journey her life had taken for what she had achieved was truly remarkable.

CHRYSTAL MACMILLAN (1872–1937)

Advocate and peace campaigner

Maggie Andrews

Chrystal Macmillan took her campaign for the vote to the House of Lords in 1908. The *Aberdeen Press and Journal* reported that:

> Miss Macmillan, the lady who conducted the hearing before the Lord Chancellor and his colleagues, is of quiet and refined manner, not at all like the representatives of "shrieking sisterhood" who have caused so much trouble recently; and the behaviour of herself and her companions showed the claim to a right, real or supposed, need not be accompanied by a species of female hooliganism.[1]

Jessie Chrystal Macmillan was one of eight children, the only daughter of John Macmillan, a tea merchant working for Melrose & Co, and his wife Jessie. Despite

THE WOMEN'S LIBRARY COLLECTION, LSE LIBRARY

her mother's death when Chrystal was young, her childhood was very comfortable. She was educated in Edinburgh until the age of sixteen. She went to St Leonards School in St Andrews, which had a forward-thinking approach to girl's education and was sympathetic to women's suffrage. She gained a First Class Honours degree in Mathematics and Moral Philosophy at the University of Edinburgh, the first women to graduate in mathematics at the university. She went on to obtain an MA in Mental and Moral Philosophy in 1900 before undertaking a period of further study in Berlin.[2] Back in Edinburgh, she quickly became involved

Chrystal Macmillan.

with suffrage societies, which, in Scotland, worked together. Chrystal was firmly committed to campaigning and persuading people to the cause of women's suffrage, and became a member of the National Union of Women's Suffrage Societies (NUWSS).

One of the quirks of the electoral system in the Edwardian era was the number of MPs elected by universities, the four Scottish universities having two MPs between them. As a graduate of the University of Edinburgh, Chrystal was a member of the university's General Council, which voted for these MPs, but as a woman she and other female graduates were denied this right by the university. Consequently, a Committee of Women Graduates (Parliamentary Franchise) was set up in 1906, and Chrystal took on the role of both honorary secretary and treasurer. Five women – Chrystal Macmillan, Elsie Inglis, Frances Simson, Frances Melville and Margaret Nairn, all Edinburgh University graduates – took legal proceedings against the university. They argued that the use of word 'person' in the 1868 act did not actually exclude them; their case, which was ultimately unsuccessful, worked its way through courts and appeal courts up to their appearance in the House of Lords in 1908.[3] The eloquence with which Chrystal Macmillan and Frances Simson argued their cause made them heroines of all the suffrage societies. On their return, the press noted:

> A women graduates' lunch was held on Saturday at the Women Student's Union, Edinburgh, in honour of Miss Chrystal Macmillan, M.A. BSc and Miss Frances Simson, M.A., in recognition of their energy, patience and ability with which they conducted the women graduates' appeal to the House of Lords, and the able manner in which they pleaded the case.[4]

In the years that followed, Chrystal became a sought after speaker in the suffrage campaigns in Scotland and London, and became increasingly involved in international suffrage movements. A local newspaper reported:

> A most successful cake and candy sale was held at Fordel, Glenfarg … under the auspices of the Glenfarg Branch of the National Union of Women's Suffrage Societies…. After a brisk sale of cakes, sweets &c., an entertainment was given.
>   After tea, Miss Chrystal Macmillan made an admirable speech, in which she described her recent visit to the International Women's Suffrage Congress at Budapest.[5]

In 1913, Chrystal moved to London to work more closely with Mrs Millicent Fawcett, and the two spoke at many suffrage meetings together. With a growing commitment to the international suffrage movement, Chrystal was horrified to see Europe slipping towards war in the summer of 1914.

She helped to draft the last minute 'International Manifesto of Women' which, on the 31 July, was signed by 'representatives of twelve million women' and delivered to Sir Edward Grey the British Foreign Secretary and Foreign Ambassadors in London entreating them to avoid 'the threatened unparalleled disaster' and instead negotiate and make concessions to maintain the peace.[6]

The women's pleas were ignored and as war began Chrystal sought to alleviate the disaster it brought to ordinary citizens. When Antwerp fell into the hands of the Germans in 1914, '… she organized the dispatch of the first food sent from this country to the Belgium refugees in Holland.'[7]

Chrystal continued to campaign for peace and was one of the organizers of the International Congress of Women held in The Hague in April 1915, which was attended by over 1,200 women from twelve countries, including Germany, Britain, the USA and France. Only four women from Britain made it to the conference, including Chrystal, who had been elected as a delegate to visit the governments of neutral nations and to try to persuade them to mediate a peaceful end to the war. The congress also led to the formation of the Women's International League for Peace and Freedom, of which she remained an active member for years to come. Chrystal maintained her commitment to internationalism throughout the war, and was among those taking part in an International Suffrage Rally in March 1918, which had representatives from many countries discussing the future of the movement.[8] As the war neared its end and the enfranchisement of some women offered potential political power, she argued that the introduction of women magistrates and that the health of babies and mothers should be quickly made political questions.[9] She wrote a leaflet, *And Shall I have a Parliamentary Vote*, to help women navigate their way through the complexity of the property qualification they had to fulfil to vote.[10]

She continued to work for the NUWSS when it became the National Union of Societies for Equal Citizenship in 1919, and became one of the very first women to train for the bar after the Sex Disqualification Removal Act was passed in 1919. She qualified in 1923 and, as a barrister, assisted women and women's organizations campaigning for justice. Her commitment to campaigning for women showed no sign of abating as she explained in a speech that year:

> the vote was only the first step in establishing the equal status of women with men. It was found that women of all countries tended to be agreed on many questions. For instance, they were at one in the demand that a mother should be equal joint guardian with the father, that men and women should have equal pay for equal work, that the married women should not be denied the right to work in the occupation of her choice and there should be an equal moral standard, that the responsibility of the father of a child born out of wedlock

should be recognized and that married women should have the same right as men to retain or to change their nationality.[11]

For the remainder of her life she dedicated herself to furthering all these causes. She was a founder of the Open Door Council, which campaigned for equal employment opportunities for women; she was on the League of Nations Committee on Married Women in 1930s; and she stood (unsuccessfully) to become an MP in 1935. Little wonder that after her death in Edinburgh in 1937, Lord Alness, writing an obituary in *The Scotsman*, said:

> It is not too much to say that Miss Macmillan dedicated her life to the emancipation of women, and that in that regard she has made the women of this country her debtors for all time. Though she is dead, her work will never die.[12]

The International Congress of Women in the Hague.

25

MARGARET BONDFIELD (1873–1953)

The first female minister in a British Cabinet

Paula Bartley

In June 1929, Margaret Bondfield became the first ever woman cabinet minister in Britain, promoted to Minister of Labour by the Labour Party Prime Minister, Ramsay MacDonald. She later commented that:

> … it touched much more than merely my own self – it was part of the great revolution in the position of women which had taken place in my lifetime.[1]

Thirteen other women were also elected as MPs in 1929, prompting the National Union of Societies for Equal Citizenship to host a lunch to celebrate their success. At this, Bondfield sat next to the Liberal Millicent Fawcett, who sat next to the Conservative Nancy Astor, party politics being forgotten in the euphoria of celebrating the progress of women.

Margaret Bondfield climbed to the top of politics from an inauspicious background. She was born on 17 March 1873, in a cottage in Chard, a small village in Somerset, the tenth of eleven children. In 1886, just before her thirteenth birthday, Margaret started work as a pupil teacher at Chard Board School, in charge of forty-two boys. In 1887, aged fourteen, she moved to Hove to work as a shop assistant. It was a hard life. The teenage Margaret worked from early in the morning until 10pm on weekdays and until the last few minutes before

THE WOMEN'S LIBRARY COLLECTION, LSE LIBRARY

Margaret Bondfield giving a speech on disarmament in 1932.

midnight on Saturdays just before the Sunday trading laws took effect (shops being forbidden to open on a Sunday). Margaret, as with over 60 per cent of shop workers, had to live in accommodation provided by her employer, accommodation that was often damp, overcrowded and lacking basic facilities.

In 1896, the Women's Industrial Council asked Margaret to act as an under-cover agent, working in a variety of shops, all the time secretly collecting evidence of the wages and conditions of work. She changed her name to Grace Dare – using the names of her grandmother and great-grandmother – and spent two years in a special investigation of London shop conditions. Her reports on the 'evils of the living in system, the fines, dismissals, bad food, low wages, long hours, restrictions on liberty and the petty tyrannies of the shops' led to widespread condemnation.[2] The results of Bondfield's inquiry led to the 1904 Shop Act, which abolished the living-in system as a condition of employment, reduced the hours of work, gave a statutory half-holiday, and regulated closing times for shop assistants. In 1898, Margaret Bondfield found a job with the Shop Assistants' Union and her rise in the trades union movement followed. Margaret Bondfield, aware of the masculine nature of trades unionism, joined the Women's Trade Union League (WTUL),[3] and later helped Mary Macarthur set up the National Federation of Women Workers (NFWW) to recruit women workers. In 1899, Margaret attended her first TUC conference: she was the only female delegate out of 382 men. It was an historic moment in other ways, too. At this conference, Margaret spoke in favour of setting up a Labour Representative Council to help elect MPs who would represent the working class. In 1906, it became the Labour Party.

A number of suffrage societies were founded to campaign for votes for women on the same terms as men, which essentially meant a property vote. The two main women's suffrage organizations focused on votes for women. Margaret Bondfield did not approve of limiting the extension of the franchise to women only. Her experience as a shop assistant and union organizer 'urged her to take up the adult suffrage rather than the limited [women's] suffrage option', and argue that she opposed 'the idea of a limited franchise on a property basis, because it seemed to me that it was tipping the scales against the workers by strengthening the political power of the propertied classes.'[4] In Bondfield's view, the 'small number of women who would be enfranchised under it did not justify the amount of energy and money'[5] spent on votes for women. 'Don't let them come', she insisted, 'and tell me that they are working for my class'.[6]

In January 1905, she helped found the Adult Suffrage Society and was its first president. The organization was open to 'all men and women in favour of the prin-ciple of Adult suffrage for men and women and against the principle of property qualification'. Bondfield engaged in a public debate with Teresa Billington-Greig, a leading suffragette and founder of the Women's Freedom League, in December 1907. Bondfield put forward the case for adult suffrage for both sexes whereas

Billington-Greig spoke in favour of a limited female suffrage. Bondfield led the debate for the adult suffrage societies and was one of the first members of the People's Suffrage Federation, which was formed in October 1909. In 1918, women over the age of thirty gained the vote, paving the way for Bondfield to become an MP in December 1923. She was fifty-three and one of the first three female Labour MPs to win a seat in Parliament.[7] In January 1924, Ramsay MacDonald became prime minister of the first Labour government. The formation of a Labour government brought new opportunities for Margaret. Within a month of taking her seat, the girl from Somerset became the first British female minister as Under-Secretary of State for the Minister of Labour.[8] It was a meteoric rise for a woman who had just been elected as an MP. A few months later there was another general election: Margaret Bondfield lost her seat, returning to Parliament in a by-election in 1926, and retaining her seat in the 1929 general election.

When Margaret Bondfield was appointed cabinet minister she was the only woman in a Labour Cabinet of twenty men. She knew that she would struggle with her new job, all too aware that the Labour government had 'taken office at a critical moment in the world's history.'[9] Britain was in financial difficulties, faced with a large national debt, an increasingly lopsided balance of payments and rising unemployment. Immediately on taking office, Margaret Bondfield was forced to tackle the troublesome question of unemployment benefits. Unfortunately, the Labour Party had only been in office for a few months when the economic bubble burst. On 29 October 1929, the Wall Street Crash precipitated a world-wide economic crisis. By the end of 1930 'the economic blizzard was then blowing with full blast'[10] and, as unemployment figures climbed towards two million, Margaret Bondfield had the unenviable task of asking Parliament to increase the lending limit of the government: in April 1930, she asked to increase borrowing for unemployment benefit to £50 million; in July 1930, to £60 million; in December 1930, to £70 million,[11] and in February 1931, as unemployment approached two and a half million, to £90 million. In June 1931, with the unemployed now totalling 2,713,000, Bondfield asked for it to be raised again to £131 million. It was, in the view of a leading trades unionist and Labour MP, 'like trying to stop an incoming tide with sandbags.'[12] The House of Commons put pressure on Bondfield to justify these increases and there was a widespread demand for a drastic reduction in unemployment pay, fuelled by bogus reports that applicants for benefits were making false claims.

The unemployment crisis intensified. When Bondfield proposed borrowing another £150 million to finance the unemployment fund, she was forced to make cuts. In July 1931, she brought in a bill to cut the benefits of casual and seasonal workers and of married women. For a woman to cut women's benefits was too much for some female MPs. A group of Labour MPs (Jenny Lee, Cynthia Mosley, Ellen Wilkinson, along with the Conservative Nancy Astor and the Independent Eleanor

Rathbone) objected to Bondfield's proposals. Their cries remained unheeded. The Bill was carried by 221 to 20 votes, and a large tranche of married women was removed from the unemployment register on the basis that these women were not 'genuinely seeking work'.

Bondfield's economies did little as unemployment continued to rise and borrowing continued to increase. At 7pm on Sunday 23 August 1931, after a number of very tense meetings, a majority of the Cabinet agreed to cuts of approximately £68,000,000, limiting unemployment benefit to twenty-six weeks, introducing a means test and cutting payment by 10 per cent.[13] However, not all the Cabinet agreed: only twelve ministers, including Bondfield, voted for the cuts. MacDonald asked the Cabinet to resign and a couple of days later formed a National Government. Margaret Bondfield wrote to MacDonald expressing approval for his decision and to:

> assure you of my deep sympathy in and admiration for the decision you have taken. May God give you the strength you need and the success you deserve in bringing the nation through this crisis.[14]

He replied that he was 'trying to involve very few of my friends in the new Government because so far as I can see it means their political death.'[15]

On 8 September 1931, Parliament re-assembled. Margaret Bondfield was not there: she was in a nursing home in Tunbridge Wells suffering from a nervous breakdown,[16] largely brought on by the pressure of her ministerial work. Two years later, in October 1931, another general election took place. The newly created National Government won a landslide victory, securing 554 seats, all at the expense of Labour, which won a humiliating fifty-two. All cabinet ministers, with the exception of George Lansbury, lost their seats. No Labour women were left in Parliament: Margaret Bondfield lost her seat to the Conservative candidate, Irene Ward.

Bondfield was fifty-eight, had never married, and was a little young to retire while being too old to start a new career. She completely collapsed after her defeat: the grief of watching all she had worked for disappear was too much. She was diagnosed with fibrositis, a chronic auto-immune condition associated with the central nervous system and which affects the muscles and makes skin painful to touch. Margaret Bondfield, forged in the fire of trades union politics, did not give up: in 1935 she again contested Wallsend, but was defeated for the second time. In 1936, Bondfield was endorsed as candidate for Reading, ready for the 1940 general election. This election was postponed because of the Second World War so Bondfield withdrew her candidature, fulfilling 'the pledge I had given myself not to stand again for Parliament after I had reached the age of seventy.'[17] On 16 June 1953 Margaret Bondfield died aged eighty at a nursing home in Surrey, a groundbreaking politician who was, regrettably, largely forgotten by then.

26

ADELINE REDFERN-WILDE (1874–1924)

A working-class activist in the Potteries

Amy Dale

In March 1912, hundreds of suffragettes, adhering to Emmeline Pankhurst's pronouncement that 'The argument of the broken window pane is the most valuable argument in modern politics',[1] wreaked havoc upon London's West End. Their hammer-wielding antics caused £5,000 worth of damage in the course of breaking 400 shop windows. Adeline Redfern-Wilde's target was the London City and Midland Bank in Mayfair:

> Mrs. Adelaide [sic] Redfern Wilde, charged with breaking windows value £20 at 129 New Bond Street, said: 'It was one more blow for freedom.' She was committed for trial.[2]

Of the 220 people arrested, custodial sentences of up to six months faced those who received a guilty verdict. The 'blow' for freedom, temporarily relieved Adeline of hers.

Adeline's participation in the campaign for suffrage had brought her to some of London's most affluent businesses, but she stemmed from far more humble beginnings. Born to Frederick Redfern and Elizabeth Thursfield in 1874, Adeline grew up in 'the Potteries', the epitome of an industrial, working-class area. Adeline was born in the small Staffordshire district of Dresden, south of the town of Longton, one of the then five towns of Stoke-on-Trent. By 1891, she was, like many working-class girls, in service, working as a domestic servant for the Heath family solicitors. In 1893, aged nineteen, she married Mr Harry Wilde, an engineer's locomotive fitter. Their marital home was in the town of Stoke. Two children quickly followed: a daughter Vera, in 1894, and their son, George, in 1898. Adeline did not continue in domestic service and the 1901 census lists her as 'housewife'. She is missing from the 1911 census; next to her name is the comment 'not in the house due to political reasons'. It is reasonable to assume that this was a consequence of the 1911 suffragette boycott of the census.

As with many industrial areas at this time, ripples of political consciousness had been stirring in the area from the latter half of the nineteenth century. In 1872, Staffordshire's first suffrage society was formed: the Stoke-on-Trent Committee of the London National Society. Although this did not last, various speakers and movements visited the town, suggesting that it was seen as a potential pool of support. For example, the North of England Society held meetings to encourage the women of the Potteries to petition for the vote in 1903. Spurred on by the increasingly political environment, women like Adeline would have been encouraged to take up individual activism.

While it was possible for the men of the Potteries to overcome their subjugation by undertaking some of the most skilled work to be found in industrial Britain, no level of skill could ever transform clay into a vote for a woman and, like the majority of industries, the pot-banks were frustratingly patriarchal. Sylvia Pankhurst observed female pottery workers during her tour of Northern England in 1907. She documented their working lives in paint and was clearly dismayed by her visit:

> In the potteries I also saw the subordination of women workers. A woman was turning the wheel for the thrower, a woman was treading the lathe for the turner: each was employed by the man she toiled for – the slave of a slave, I thought![3]

It is unsurprising that some of these 'slaves of slaves' were encouraged to move away from turning the wheel of the potter to turning the wheel of change:

> I thought that women should have the same rights as men. Several of us, who wanted votes for women, we used to get up in Hanley Market square, and spout a bit but, in those days, if it got too rowdy the police would come and move us off – but we still used to say what we thought.[4]

There was a Stoke-on-Trent and a Newcastle-under-Lyme Suffrage Society and, eventually, a branch of the Women's Freedom League (WFL), but it was Adeline, along with her sisters, Elizabeth and Emily, who formed Stoke-on-Trent's branch of the Women's Social and Political Union (WSPU) in September 1908. This was a space for like-minded women to be heard above the billowing smoke of the bottle ovens that engulfed them. They had all previously been involved in the suffragette movement in Birmingham, where Adeline had become a founder member of WSPU branch set up there.[5] Sylvia Pankhurst returned to Stoke to hold a WSPU branch meeting there in September 1908. Sylvia regarded the activism of the working class as the cornerstone of the suffrage movement, one of the reasons for her expulsion from the WSPU in 1914. Sylvia's relationship with Adeline and her sisters is also evidenced in an autograph album that was recently discovered in a house in Hanley. Compiled by either Adeline or one of her sisters, it contains the autographs and comments of the prisoners involved in the window-breaking campaign of March 1912. Approximately fifty suffragettes (including Sylvia Pankhurst) signed the book in which Adeline argues:

> The women's movement is a revolution of the highest order; it is a moral revolution which marks a crisis in human evolution, and which will tend to arrest the physical and national decay which has set in.[6]

In 1908, Adeline was involved in one of the more droll moments in the Suffragette movement – the Trojan Horse. Although unsuccessful in the aim of storming parliament, it received widespread media attention both at home and abroad. The New Zealand *Auckland Star* relished in the boldness of the plan that saw women hiding in the back of two furniture vans:

> Following the famous precedent of the Greeks who entered Troy concealed in a wooden horse, the Suffragettes outwitted the police this week in the Old Palace Yard in a fashion that was both humorous and effective. Things have come to such a pass that Parliament has now to be protected from a band of resolute women by hundreds of police. Strong men watch the gates of Parliament to protect the trembling legislators from the womenfolk … But the Suffragettes can be as wily as Ulysses of old … In a contest of wits the police were no match for the women … The back of the covered van was let down, and out jumped twenty-one women and girls, who made an instant dash for the Stranger's Entrance to the House of Commons. … The women outside the door, unable to charge the entrance, refused to go away and insisted on being arrested.[7]

Farcical though it was, it must not be forgotten that such clashes with the authorities were often brutal, although, if the account of this attending policeman was to be believed, such brutality was a consequence of misplaced femininity. As a report in the *Birmingham Gazette and Express* noted on 12 February 1908:

> The stalwart guardians of the peace presented a firm barrier, but the 'light brigade' made a most determined attack, and it was with difficulty that the ladies were kept back … 'They clung round our necks with their arms', said one of the policemen … 'We treated them, however, as gently as we could', said another tall, strapping policeman, 'but possibly some of them got a little bit bruised. Women are such tender, fragile beings that you can hardly touch them without bruising them.'[8]

Adeline was in the thick of the action. The *Daily Mail* listed the twenty-one names under the heading 'The Martyrs', amongst them: 'Adeline Redfern, 33, married … Stoke-on-Trent.'[9]

Adeline died on 4 April 1924, at her home in West Street, Stoke-on-Trent. She did not live to see the extension of female suffrage in 1928 to working-class women, but without the efforts of often forgotten working-class campaigners like Adeline, women would never have won the vote.

27

ALICE CLARK (1874–1934)

Historian and shoe company executive

Maggie Andrews

On 23 February 1907, Alice Clark wrote the following letter to the collector of the Inland Revenue:

Dear Sir,

I regret my delay in replying to your letter of February 15th gave you the trouble of calling upon me. A parliament in which no women are represented has no right to levy taxes upon women without their consent. After most careful consideration I have come to the conclusion, therefore, that it will not be right for me to pay any tax.

Yours faithfully [signed] Alice Clark[1]

Alice Clark, the fourth of William Stephen Clark and Helen Priestman Bright's six children, was born in Bridgwater in Somerset. The family were Quakers, liberals, radical social reformers, and manufacturers of shoes. She spent only one year in formal education, at a school in Southport. Alice's three sisters went to university and she had plans to go to Newnham College, Cambridge, but instead, in 1893, Alice entered the family firm of C and J Clarke Manufacturer of boots, shoes & sheepskin rugs, which had been founded in Street, Somerset, in 1825. Alice worked initially in the women's room where topstitching was undertaken, then progressed to cutting in the men's rooms and working as an assistant in the firm's Edinburgh shop, thereby gaining a thorough apprenticeship in shoe manufacturing and retailing.[2] C and J Clarke sought to modernize its production techniques, materials' technologies and organization, and Alice was one of its first directors – and the only female director – when the family firm became a private limited company in 1904.[3]

The company sought to improve the lives of its workers: it established a school to enable younger workers to combine work and education; a theatre, library, swimming pool, town hall, and low-cost family housing were provided for employees. However, there were also expectations of sobriety and Alice was a strong supporter of the temperance movement. At a meeting in 1908, she emphasized the importance of total abstinence and how this could provide a tremendous protection for young people's welfare. She went on to explain to her audience that:

> Unfortunately women were not all temperate, but it was partly for that very reason that they wanted to make haste and give women more power in the government of the country. There was an increasing amount of drunkenness amongst many women in large towns, but that sad state of affairs, which was, perhaps one of the greatest dangers of the country, which was largely caused by the terrible circumstances in which so many women had to live.[4]

Alice's political involvement grew in the years that she worked in the factory. In 1890, she became secretary of the local Liberal Association, a post she held for eleven years. She was a keen supporter of women's suffrage; initially working through the Liberal Association, but then taking an active role in suffrage societies. She spoke at meetings organized by the National Union of Women's Suffrage Societies (NUWSS), participated in the WSPU's first raid on the House of Commons in 1907, subscribed to the WFL and undertook a much publicized campaign to resist taxation without representation. Not only did she write to the Inland Revenue to explain why she would not pay her taxes, but she sent copies of her letter to numerous local newspapers. However, in 1909 Alice developed tuberculosis and, after spending time in a sanatorium, was bedridden and forbidden to speak for many months in 1910. During this time, letters to her friends suggest that she supported the WSPU's window-smashing campaigns and, as her health slowly improved in 1911, she began again to distribute suffrage literature in the towns and villages around her home in Somerset.[5]

When Alice finally recovered, at the age of thirty-eight, although she had no formal academic training, she undertook a study of women's history and was awarded the Mrs George Bernard Shaw Research Fellowship at the London School of Economics. In London, she once again became involved in suffrage activities, taking an active role in the National Union of

Tax Resistance League march, October 1911.

Women's Suffrage Societies and in 1912 she helped to set up the Friends League for Women's Suffrage with her brother Roger Clark. As Quakers, Alice and her family opposed the First World War and she began her lifetime support of the Women's International League for Peace and Freedom. She also joined her sister Hilda in working for the Quaker War Relief campaigns. Alice herself undertook midwifery training to assist her sister, a trained doctor, care for war-refugees.[6] Long-term consequences of her illness meant that she was not well enough for such work, but she continued to help with the organization of the relief effort, combining work at its London headquarters with her studies. In the immediate post-war era, the sisters worked with the newly established Save the Children Fund to ensure that the starving children of Vienna received milk.

In 1919, Alice published the *Working Life of Women in the Seventeenth Century* – still regarded as a ground-breaking and classic women's history book. Alice's research relied upon a painstaking examination of letters, diaries, wills, account books, magistrates' wage rate assessments, parish records, guild and municipal records, tax returns and workhouse records to understand the lives of ordinary working women. Her book argues that the seventeenth century was pivotal in English women's lives and that many of the better-paid skilled crafts that women worked at were destroyed, to be replaced by low-paid and low-skilled jobs. Alice Clark presents a pessimistic view of the changes of industrialization in this era and perhaps idealizes women's lives in pre-industrial, family-based economies. In attempting to write a history that covered the whole of the seventeenth century perhaps some generalization crept into Clark's volume. Nevertheless, importantly her exploration of women's day-to-day lives demonstrates that the 'non-working' housewife was a very modern invention. Women have always made an economic contribution to society.

Alice Clark planned to write a second volume to her history of women in the seventeenth century. Instead, in the inter-war era she returned to her family home. She worked in her family's shoe company, which was by 1922 employing 1,200 people, and taught in a local adult education school. Her spiritual and religious affiliations shifted from her families' Quakerism to Christian Science, and when her tuberculosis returned in the 1930s this created difficulties for her family and friends. Mary Baker, the founder of this particular religious movement, had argued in her book *Science and Health* (1875) that sickness is an illusion, which can be overcome by prayer. Adhering to this ideology, Alice suffered a slow and painful death.

28

MRS ARTHUR WEBB (1874–1957)

Suffragist domestic goddess

Maggie Andrews

On 4 May 1907, a meeting in Worple Hall, Wimbledon, to support the candidacy of Bertrand Russell, who was standing as a pro-women's suffrage candidate for Parliament, was apparently disrupted by rats being released into the hall. In the pandemonium that ensued, Mabel Webb was one of a number of women's suffrage speakers who struggled to make themselves heard.

Mrs Arthur Webb, as she was known, began life in 1874 as Mabel Elizabeth Edwards, the daughter of a Welsh farmer. She grew up in Knighton, in the county of Radnorshire, very close to the English border, but lived in the London suburbs after her marriage, in 1899, to Arthur Webb, secretary to the Co-Operative Building Society. Arthur came from a respectable, middle-class family and the newly married couple appear to have supported both the co-operative movement and social reforms such as women's suffrage. By 1906, the couple had four children – Gwynnett, Rhonna, Seymour and Harold – and had settled in Wimbledon, where they were seen to have been comfortably off rather than wealthy. According to the 1911 census, they only had one live-in 'lady-help'. Mabel's life would have involved a significant amount of housework, with four small children to care for and little in the way of labour-saving devices, even if perhaps a woman came to assist with the weekly washing on a Monday. Nevertheless, she became active in the Wimbledon branch of the London Society for Women's Suffrage,

Cover of Mrs Arthur Webb's *Farmhouse Cookery* book, which accompanied her BBC series of the same name.

affiliated to the NUWSS. Like so many of the women who supported the suffrage campaigns, Mabel's contribution to the movement is in many ways hidden from history.

Wimbledon according to Elizabeth Crawford became a suffrage stronghold both of the NUWSS and the WSPU.[1] Perhaps this explains why, in 1907, when Eric Hambro, the then Conservative MP, resigned to pay more attention to his expanding business interests, the constituency became the first place to field a women's suffrage candidate, backed by the NUWSS. Bertrand Russell, a philosopher and mathematician of aristocratic lineage, was, it seems, persuaded to stand by his very pro-suffrage American Quaker wife, Alys Russell. It is in reports of Russell's campaign meeting that Mabel Webb's involvement in suffrage activities can be identified. On 4 May 1907, she shared a platform both with Bertrand and Alys Russell, Mrs Philip Snowden, a Socialist and supporter of the NUWSS, and Mrs Allison Garland. Even before two rats were spotted in the hall, many of the speakers were already struggling to make themselves heard amidst the commotion, which included boos and shouts of 'We don't want a petticoat government'. This line of heckling was taken up by another voice, which yelled 'Do we want petticoats?' to be greeted with shouts of 'No'. Other members of the audience turned their backs on the speakers on the stage and seemed to hold another meeting among themselves, or got hold of the springs on roller-blinds at the windows, pulled them down and then let them fly back to cause more disturbance.[2]

Such scenes were not unique; baiting and jeering at suffrage speakers seems to have been something of a sport for many men. In this instance, it seems that many of the audience of nearly 2,000 had chosen to attend the meeting as a result of encountering an open-air demonstration in favour of women's suffrage and accepting the invitation to hear more. They were predisposed towards causing a disturbance and later were referred to as 'Cowards', 'Cads' and 'Hooligans' in some local newspapers. In the days that followed there was some debate about whether the rats had been deliberately brought into the hall, concealed in a bag to disrupt the meeting, or the hall was already infested with rats. At a meeting the following week, an egg was thrown, which hit Alys Russell on the cheek, and the rest of Russell's brief campaign met with similar opposition. His pro-suffrage candidacy managed to obtain 3,298 votes while the Wimbledon Conservative Parliamentary Party candidate, Henry Chaplin, polled 10,262 votes and achieved a record majority of 6,964. The women's suffrage campaign in Wimbledon, however, continued undeterred: a WSPU branch was set up in 1908 and this became well known for its militancy, often led by Mrs Rose Lamartine Yates. In 1911, women boycotting the census spent the night on Wimbledon Common, arriving in horse-drawn caravans adorned with signs announcing 'If women don't count, neither shall they be counted' and participating in a picnic of roast fowl, sweetmeats and tea.[3]

The inhospitable and confrontational audiences she encountered at suffrage meetings do not seem to have dissuaded Mabel Webb from public speaking; during the First World War she both managed a farm and lectured on food production.[4] Such wartime activities propelled her into a highly successful career as a journalist, cookery book writer, WI lecturer and general expert on cookery and food preservation, giving advice particularly to those with gardens, allotments, smallholdings and farms. Her status as a domestic goddess in the inter-war years was confirmed when, on 11 January 1932, she presented her first broadcast talk on Marmalade-Making in the BBC's lunchtime radio programme Hints from Other Cooks. Her next broadcast was in March and by September that year the *Radio Times* announced that:

> Mrs Webb will give practical advice on how to catch and then preserve the bilberry, the whortleberry, the sloe, the wild raspberry, the wilder strawberry, the elusive blackberry, and the shy cranberry.

Suffragette campaigners had frequently made and sold jams and marmalades to raise money for their cause. Mrs Webb's broadcasts propelled such skills into the public sphere via the new medium of the wireless. Her advice was down-to-earth, informal, economical and intended to help hard-pressed housewives make ends meet. She included recipes for pot roasts, pig's head and tail soup, and how to cover half a pig's head with pastry to make a roast.

In 1935, Mrs Webb travelled the country in her car, at the behest of the BBC, to accumulate recipes for a new broadcast series, Farmhouse Cookery, for which she received £7 for the series. This would have been a substantial sum of money. By this time she was writing regular columns for *Farmer's Weekly* and the series highlighted the skills of rural housewives and regional specialities. In the best-selling accompanying cookbook, Shropshire was described as a county 'possessing skilled cooks', while Leicestershire was praised for being 'the proud home of the wonderful Melton Mowbray pork pie'. The down-to-earth, folksy nature of *Farmhouse Cookery* cemented not only Mrs Arthur Webb's skills and expertise, but those of ordinary rural women whom she interviewed to make the series.

In the Second World War, Mrs Webb was quickly called upon once again to provide guidance and advice to the nation. Her first programme, Making the Most of the Wartime Larder, was broadcast within days of the outbreak of war. She published her first wartime cookery book before the end of 1939; a second edition followed in 1940, and she continued to publish and broadcast into the 1950s. Like many suffrage campaigners, Mrs Arthur Webb's fight for the vote was not about a rejection of women's domestic skills. The career that she created for herself in the aftermath of the suffrage campaigns had many continuities with traditional ideas of femininity, but it provided her with a good income while giving the domestic lives of ordinary women a national media profile.[5]

Campaigners from All Walks of Life

29

GRACE HADOW (1875–1940)

Oxford don and NFWI Vice Chairman

Elspeth King

Grace Hadow, a young don and English scholar at Somerville College, Oxford, edited *The Oxford Treasury of English Literature* with her brother in 1906. She was also a founder member of the Oxford Women's Students Society for Women's Suffrage, and was present when members carried the banner into the Royal Albert Hall, London, at the end of the 1908 procession for Women's Suffrage.

Born in 1875, Grace lived in South Cerney, in Gloucestershire, where her father was the local vicar. She had five siblings and after initially being educated at home and having some experience as a junior teacher at Cheltenham Ladies College, she studied at Somerville College, Oxford. Like other women at the time, when she passed her degree she was not able to graduate. After a year teaching at Bryn Mawr College in the USA, she returned to Somerville, but when her mother became frail after being widowed, she became a visiting lecturer. It was while caring for her mother in Gloucestershire that she became a suffragist.[1]

Grace later described Cirencester as 'very much cut off from the outer world … [where] brains were disliked, especially in women', but it was during this period she became involved in the Cirencester branch of the National Union of Women's Suffrage Societies (NUWSS), becoming its honorary secretary and also the honorary secretary of the local Conservative and Unionist Women's Franchise Association (CUWFA),[2] which became the third largest suffrage organization with sixty-eight branches in 1913.[3] Her Conservative political affiliations were also evident when she addressed the Cirencester 'juvenile' branch of the Primrose League on the subject of the British Empire.[4] In 1913, the non-militant, non-party suffrage pilgrimage entered Cirencester en route to London, and Grace acquired the distinction of organizing what was apparently the town's largest ever crowd. She arranged a rally to cleverly coincide with a group of 500 people setting off for Gloucester to protest against the Welsh Church Bill, and these protesters also became part of the large gathering that congregated in the Market Place to see the suffragists. Grace sat in a break (a style of carriage) from where Mr Ainsworth explained the object of the pilgrimage. The meeting was not without interruptions and events got a little rough when at one point:

> ladies lost their hats and other portions of attire. The disturbance was not caused by the suffragists and was not quite in keeping with their ethos of peaceful protest. After the pilgrimage left the town and travelled about two miles to Siddington, a further commotion broke out and suffragist ladies were forced to take shelter in local cottages. It was 11 pm before, accompanied by the police, they got on their way. The enormous publicity raised the profile of the local suffrage cause.[5]

During the First World War, Grace Hadow, like many women, was involved in multiple local organizations: she worked with Belgian refugees and served on the women's subcommittee of the County War Agricultural Committee. In 1916, after hearing Madge Watt speak, she was galvanized to join the fledgling Women's Institute movement (WI). She became president of the WI in Gloucestershire and remarked that 'the movement ought to do a great deal not only to promote thrift but to educate country women and to improve conditions of country life',[6] an indication of the future direction her life would take. After the death of her mother, Grace worked with the Ministry of Munitions, focusing on the 'health and happiness' of women munitions workers. Her work covered lodgings for workers, their housing outside the factory, getting to work, crèches, maternity homes and clubs. Some of her work was quite revolutionary at the time and suggested a new approach

Oxford Suffrage campaigners joining the 1913 Pilgrimage.

The NFWI in 1937 with Mrs Wintringham, Hon. Mrs Mottram, Mrs Munro, Miss Hilda Chamberlain, Mrs Huxley, Mrs Neville Smith (front row), Lady Denman, Miss Hadow and Mrs Watt.

to welfare in the workplace, laying the foundations for more permanent reforms later. One account noted that her 'strangely assorted team' were bowled over by her 'clear, fine, buoyant personality' and became one of the 'best working teams I have ever seen'.[7] She was apparently quite single-minded in her work – a trait she shared with others in the suffrage movement. While by nature a bit of a rebel, her time working for the ministry developed her understanding of public affairs and how government departments worked. When the Representation of the People Act 1918 gave some women the suffrage, Grace Hadow wrote to congratulate Mrs Fawcett, and she kept the reply she received for the rest of her life.[8]

By the end of the First World War, Grace Hadow had become vice-chairman of the National Federation of Women's Institutes, where she was not only responsible for writing the first edition of the *National Federation of Women's Institutes (NFWI)* handbook, but also for the choice of 'Jerusalem' as an anthem. It was only after a competition for an official song had produced nothing original that was worth using that Grace hit upon the idea of using 'Jerusalem'. The anthem was adopted by the suffrage movement to celebrate women's enfranchisement in 1918 and, as many suffrage supporters were also WI members, it seemed a logical move. Since 1924, it has endured as one of the most recognizable aspects of the WI move-ment.[9] Grace also held the position of NFWI vice-chairman for more than twenty years, alongside a growing professional life as principal of the Society of Oxford Home Students (later St Anne's College) from 1929 to 1940. Her commitment to numerous national bodies included the executive committee of the National Council for Social Services, and the Adult Education Committee of the Board of Education. From 1920 to 1929, she became secretary of Barnet House (Oxford University's centre for social work and social studies training), and was key in starting the Oxfordshire Rural Community Council. She worked for many other organizations: from 1929 until her death in 1940 when she was principal of the Society of Home Students. Even after all women were enfranchised in 1928, there was no let-up in Grace's promotion of women being equal to men.

Grace's accomplishments were not limited to these commitments. She discovered a passion for mountaineering on a holiday in Scotland. Due to her other commitments, it was some years later before she was able to take it seriously, but she enjoyed several climbing holidays in Switzerland using the services of a guide to climb on glaciers and other mountains, including the lower levels of the Weissmies. Her climbing reached its peak when she ascended the Fletschhorn several times and apparently the Matterhorn in the early 1920s.[10] After climbing the Fletschhorn using a route previously never climbed by a woman, she wrote in a letter to her brother: 'I've done my climb no woman has done before – but I can't boast of it' (she had, it seems, suffered from terrible mountain sickness).[11]

Grace was not a person to get in the way of progress and she embraced the new medium of radio with enthusiasm. She served on the BBC Advisory Council, and her interest in books and adult education led her in 1928 to turn her hand to broadcasting. She was regarded as one of the better women speakers in the country on a wide range of topics. In July 1939, she spoke on 'The Constructive Sex', arguing that it was '… our [Women's] business to build up homes in every land. It is largely in the hands of women … that the health and happiness of mankind rests.'[12]

That Grace should have had such a full and prominent life involving many organizations, including the suffrage movement, should be no surprise at all. Both the WI and suffrage movements were about empowering women and showing they were the equals of any man. This idea permeated Grace's work until her death in 1940 from pneumonia.

30

ROSA MAY BILLINGHURST (1875–1953)

Disabled militant suffragette

Janis Lomas

Rosa May Billinghurst recalled:

> It was gradually unfolded to me that the unequal laws which made women appear inferior to men were the main cause of these evils. I found that the man-made laws of marriage, parentage and divorce placed women in every way in a condition of slavery – and were as harmful to men by giving them power to be tyrants.[1]

Rosa May Billinghurst, known as May, was born into a well-to-do, middle-class family in Kent. The second of five children, she was paralysed at the age of five months, possibly from polio. She also suffered from chronic hay fever and in her teens she spent over a year unable to swallow liquid because of a paralysis of her throat. She could only stand using crutches, but all these health issues did not stop her from taking a full part in suffrage activities. She was one of the first members of the Lewisham branch of the Women's Social and Political Union (WSPU); her sister joined, as did her father and mother; they also donated money and allowed their house to be used

Rosa May Billinghurst on a suffrage demonstration.

THE WOMEN'S LIBRARY COLLECTION, LSE LIBRARY

for 'at WSPU, homes.' Her brother, Alf, was an active member of the men's campaign for women's suffrage.

As well as taking part in militant activities, she was also one of the members who kept the grassroots of the movement working and her disability gave the movement a distinct propaganda advantage. She was fearless and sometimes used her disabled tricycle as a battering ram to attack the police lines. She took part in many militant activities, despite her fragile health. As Fran Abrams has suggested:

> It made it difficult, if not impossible, for the media to portray May as a howling harridan with little care for the safety of others. At its least effective the sight of her at a demonstration was a picturesque one ... At best, it served to underline in bold the brutal tactics of the police and the vulnerability of the suffrage demonstrators.[2]

She joined the Women's Social and Political Union (WSPU) in 1907 after having seen at first hand the conditions in Greenwich Workhouse through her voluntary work. This led her to feel that it was only by gaining the vote that women would be able to change the terrible conditions being suffered by the poorest in society. She is recorded as having donated money to the WSPU from the first edition of the suffragette newspaper, *Votes for Women*, and also managed to take part in rallies and marches with the use of her specially adapted tricycle, operated by hand-controlled pedals. The tricycle was decked out in the WSPU colours of purple, white and green, with ribbons proclaiming Votes for Women attached.

By 1908, May was being sent all over the country. In April 1908, in Manchester, she canvassed against Winston Churchill, who was standing for election for the North-West Manchester seat. She stayed in a hotel for the duration of the campaign and toured the streets in her tricycle. One local newspaper dubbed her the star attraction of the militant campaign; the meetings she helped to organize drew bigger audiences than Churchill's official meetings and Churchill was defeated in the election. She was tireless in helping to organize fundraising events, house-to-house canvassing and leafleting in the street to gain support for the WSPU. In 1910, she became secretary of the Greenwich branch of the WSPU and attended the 'Black Friday' demonstrations in November 1910; during this she was so outraged by the brutal police tactics that she attempted to use her tricycle as a battering ram to charge the police lines, resulting in her being thrown off her tricycle. In retaliation, the police put her back onto her tricycle and took her to a side road, let down her tyres and pocketed the valves, leaving her quite helpless in the midst of a hostile crowd.

She was arrested several times over the following years and was often in the forefront of militant activities. At first the courts seemed loathe to imprison her; perhaps aware of the negative publicity that would inevitably result. However, in March 1912 she was finally imprisoned after taking part in the mass window smashing of Oxford and Regent Street shops. During this raid she once again utilized her tricycle to best advantage by using it to hide under the blanket that covered her knees all the bricks, stones and hammers to be used in the window-breaking raid. She was sentenced to one month with hard labour, but due to her infirmity the hard labour part of the sentence was not enforced. After her release, May began to take part in more serious offences, in her case damaging pillar boxes and destroying the contents. Fellow militant suffragette Lilian Lenton reported on May's *modus operandi* years later when she wrote:

> She would set out in her chair with many little packages from which, when turned upside down, there flowed a dark brown sticky fluid, concealed under the rug which covered her legs. She went undeviating from one pillar box to another … dropping a package in each one.[3]

This time she was remanded on bail, with two other suffragettes, for trial at the Old Bailey. She gave an eloquent speech in her defence, which seems to have impressed the Recorder, Sir Forrest Fulton. It was reported that before passing sentence he said that he realized that the prisoners did not belong to the class of hysterical women who were motivated by a desire for notoriety. He also referred to her threat to go on hunger strike, saying that 'he wished he could induce her to desist from that lamentable course of conduct'.[4] May was sentenced to eight months' imprisonment. Due to her poor health she was imprisoned in the first division, which gave her something of a dilemma, as not being placed in the first division was the usual excuse to go on hunger strike. Despite this, May decided to carry through her plan and began a hunger strike. After three days, the authorities attempted to force-feed her, but withdrew when it proved almost impossible to insert the tube. The following day, however, the doctor decided to make an even more determined effort. He found her nostrils were tiny and tried first one and then the other before deciding that the first one was the best. He then used great force to insert the tube after which her mouth was forced open using iron pincers, which broke one of her teeth. She said that the procedure was agonising and even the wardresses who held her down had tears in their eyes. She suffered damage to her nostrils and throat and her own doctor later stated that a medical examination before would have shown that forced feeding should not have been attempted. She was released on 18 January as her heart was showing signs of stress.

Her forced-feeding received wide publicity with many being outraged. The newspapers overwhelmingly condemned her treatment, although her family did also receive threats to their safety. This did not stop them opening their home to suffragettes who needed somewhere to recover after being released from hunger striking and forced-feeding. Lilian Lenton went there to recover after nearly dying when she had liquid poured into her lung rather than her stomach. While she was still weak, Lilian sat in May's tricycle in disguise with May walking with crutches beside her, and they went for an airing around the neighbourhood, somehow avoiding the police who were looking to re-arrest Lilian under the terms of the 'Cat and Mouse Act'.

By early 1914, public opinion had been soured by militant action and suffragettes faced increasing violence from hostile crowds and the police. On 23 May, at the last demonstration before war broke out, 1,500 police were deployed and they, once again, used a great deal of violence to hold back women who were trying to reach Buckingham Palace to speak directly to King George V. As usual, May was in the midst of it all and drove her tricycle into a line of mounted police, whereupon two policemen turned her vehicle over and knocked her to the ground. Another suffragette picked her up and put her back. Despite being bruised and battered, she managed to reach the palace gates and chain her tricycle to the railings. On this occasion the police refused to arrest her, much to May's annoyance.

When war began May loyally supported the suspension of all WSPU militancy and supported Emmeline Pankhurst at rallies for the war effort. In 1918, she went to Smethwick to support Christabel Pankhurst's candidacy in the election. After the war, she went to live in the basement of her brother's house, bought a car and travelled extensively. She attended Emmeline's funeral in 1928 and is thought to have fostered a child in the 1930s. When the Second World War broke out, she moved from London and settled in Weybridge, Surrey, where she lived until her death in 1953.

31

MRS AUBREY DOWSON (1876–1944)

Editor of *The Women's Suffrage Cookery Book*

Jenni Waugh

Mrs Aubrey Dowson has edited a cookery book containing 230 cookery and still room recipes by Suffragists. It is published by the Women's Printing Society in paper board, price 1s 3d post free and can be obtained from Mrs Aubrey Dowson, Yew Tree Cottage, Lapworth, Warwickshire or Miss E. M. Gardner, 10 Easy Row, Birmingham. The recipes are good and some of them are distinctly original. The proceeds of the sale are to go to the National Union.[1]

Mrs Aubrey Dowson was born Phillis Ellen Heaton Atkinson in Frimley, Surrey, in October 1876, to Mary Lang (née Thomas) and Edmund Atkinson, who was at that time employed as Professor of Experimental Science at the Royal Military College. She was their second daughter and the third of six children. Her middle name, Heaton, was the maiden name of her paternal grandmother. On 26 May 1903, Phillis married Aubrey Osler Dowson in Guildford, Surrey. Following their marriage, the couple moved into their own home, Yew Tree Cottage, Lapworth, Birmingham. They had no children.

Phillis' husband was born in 1875 in Gee Cross, Cheshire. After graduating from New College, Oxford, in 1897,[2] he moved to Edgbaston to live with his maternal grandfather, Abraham Follett Osler, and to begin working for

The Women's Suffrage Cookery Book, edited by Mrs Dowson.

the family glass manufactory on Broad Street, in Birmingham. Having excelled
as a sportsman while at Rugby School and the University of Oxford, Aubrey
joined Moseley Rugby Football Club during the 1897–98 season,[3] and continued
to play top level cricket. Given their geographical separation, it is a wonder that
the two ever met, but it is possible that Phillis met Aubrey through her brother,
Christopher Atkinson, who was a fellow of Exeter College, Oxford.[4] As contemporaries at Oxford, the two men both read Modern History. That the families were
acquainted is certain: on the night of the 1901 census, Aubrey's youngest brother
Oscar Dowson is recorded as a visitor at the Atkinson family home, Portesberry
Hill, Camberley, where Phillis and Christopher were listed as resident.[5]

Science, industry, non-conformism, civic duty and activism were strong influ-
ences in the families of both husband and wife. Aubrey's father was a Unitarian
minister; Phillis' mother, a Baptist. Phillis' father was a Surrey justice of the
peace; her maternal grandfather a Bristol Town councillor. Through the Osler
line, her husband Aubrey was connected to the campaign for Women's Suffrage:
his aunt by marriage was Catherine Courtauld Osler (née Taylor), a significant
figure in Birmingham suffrage campaigns. She was descended from a Unitarian
family and her parents had been members of the Birmingham Women's Suffrage
Society (BWSS) since its formation in 1868. Catherine's own commitment to
suffrage activism did not stop when she married Alfred Clarkson Osler in 1873;
she went on to found the Birmingham Ladies Debating Society in 1881, before
becoming secretary of the Birmingham Women's Suffrage Society (BWSS) in
1885.[6] Catherine involved her son, Julian, and two daughters in the campaigning societies and, by 1909, Phillis had joined the BWSS, and been appointed the
first secretary of the Midland Federation of National Union of Women's Suffrage
Societies (NUWSS).[7]

In 1910, as Mrs Aubrey Dowson, Phillis edited *The Women's Suffrage Cookery
Book*, published by the BWSS to raise funds for the NUWSS. The book went
through several editions and included recipes from suffrage campaigners across
the country, including her cousin by marriage, Mrs Julian Osler, as well as Mrs
Millicent Fawcett and at least one Pankhurst.[8] Linda Schlossberg describes how the
recipes comprised 'traditional English dishes as well as dishes that might be made
more swiftly or at non-traditional times of day – that is, recipes that accommo-
dated the busy schedules of women campaigning for the vote.' Its political message
was made clear in the final section, 'Menus for Meals for Suffrage Workers', which
states that 'it is not always easy to provide suitable food for workers who have to get
their meals as best they can during a day's hard and exacting work often lasting for
12 hours or more'. The section included a recipe from Mrs Bertrand Russell entitled
'Cooking and Preserving a Good Suffrage Speaker … [grease] the dish by paying
all the speaker's expenses … [beat] her to a froth with an optimistic spoon … [and
avoid] too strong a flavour of apologies'.[9]

Phillis appears on the 1911 census return for the marital home of Yew Tree Cottage, giving her occupation as 'Women's Suffrage Worker'. Her mother, Mary Lang Atkinson, and sister, Evelyn, noted on their census return for Portesberry Hill, Camberley, that they both had an infirmity: 'No Vote at 21'. By 1912, Phillis is listed as a member of the Solihull & District Branch of the NUWSS,[10] and helps to run the 'Foreign Stall' at the Leamington Franchise Fair on 17 April 1912.[11] She appears to have moved to Stratford-upon-Avon in late 1912,[12] and from 1913 reports in the local press place her at county suffrage and Conservative Unionist society meetings and fundraisers for Stratford-Upon-Avon Hospital. In May 1915, following the outbreak of the First World War, Aubrey Dowson joined the 12th Rifle Brigade, despite being aged nearly forty. In 1917 he was mentioned in despatches for his work as the brigade transport officer and on 1 January 1918 he was awarded the Military Cross.[13] In the post-war world, the couple seems to have settled down to a quiet rural life on their farm at Hanging Langford, near Salisbury, where Aubrey died in 1940, followed by Phillis' death four years later.

32

PRINCESS SOPHIA DULEEP SINGH (1876–1948)

The suffragette princess

Carol Frankish

Sophia Duleep Singh twice had her jewels seized by bailiffs as a result of her refusal to pay taxes during the 'No taxation without Representation' campaign. On both occasions suffragette friends bought back the jewels and returned them to her.

Princess Sophia Duleep Singh was the daughter of a deposed maharajah and a goddaughter of Queen Victoria. Her early life was one of royal patronage and privilege. Her social life took place in the higher echelons of society, and it was through her contact with the women of the upper classes that she met socialite Una Dugdale, a prominent and charismatic member of the Women's Social and Political Union (WSPU). In 1908, Sophia heard Una speak of (what seemed to Sophia) the wildly exciting exploits of the WSPU, at an event at the Dugdale's family home. Sophia signed up as a member of the WSPU the same day, joining her local branch in Kingston-on-Thames,[1] and in the early days of Sophia's membership her contribution was mainly fund-raising. She organized fêtes and bazaars, and lent her name to the cause by donating jams and preserves labelled 'Made by the Princess'. Gradually, she started to attend suffragette 'At Homes', where women were recruited and donations to the cause were encouraged. Sophia's celebrity and wealth proved useful: women would attend the events just to meet the exotic princess. Eventually,

MARY EVANS PICTURE LIBRARY

Princess Sophia Duleep Singh during the First World War.

Sophia came to the attention of Emmeline Pankhurst, who, as well as being intrigued by this unlikely, extremely avid, new recruit to the cause, was quick to realize the advantages of Sophia's status. She recognized that her newsworthiness, especially, was a tool that could only further the aims of the campaign. Sophia soon became a member of the suffragette inner circle, delighting in the exalted company of Emmeline Pethick Lawrence, Annie Kenney and Ethel Smyth as her commitment to the movement intensified and she enthusiastically took part in protest marches.

At the State Opening of Parliament on 18 November 1910, Sophia joined her fellow suffragettes at Caxton Hall, and the different ranks of the WSPU moved outside to march to the Palace of Westminster. Sophia was one of the nine women in the elite first group who surrounded Emmeline Pankhurst. What started as a peaceful protest, with suffragettes carrying their purple and white banners and chanting their slogans, soon got out of hand. Sophia and the first deputation could do nothing but helplessly watch the violence meted out to their members. Eventually, horrified as she watched a police officer repeatedly throwing a woman to the ground until she seemed to be losing consciousness, Sophia forced her way through the crowds and placed herself between the woman and the officer. In her high pitched, cultured voice she ordered him to stop. Shocked at the sight of this small, vociferous harridan, he stepped away. Sophia followed him and caught sight of his identification number, V700, which she committed to memory. Her name appears on the Home Office list of the hundreds of suffragettes arrested that day. Beneath her entry in the list 'Singh Princess A Duleep' was the legend 'complaints of police conduct'.[2] Once released, without charge, Sophia wrote to Winston Churchill, then the Home Secretary, complaining about the brutality of Constable V700. The letter was forwarded to the Metropolitan Police. No further action was taken against Constable V700 and, although Sophia continued to press her complaint, Winston Churchill wrote tersely on her file 'Send no further reply to her',[3] and the case was closed.

Sophia's militancy was not restricted to the WSPU activities. In October 1909, she also joined the Women's Tax Resistance League (WTRL) and supported the Women's Freedom League's Census Boycott, writing across her census return, 'If women don't count, neither should they be counted'.[4] Her resistance to paying tax led to a summons to appear in court in 1911 and then the bailiffs seizing some of her property to offset the taxes she owed. Such was her prestige in the WSPU that her property – on this occasion, jewels – sent for auction were bid for and won by her wealthy suffragette colleagues. She continued to defy the taxation laws. On the second occasion of her summons to court in 1913, the *Daily Mail* reported that '… she came to court wearing the badge and medal of the Tax Resistance League and was accompanied by six other ladies, including the secretary of the League.'[5] She told the judge: 'When the women of England are enfranchised and the State

THE WOMEN'S LIBRARY COLLECTION, LSE LIBRARY

Women's Tax Resistance League.

No
Taxation
Without
Representation.

TELEPHONE: 3335 CITY.
10, TALBOT HOUSE,
98, St. MARTIN'S LANE,
W.C.

The Princess Sophia Duleep Singh's

Goods will be sold for Tax Resistance,

on Tues. July 25th at Hick's, Station Rd. Ashford

Meeting to be held in Auction Rooms after Sale

Please come and bring friends to support Protest
Meeting at 4 *o'clock.*

Waterloo 2.10 to Ashford — 2/6 return

Notice of sale from goods seized for non-payment of taxes.

acknowledges me as a citizen I shall, of course, willingly pay my share towards its upkeep.'[6] The judge was unimpressed and fined her £12 10s for the unpaid taxes. When Sophia replied that she had no intention of paying, she was told to expect the bailiffs, who once again seized jewels deemed to be the value of her tax and fines. Once again, when these were sent for auction, they were purchased by a fellow suffragette and handed back to Sophia.

Sophia and the WSPU were also incensed by the opinions of the former Viceroy of India, Lord Curzon, an outspoken opponent of women's suffrage, who formed The National League for Opposing Women's Suffrage and who suggested that women's suffrage would jeopardize the very foundation of the British Empire. Suffragette publications vilified Curzon at every opportunity. On 6 February, WSPU members stationed themselves at the homes of prominent cabinet ministers. They held their banners and slogans high so that these would be the first thing the ministers saw on their way to Parliament. Sophia and one other suffragette made their way to stand outside 10 Downing Street and waited quietly until Herbert Asquith emerged. As he got into his chauffeur-driven car, Sophia hurled herself at his window, shouting slogans and waving a poster that declared 'Give women the vote!' Although arrested, embarrassment at having Queen Victoria's goddaughter detained meant she was released without charge, although her exploits were reported in newspapers in Britain and the Empire.

Sophia, however, remained a steadfast supporter of the WSPU even when the militancy increased, giving £30 (an enormous amount) in 1913; in 1914 she gave £51 of her £600 annual income.[7] She continued to sell *The Suffragette* outside her Hampton Court home, spoke at meetings, drove press carts through London, loaded with suffragette leaflets, and tried to exploit her fame for the movement whenever she could. On 18 February on one well-documented occasion, Sophia acted as one of the bodyguards and decoys that allowed Emmeline to escape from the police. When war was declared in 1914, Sophia's suffragette militancy came to an end and her energies turned to the war effort.

In 1914, more than 40,000 Indian troops, many of them Sikhs, were deployed to Europe to fight in the trenches of the Somme, and Sophia became involved in the welfare of Indian wounded soldiers. On a visit to India with her sisters, Sophia had been horrified by the poverty and deprivation of the people she encountered there. On her return to England, with those experiences fresh in her mind, she turned her attention to the plight of the Lascars, Indian merchant seamen (most of them originating from the Punjab) who worked on British cargo ships. These men were treated appallingly by the British merchant service, many living as virtual slaves in hovels in the East End of London. Sophia decided to alleviate their circumstances. Through her contacts with the wealthy and influential and her own contributions, she succeeded in constructing a safe house for the Lascars, where they could be fed and decently sheltered. She continued her commitment to India alongside her suffrage campaigning. In 1907, on a visit to India to see her sister Bamba, she, with her sister, attended several rallies at Lucknow University and heard Gopa Krishna Gokhale and Lajpat Rai, members of the burgeoning Indian National Congress express their nationalist views. Sophia was impressed by both men's oratory and began to study the Indian Nationalist arguments in detail. Her interest in and loyalty to their cause for self-determination politicized her, but, as her political destiny lay, not in India, but in England, she threw her support into a political cause of her own.

By December 1914, the dead and the wounded Indian troops numbered thousands. The wounded were sent back to England. In Brighton, The Lady Hardinge Hospital was founded to house them. It was administered by a charity and run by volunteers. Sophia volunteered her services very early on. At first she just visited the soldiers, but later became a Red Cross nurse. She completely mystified the Indian soldiers as she appeared to be an Indian, but could not speak their language. The wounded Sikhs, however, were delighted and honoured that an Indian princess called Duleep Singh was attending them. Sophie furthered her war effort by fundraising to help sepoys at the Front, supplying them with warm clothes, stout shoes, chocolates and cigarettes.

The years between the wars saw Sophia's fortunes changed. No longer regarded in such high esteem by the socialites and, as the government and the Royal family no longer saw any need to pander to Duleep Singh's heirs, she was struggling financially. Her later years were spent in quiet domesticity with her housekeeper's family and Catherine, her sister. Sophia always remained faithful to her suffragette roots and was delighted in 1928 when the Representation of the People (Equal

Franchise) Act came into being, seeing it as a just reward for the suffering of her fellow suffragettes. As a member of the Suffragette Fellowship, she and her fellow suffragettes held occasional meetings to talk about past triumphs and hardships. Although the membership was really restricted to those suffragettes who had been force-fed in prison, they allowed Sophia to join, perhaps realizing that she had done everything in her power to get herself imprisoned. Sophia was among the hundreds of suffragettes who watched Emmeline Pankhurst's statue being unveiled in Victoria Tower Gardens, London, on 6 March 1930. The floral bouquets that were laid at the feet of the statue had been organized by Princess Sophia in a last tribute to a woman she regarded not only as a heroine, but also a true friend.[8]

33

MURIEL MATTERS 1877–1969

Campaigner and Montessori teacher

Janis Lomas

Muriel Matters was one of the founding members of the Women's Freedom League (WFL) and took a leading role in three of the most innovative non-violent protest actions during those years: travelling to the outlying villages and towns of southern England in a horse-drawn caravan, chaining herself to the House of Commons' grille in the Ladies' Gallery, and staging the first ever aerial protest in the world.

Muriel Matters was born in Adelaide, Australia, one of ten children of a cabinetmaker. She studied music and enjoyed success in dramatic productions and declaiming dramatic poems and prose in public performances. Her success encouraged her to try her luck as an actress and elocutionist in England, where she was to spend most of the rest of her life. All thoughts of a stage career were rapidly put on hold when she joined the Women's Social and Political Union (WSPU). In 1907, she was one of the many WSPU followers who left to form the WFL after determining that the WSPU had become autocratic. In 1908, the fledgling WFL needed publicity, members and funds and the WFL leadership felt that they needed to promote themselves beyond London to set up new branches and get their message of non-violent action across to a wider public. One of the WFL leaders, Charlotte Despard, came up with the idea of a gypsy-style caravan travelling the countryside, and Muriel was one of the leaders of this venture. For three months in 1908 the caravan, pulled by a horse called Asquith, moved through the towns and villages of southern England, encountering occasional cheering crowds and packed halls, sometimes puzzled indifference, and sometimes heckling, rotten fruit and eggs, rowdy behaviour and violence. Several times the police had to step in to prevent the women being attacked. In her memoirs, Margaret Newinson, a fellow caravanner, recalled:

> At Herne Bay, we had a very hostile reception, and finally our lorry was pushed along the parade with loud cries of 'Chuck 'em in the sea'. A bodyguard of

Muriel Matters in the Suffrage Caravan.

fishermen came to our help and escorted us to … where our caravan was parked. They stood as sentinels by the gate, whilst outside the mob howled like wild beasts till a late hour.[1]

At the end of the summer, Muriel returned to London and was asked to take part in a carefully planned daring action within the House of Commons itself. This was to gain her widespread notoriety as it led to her being the first woman to give a speech in the House of Commons. She was chosen to lead the protest because the WFL leadership were all well known to security staff in the House of Commons, whereas Muriel was relatively unknown in London so it would be easier for her to gain access to the Ladies' Gallery. The gallery was a small room two flights up and directly above the Speaker's chair. Fitted with a heavy grille, the gallery restricted the view female visitors had of the floor of the House, rendering them almost invisible to the MPs below. Consequently, it was seen by suffragettes as being a symbol of their oppression and exclusion from politics. On 28 October 1908, three hours after Muriel and another suffragette, Helen Fox, had entered the gallery, the two women saw their chance and chained themselves to the grille with heavy chains, which they had concealed under their coats. The keys to the sturdy padlocks that secured the chains they dropped down their backs. While supporters in the men only Strangers' Gallery showered suffrage leaflets onto the floor of the Commons, Helen shouted 'The women of the country demand the vote'. Muriel then used her elocution training to project her voice, as she proclaimed:

Mr Speaker, members of the Liberal government, we have sat behind this insulting grille for too long ... You are discussing a domestic question, and it is time that the women of England were given a voice in legislation which affects them as much as it affects men. We demand the vote ...[2]

Uproar followed, but Muriel's voice could still be heard as she continued her speech. Two men appeared and tried to drag her away; more men followed but eventually the grille had to be removed and the two women, still firmly attached, were taken away to a committee room. There, finally a smithy succeeded in filing the chains away from the grille. News of the escapade caused a sensation and was reported in newspapers around the world. In total, fourteen WFL members were arrested that evening, with the harshest punishment reserved for Muriel and Helen, who were sentenced to one month's imprisonment in the third division, reserved for the most hardened criminals. This meant no visitors, worse food, exercise only three times weekly, harder work than other prisoners and, except for chapel, no contact with others for twenty-two hours a day. Newspapers in both Australia and England had mixed reactions to her sentence: many condemned the actions of the women, while others felt that it was unjust to imprison the activists with drunkards and vagrants. Muriel was deeply affected by what she saw in prison. On her release, she described the regime in Holloway as: 'a system of hopelessness that made no attempt to raise the spiritual or moral standard of the inmates, but rather to depress and deprave them'.[3] Muriel's notoriety certainly helped promote the WFL and raised much-needed funds. When, a few weeks later, Muriel spoke in St James' Hall, London, a packed audience donated £2,000. Muriel was now given a paid position within the WFL, tasked with branch development and formation. She helped to found the Actresses' Franchise League (AFL) the same year.

In February 1909, Muriel carried out her most daring escapade and became one of only a handful of women in Britain to have flown in an airship. The WFL hired an airship and pilot for £75 to fly over London and Muriel dropped leaflets near to the king's state coach as he made his way to the State Opening of Parliament. The airship had *Votes for Women* painted on one side and *Women's Franchise League* on the other. Although armed with 65lb of leaflets, as the wind was against them, she did not manage to shower the royal procession with leaflets, although many leaflets were dropped all over London. The escapade was the first aerial protest ever staged, and hailed as a great success; news of it reached around the world. Muriel's fame now meant that she and her close friend and fellow suffragist, Violet Tilliard, were invited to travel back to Australia to go on a speaking tour. In the four months she spent in Australia, she crossed the continent twice, spoke to thousands at packed public meetings, attracted crowds and gained publicity for women's suffrage in the United Kingdom. Australia gave women the vote in 1911, although it was to be a few more years until women were allowed to stand for election in some states of Australia. On her return to the UK, Muriel became disturbed by the violent tactics used by the militants and her support for the WFL waned. She turned her attention to issues of social injustice, although she continued to speak from time to time for the AFL, the New Constitutional Society for Women's Suffrage and the Church League for Women's Suffrage. She also undertook another caravanning tour with Violet for the Tax Resistance League and in 1914 she spoke on behalf of the NUWSS.

In 1914 after several months of indecision Muriel married William Porter, an American dentist living in London. As a pacifist, during the war years Muriel spoke at peace conferences and attended the International Congress of Women in The Hague. When she heard that Maria Montessori had opened a school in Barcelona and was running an intensive teachers' training course on her methods, she travelled there to attend the course. On her return, Sylvia Pankhurst asked her to use the Montessori method to teach at a school she had set up in a disused pub in the East End to be called 'The Mother's Arms'. The school was a success and Muriel was soon also running courses and lectures to teach 'Montessorianism'.

After the war, Muriel travelled to Australia for the last time and undertook speaking engagements in Perth, Adelaide, Melbourne, Sydney and Brisbane. On her return, she continued to write and lecture on early years' education. In 1924, she stood unsuccessfully as the Labour Party candidate for Hastings, despite knowing that she had very little chance of securing the seat. She and her husband seemed to have led fairly independent lives and she had no children of her own. In the 1920s and 1930s, she campaigned for equal pay for women teachers and was a member of the Committee of the Women's Guild of Empire, which had been set up by Flora Drummond to campaign against both Fascism and Communism. After her husband's death, she moved to a small house on Hastings seafront for the last twenty years of her life, and died in 1969.

34

MABEL LIDA RAMSAY (1878–1954)

A doctor and suffragist in Plymouth

Maggie Andrews

At a meeting in Saltash Guildhall in September 1910, Mabel Ramsay, a doctor and committed suffragist, explained that in England:

> infantile mortality was 147 per 1,000 per annum, in Scotland it was 125 per 1,000; but in New Zealand and Victoria, where women had the suffrage, the infantile mortality was only 77, per 1,000.[1]

For Mabel, and the audience who responded to her speech with rapturous applause, women should be enfranchised to bolster their roles as wives, mothers and carers.

Mabel Ramsay was born in London. Her mother was committed to women's suffrage and supported her in studying medicine at the University of Edinburgh. She apparently preceded her studies by two years' training as a gymnast to deepen her understanding of the human body. By 1906, she was qualified as a doctor and a surgeon and went on to work in Glasgow, Leeds and Huddersfield, before moving to Plymouth in 1908. However, as one of very few trained women doctors in Edwardian Britain, it was difficult to obtain a hospital post and so she set up her own practice.

By 1909, a branch of the National Society for Women's Suffrage had formed in Plymouth and Mabel Ramsay took on the role of secretary.[2] For the next five years she combined her developing medical career with her commitment to women's suffrage, arranging meetings and campaigning. In 1911, Mabel and her mother hosted 'a large party of census invaders', at the home they shared in Plymouth.[3] For Mabel, suffrage campaigning was intrinsically entwined with social welfare for mothers and children. In early 1912, Mabel argued at a public meeting that 'They should do everything in their power to keep mothers in their homes if possible', but promoted the setting up of a crèche for mothers and children for whom this was not possible.[4]

THE WOMEN'S LIBRARY COLLECTION, LSE LIBRARY

MAY, 1913.

National Union of Women's Suffrage Societies,
14, GREAT SMITH STREET, WESTMINSTER, LONDON, S.W.
NON-MILITANT.   NON-PARTY.
President   -   -   Mrs. HENRY FAWCETT, LL.D.
Colours: Red, White, and Green.

WOMEN'S SUFFRAGE PILGRIMAGE

CONSTITUTIONAL SUFFRAGISTS,

Join the Great March to London

from North, South, East, or West, and show that Men and Women
are dedicating themselves afresh to the great cause of the

FREEDOM OF WOMEN.

What are the Objects of this Pilgrimage?

THE OBJECTS ARE TWOFOLD:—

1. To prove throughout the length and breadth of the country
   the extent of the demand for the Vote by Constitutional
   Suffragists, and to demonstrate the determination of
   law-abiding citizens—both men and women—to win the
   political freedom of women.

2. To collect a large sum of money to hand into the Treasury
   of the National Union on July 26th when the Pilgrims
   will march into London.

[P.T.O.

Details of the 1913 Suffrage Pilgrimage in which both Mabel
and her mother took part.

Mabel Ramsay was not a militant, but rather someone who by less dramatic methods, such as collecting signatures and making speeches, sought to persuade people to support women's suffrage. She presided at the annual meeting of the South Western Federation of Women's Societies at Clarence Chambers in Plymouth, where they heard about the work of a number of branches, including those in Truro, Launceston and St Ives on 18 November 1912.[5] Mabel Ramsay spoke in favour of women being enfranchised on the same terms as men, sometimes facing fierce opposition from those who were concerned that if this occurred women voters would outnumber men, or who, alternatively, argued that the actions of militant suffragettes proved that women were unfit to be enfranchised.[6] She and her mother took part in the great Suffrage Pilgrimage of 1913 when her mother was the eldest of the thirteen women who marched on foot all the way from Land's End to London.

When the First World War began in 1914, there were approximately 500 trained female doctors. They were seen as a vital resource, but it was expected that their role would be on the home front, replacing men in looking after the civilian population.[7] Many women in the suffrage organizations thought otherwise. By 20 September, Mabel was working at a hospital close to the lines in Antwerp, Belgium. She later recalled:

> I was invited to join the unit on Thursday September 18th and … I left Plymouth on Sunday morning September 20th arriving at Fenchurch Street Station … We arrived at the Scheldt at 10 pm.
>
> Within two hours we had all set to work and cleaned up the hospital and the beds we had brought were set up and we were ready to receive patients. The operating theatre was ready and two days later the X-ray room in working order. After being inspected by Sir Cecil Hertzlit and the Chief of the Belgian Croix Rouge, and the chief doctor of the Belgian Army, the hospital was passed and accepted as an Auxiliary Red Cross Hospital under the Belgian Red Cross.

However, as the Allied army retreated, the fighting got closer and she recalled:

Lights are out earlier and earlier as the bomb habit is developing. Nursing and operating done under great difficulties. We took in two English Marines who were wounded today. The position of Antwerp is very serious. Town is full of rumours but no official news. Many forts have fallen.[8]

She was decorated with the Mons Star with Bar for caring for the wounded during the Allied retreat from Belgium. She briefly returned to England, but was soon in France as Chief Medical Officer of the No. 2 Anglo-French Hospital at Chateau Tourlaville in Cherbourg. The Women's Imperial Service League organized the hospital, but accommodation in a chateau was less than ideal as she telegraphed London to explain:

Sanitation imperfect. Help urgent. Wanted Primus and oil stoves. Electricity. No gas. Nothing prepared. Croix Rouge poor. Come as soon as possible. Difficulties surmountable.

A visit to the quays to see the arrival of the wounded confirmed the opinion that help was urgently needed.

In 1915, she and fellow doctor Florence Stoney described some of their practices in the *British Medical Journal*, providing details of how they managed all manner of injuries and diseases including fractures of the jaw, pelvis and feet, femur and injuries to the lungs and nerves.[9] In 1921, she became the third woman to become a Fellow of the Royal College of Surgeons in the UK.

True to her suffragist commitment to women, Mabel's post-war outstanding career was focused upon women as both doctors and patients. In 1922, she was part of the British delegation to the Medical Women's International Association in Geneva. Following their wartime service and the Sex Disqualification Removal Act in 1919, women doctors found it easier to get hospital appointments in the inter-war years when Mabel focused on gynaecology, obstetrics and maternity care. From 1929, she was a member of the Royal College of Obstetricians and Gynaecologists and became a consulting gynaecologist and obstetrician at several hospitals and clinics in the west of England. She published a number of papers on her work, including 'A Case of Puerperal Sepsis and Sloughing Fibroid and Subsequent Pregnancy' (1932). She became president of the Women's Medical Association from 1933 to 1934.

She continued to live and work in Plymouth and was the first woman to become president of the Plymouth Medical Society in 1930, the same year she became a founder member of the Plymouth branch of Soroptimist International. In 2014, she also became the first women to have a blue plaque put up to her in Plymouth.

35

MARGARET COUSINS (1878–1954)

Irish Nationalist, Theosophist and magistrate

Leah Susans

In 1913, after being sentenced to a month's imprisonment in Tullamore Prison in Ireland, Margaret Cousins went on hunger strike and wrote to the chairman of the Prison Board:

> I am not a criminal but a political prisoner – my motives were neither criminal nor personal – being wholly associated with the agitation to obtain the Votes for Women.[1]

Margaret Gillespie was born in Boyle, County Roscommon, in 1878 and brought up in a Unionist and Protestant household. Her father was a legal clerk. The oldest of fifteen children, she was awarded a scholarship to the Victoria High School for Girls in Derry and matriculated with distinction in 1898.[2] Later, she studied at the Royal Academy of Music in Dublin and became a music teacher, something she continued to do after she married James Cousins in 1903. He was a poet and play-wright who later took on the role of editor for the *Irish Citizen* newspaper. At their wedding, Margaret announced her commitment to vegetarianism, as practised by her husband, and later became honorary secretary of the Irish Vegetarian Society. The couple became involved in a social milieu within Dublin's society, which was interested in nationalism and naturalism and included the Celtic literary move-ment. They associated with famous writers such as Y. B. Yeats, George Russell and James Joyce and became interested in topics such as food reform, anti-vivisection, temperance, Socialism and Eastern philosophies including Theosophy. The couple never had children and Catherine Candy has suggested that there is an indication in their joint autobiography that they 'eschewed sexual intercourse', something that was influenced by Margaret's 'earnest studies in Buddhist and Hindu metasexual narratives'.[3]

Margaret joined the Irish Women's Suffrage and the Local Government

Association in 1906 and co-founded the Irish Women's Franchise League (IWFL)
with Hanna Sheehy Skeffington after a meeting held on 4 November 1908. Most of
the women in this organization were well-educated, middle class and Protestant.[4]
There was in the IWFL a sense of frustration at how women's issues were sidelined
by some of those with a commitment to the nationalist cause as Margaret Cousins
explained later in her autobiography:

> We were as keen as men on the freedom of Ireland, but we saw the men
> clamoring for amendments, which suited their own interests and made no
> recognition of the existence of women as fellow citizens.[5]

Margaret was a leading speaker for the Irish Women's Franchise League and regularly addressed its open-air meetings across Dublin. When the IWFL established
links with the WSPU in 1909, Margaret Cousins spent three weeks at the WSPU
London headquarters at Clements Inn. She learned militant tactics and invited
Mrs Pankhurst to come to Ireland to speak. Margaret was also involved in militant
campaigns herself while on a visit to Britain; she was present at the Black Friday
demonstration on 18 November 1910, and was imprisoned for breaking windows
in Downing Street three days later.

Back in Ireland, Margaret Cousins accompanied Emmeline Pankhurst on a
speaking tour of Irish towns, including Derry and Cork in October 1910. However,
the IWFL focused their campaigns on trying to get votes for women included in
proposals for Irish Home Rule. Consequently, their priorities, concerns and policies
differed from the suffrage campaigns in London and the relationship between the
two organizations became rather tetchy and shortly after broke down. By January
1913, it seemed likely that a second reading of an Irish Home Rule bill would pass
its second reading, without an amendment to include women's enfranchisement.
Margaret Cousins and other Irish suffragettes were unimpressed and in protest
broke a number of windows at Dublin Castle. This led to another term of impris-

onment: this time for
a month in Tullamore
Jail, where she success-
fully fought for politi-
cal status after a brief
and well-publicized
hunger strike.[6]

In 1913, Margaret
and her husband left
Ireland; his less than
successful financial
investments, tensions

WSPU offices.

with W. B. Yeats and the Abbey Theatre and their growing interest in Theosophy all contributed to their decision to leave. Initially, they went to Liverpool, but in 1915 set off to the Theosophical Society's Headquarters in Adjar, Madras. Annie Besant, the British Socialist and women's rights advocate who had taken a leading role in the Matchgirls' Strike in 1888, was by then the president of the Theosophy Society in India, where James became the editor of the Theosophy newspaper *New India*. In India, Margaret's spiritualism and politics sat comfortably together. She was actively involved in feminist campaigns for women's education and women's right to take up political and legal office; in 1922, she became India's first female magistrate. She sought to revive indigenous crafts and industries, raise the age of consent for young girls, promote birth control and oppose child marriage. She founded the Women's Indian Association in 1917, a network of groups to promote women's suffrage, and edited its monthly journal. She worked on campaigns to mobilize Indian women to use their vote after provisional legislatures began to enfranchise women in 1921. She took a major role in organizing the All-India Women's Conference in 1926 and the All-Asia Women's Conference in 1931, and was president of the All India Women's Conference in 1938.[7]

Margaret shared a commitment to improving education and child welfare with many suffrage campaigners, which led her to become the first non-Indian member of the Indian Women's University at Poona in 1916 and to take up a position as headmistress of a girls' school in Mangalore. She supported the Children's Aid Society, the Women's Homes of Service and 'baby welcomes'. In India, as in Ireland, Margaret was part of a middle-class milieu, seeing those she sought to help through the prism of her own values, oblivious, for example, of the Indian caste system.[8] Nevertheless, she published three books on Indian women's rights. For Irish women, like Margaret Cousins, there were parallels in India's experience of British colonial rule and that of Ireland. Hence, she supported the Indian liberation movement and, in 1932, spent a year in Vellore Women's Jail as a consequence of her support of Ghandi's free speech campaign.

Margaret also assisted with campaigns for women's political candidates in southern India in 1937. However, by the 1940s, bad health, high blood pressure and then a stroke, slowed Margaret down. She lived to see Indian Independence in 1947, cared for by her husband and friends. The new Indian government recognized her contributions to the state by awarding her five thousand rupees in 1949, a great help to the financially strapped couple for the remaining years of their lives until, on 1 March 1954, Margaret died in Adyar, India.

36

KATE PARRY FRYE 1878–1959

Impoverished suffrage organizer and palm reader

Janis Lomas

As a paid organizer for the newly formed New Constitutional Society for Women's Suffrage, Kate Parry Frye undertook work that was by no means easy. In 1914, she wrote in her diary:

> As for this work I am completely fed up with it. It is people's own loss if they are not Suffrage but I seem to have lost the knack of converting them. Personally I am keener than ever but I feel I loathe and detest the work of it.[1]

Kate Parry Frye enjoyed an idyllic, middle-class childhood. Her father, Frederick Frye, was Liberal MP for Kensington North and owner of a seemingly successful chain of grocers' shops. In 1893, they moved to a substantial six-storey house in Arundel Gardens, London, and their summer house on the Thames called The Plat, in Bourne End, Buckinghamshire. The position of The Plat on the banks of the Thames meant that Kate and her sister Agnes could enjoy regattas, canoeing, punting and cycling. Although Kate, as an unmarried middle-class daughter, could have stayed at home, she was keen to pursue a theatrical career and tried to earn her living as an actress from around 1903 onwards. It was while touring in a production of *Quality Street* by J. M. Barrie in 1903 that she met a young actor called John Collins. Two years later, they became engaged although John had little prospects and her family was quite disapproving of the match. Kate and John were to be engaged for ten years, and Kate was not nearly as infatuated with him as he was with her. Between theatrical work, she could always live comfortably at home, and she frequently needed to do so as she found it almost impossible to live on the pittance paid to a minor repertory actress who was only in sporadic demand.

Her interest in politics stemmed from her father's time as an MP from 1892, although he served for only one term, losing his seat in 1895. Kate's diaries mention attending meetings of the National Union of Women's Suffrage Societies

(NUWSS) from around 1906,[2] and working on a voluntary basis for the suffrage cause. By 1908, it became clear that her father's business was not doing well and economies would have to be made. The family was forced to leave their Arundel Gardens house and move into a flat. It did not solve their financial problems, and matters came to a head in 1911 when her father could no longer hide the extent of his debts. It now became imperative that Kate support herself and she realized that the stage was not going to provide her with a regular income.

The discovery that her father had accumulated substantial debts, which he was unable to pay, quickly resulted in the family descending into genteel poverty. Where she had once occupied a certain position in middle-class society, as the daughter of a business owner and former MP, Kate was now reliant on the patronage of others, which she found very difficult to bear at times. She, therefore, felt both resentful and grateful when through her friends, Alexandra and Gladys Wright, she was offered the position of paid organizer for the newly formed New Constitutional Society for Women's Suffrage (NCSWS) in 1911. The NCSWS had been formed the previous year by some of the leaders of the London Society for Women's Suffrage (LSWS), an organization affiliated to the NUWSS. These ex-LSWS members had become disillusioned by what Kate called the NUWSS's 'half-hearted and perplexing counsels', but also felt unable to take part in the law-breaking militancy of the WSPU. The NCSWS saw itself as a half-way house between the two organizations, having adopted an anti-government policy, which went further than the NUWSS; the NCSWS aimed to:

> unite all suffragists who believe in the anti-government election policy, who desire to work by constitutional means and to abstain from public criticism of other suffragists whose conscience leads them to adopt other methods.[3]

The Wright sisters were leading members of the NCSWS from the beginning.

The work that Kate Parry Frye now undertook was by no means easy. Her salary of £2 weekly had to cover her 'digs', which could often cost a guinea (£1.05). She had to find speakers for meetings, publicize them, and try to get a good crowd to attend. Attendance at her meetings often depended on the weather, or whatever else was happening in the town and the particular speakers she had been able to persuade to appear. She frequently had to position herself at the door of the hall to try to prevent rowdy youths disrupting the speakers. On occasions she had a good attendance, but sometimes the numbers were low and the collection for the society resulted in just a few shillings, which neither covered the costs of the meeting nor justified her salary.

On 1 June 1911, Kate began to canvass for a London meeting to be held a week later on 8 June. This meeting was a fairly typical one and necessitated a whole week of canvassing. To save money, she had been staying with her parents and sister at The Plat the evening before. This meant that she had to catch two buses into London to canvass all morning, then travel to the NCSWS office to collect everything needed, then travel to Chelsea where the meeting would be held. After getting the hall ready, she went out canvassing again for an hour and a half. By the appointed time she had three stewards, three speakers and a singer booked for the meeting. After all that she records that:

> Alexandra and Gladys came and five or at most seven other people. It was hopeless ... I stood outside trying to get people in ... I was so vexed. I had to leave at 9.15 as arranged, for my train at 10pm. I was dead tired.[4]

She often felt very lonely, especially when exhausted or unwell. On Census Day in 1911, she was in Maldon and had a cold. She wrote in her diary:

> It poured with rain all day – and I stayed in bed in my little room 6 feet square. Not a happy day, my cold was so violent I ached all over ... I did feel miserable.[5]

She also worried about her family whose finances were going from bad to worse. After giving up their London flat and moving permanently to The Plat, they then had to leave that place and move to rented rooms in Worthing. In October 1913 came the final humiliation: the sale of all their furniture and effects. Kate was now, in effect, homeless and totally reliant on her salary, so despite the difficulties she faced she had no option but to continue her work. She was now in the same position as most working women, but one to which she was totally unaccustomed.

By 1913, the WSPU's arson attacks on public buildings, letter boxes and window-smashing campaigns had turned a great deal of public opinion against the suffrage campaigners. Subsequently, meetings became increasingly rowdy, and even dangerous. Kate seems to have taken these dangers in her stride, even when, while selling *Votes for Women* she nearly got knocked down and was struck a savage blow from one youth. On another occasion when the NCSWS were sharing a Waggonette as a platform with the WSPU, she wrote of the crowd:

> but, oh it was so rowdy – the Hooligans with squibs, and crackers and tin trumpets and rattles – oh it was a noise. The WSPU had a good crowd but the boys were so awful and put fireworks under the Waggonette – so eventually a policeman came up and they stopped – so we got their crowd ... I shall never forget that firework night ... I had a horrid wad of something soft and squishy strike me on the mouth, but I just took my handkerchief and wiped it off ... The boys never got a squib (a small firework) under my skirts – I walked away in time. Well, it was exciting.[6]

Attendances at meetings seem to have got even worse and, after one meeting in February 1914, she wrote in her organizer's book that the collection came to 6d (two and a half pence) and the sale of literature 7d (three pence).[7] She somewhat reluctantly offered to read the palms of people attending NCSWS Bazaars and 'At Homes' in a somewhat desperate measure to get people to attend and to raise funds for the society. As the First World War approached Kate was worried that her work would end while her responsibilities increased when her father died in March 1914 and she had to sort out the family finances. Her aunt helped the family out by giving her mother £150 a year to add to the £150 a year she had already been given by her father's business associates; she also promised Kate and her sister Agnes £50 a year for life in her will.

In January 1915, when she was thirty-seven, Kate finally married John Collins. Perhaps the uncertainties of war and her own future, his commission as an officer and his imminent departure for the Western Front were the deciding factors that persuaded Kate to finally marry him. She continued to work for the NCSWS in 1914–15 as they opened a workroom for unemployed seamstresses in the early months of the war, and then she helped to run an NCSWS canteen. She appears to have had some sort of breakdown shortly after her marriage. When she recovered, she never returned to work, although she kept in contact with the NCSWS. The organization was finally disbanded when the Representation of the People Act was passed in 1918, finally giving women householders aged over thirty the vote for the first time.

Luckily, John came through the war unscathed and, having distinguished himself in his war service by being awarded the Military Cross, the couple were able to settle down to married life. John returned to acting, but, as Kate had feared, he enjoyed very little success on the stage. From the 1920s, they lived in a cottage next door to her mother and sister Agnes. Kate's last suffrage-related activity was attending the funeral of Emmeline Pankhurst in 1928. She continued to write her diaries for the rest of her life and died aged eighty-one, five months after the death of her husband in 1959.

37

NORA DACRE FOX (1878–1961)

Suffragette and Fascist

Maggie Andrews

On 14 May 1914, newspapers reported that Mrs Norah Dacre Fox was arrested 'for making speeches advocating acts of militancy and violence', and subsequently brought before the Westminster Police Court. She indicated to the magistrate that she had no intention of taking part in proceedings, later saying, 'I am not going to allow you to talk to me. You know the whole thing is ridiculous, and that before we women enter the dock you have a rope around our necks.'

Norah was born in Dublin in 1878, the oldest child of Charlotte and John Doherty. She had two elder half-sisters from her father's first marriage, which ended when his wife died. Nora was ten years old when the whole family, which now also included two young boys, moved to London. Her father was well off, a Liberal, a justice of the peace, a local councillor, an Irish Nationalist and, it appears, a harsh disciplinarian with a tempestuous nature who was ready to use his fists. At the age of thirty-one, in 1909, Norah married Richard Dacre Fox, who ran a printing press, but the marriage was not a success.[1] By this time, she was already a member of the London and Provincial Anti-Vivisection Society and held strong views against vivisection.

Nora may have been a member and financial contributor to the Women's Social and Political Union (WSPU) before she married, but her truly active participation in the organization's activities seems to have coincided with the beginning of the disintegration of her marriage and the WSPU's greater militancy around 1912. She was the honorable secretary of the Kingston and District division of the WSPU, writing reports of their activities for the *Suffragette* magazine, organizing speakers and weekly recruitment meetings as well as raising

Nora with Oswald Mosley in 1936.

funds. She must have been an apt organizer because by March 1913 she was the general secretary of the WSPU, based in the London headquarters. She was also it seems a lively, dramatic and confrontational public speaker, much in demand in London and beyond, who has been described as being a 'defiant and unapologetic voice of the extreme activities of the WSPU'.[2]

An active campaigner against force-feeding, she wrote to the bishops of Winchester, London, Croydon and Lewes on the matter. The Church Suffrage League had been formed in 1909, but the organization was split in its attitudes to militancy and church leaders failed to condemn the treatment of women in prisons. Even after the Bishop of London paid a visit to women prisoners in Holloway, the Church of England still backed the government's treatment of women prisoners. On 29 January 1914, Nora and a group of suffragettes laid siege to Lambeth Palace; she was eventually admitted to speak to the Archbishop of Canterbury. All to no avail, the opinion of many church leaders was that suffragettes were not behaving in an appropriately Christian manner.

As the daughter of an Irish Nationalist, Nora had little sympathy for the Ulster Unionists, who were trying to prevent Irish independence and argued for the creation of Northern Ireland. Many in the WSPU believed suffragettes were treated harshly by the government and lesser force was used towards those who protested, demonstrated and threatened violence in support of Unionism. In May 1914, Nora was one of the suffragettes who laid siege to the houses of Unionist leaders such as Sir Edward Carson and Lord Lansdowne. Nora arrived at Lansdowne House before 9am on 14 May. The police removed the suffragettes within a couple of hours after much speech-making, bell-ringing and knocking at the gate. These activities led to one of Nora's three terms of imprisonment. Her hunger strike, refusal to undress and the breaking of two cell windows, resulted in her spending time in solitary confinement; her thirst strike led to her release from Holloway.

When the First World War broke out, Nora joined Emmeline and Christabel Pankhurst in their patriotic support of the war and efforts to recruit women to undertake war work. Her speeches backing the government were as ferocious as those criticizing the government for its failure to enfranchise women had been before the war. She became a strong anti-alien campaigner, speaking and writing in rallies organized by groups such as the British Empire Union in 1918. Among their requests was the demand that no person of enemy origin, whether naturalized or not, should be allowed to live in the British Empire for at least ten years after the war had ended.

Like a number of suffrage campaigners, Nora stood unsuccessfully as a candidate in the general election of 1918. She was an independent candidate in Richmond and came second, gaining only 3,165 votes. Her political activities were less prominent in the 1920s, and she unexpectedly gave birth to an illegitimate child in 1922. She had believed herself to be infertile, but it seemed that it was her

husband who suffered from infertility. Nora does not seem to have taken to motherhood enthusiastically. Her son's father was Edward Descou Dudley Vallance
Elam and, by the end of 1920s, Nora was calling herself Nora Elam and living with
Dudley at the Old Forge, Northchapel, in West Sussex. Neither Nora nor Dudley
divorced their first marriage partners, but presented themselves as a married couple
and took a very active role in the West Sussex Conservative Party.

By 1934, Nora and Dudley had transferred their political allegiance to the
British Union of Fascists (BUF), which was active in West Sussex. Nora spoke at
the Chichester Assembly rooms in April that year alongside William Joyce (later
shot as a war criminal after his infamous radio broadcasts as 'Lord Haw Haw'
made from Germany during the Second World War). The BUF's membership was
approximately 50,000 by this point and Rothermere's *Daily Mail* had endorsed the
movement under the heading 'Hurrah for the Blackshirts'.[3] Nora was not the only
suffragette to become a supporter of Fascism. Others include Sophia Allen and
Mary Richardson, the woman who had slashed the Rokeby Venus and had been
imprisoned nine times during the suffrage campaigns. Indeed, Richardson wrote:

> I was first attracted to the Blackshirts because I saw in them the courage, the
> action, the loyalty, the gift of service and the ability to serve which I had known
> in the Suffragette movement.[4]

Mary quickly rose to prominence and became, for a while, the organizing secretary
of the women's section of the BUF.

Nora became the BUF women's officer for West Sussex and Hampshire and was
adopted as the BUF parliamentary candidate for Northampton in 1936. According
to the *Mercury and Herald* on 27 November 1936, when her candidature was
announced, much was made of Nora's suffragette past. The leader of the BUF,
Oswald Mosley, announced that he was '... glad to introduce a woman as the
prospective candidate in Northampton because it killed the silliest of all stories
that the Fascists were against women'. Martin Durham has pointed out that of
'the eighty prospective parliamentary candidates chosen by Mosley between 1936
and 1938, eleven were women ... 10% of their candidates were women, higher
than any other party.'[5] Even so, after two years, Mary Richardson left the BUF,
disillusioned with its policies towards women. Other suffrage campaigners, such
as Cicely Hamilton, were upset to see the number of women on fascist marches in
1930s and many campaigned against Fascism, but Nora was unflinching in her
support for the movement and for Oswald Mosley.

Consequently, in 1940, Nora and her 'husband', Dudley, were arrested under
the Defence Regulation 18B and she was once again interned in Holloway, this time
with Diana Mosley. Nora was released in early 1942, shortly after her husband. For
a while, they looked after Diana's sister, Unity Mitford, and were one of the few

people to visit Mosley in prison before he was released in 1943. The years that followed the Second World War, until her death in 1961, seem to have brought Nora little peace or happiness. Her relationships with her son and other relatives were far from cordial; her grandchildren describe her as a racist and Holocaust denier.

Women of many different political beliefs, values and ideals came together in the suffrage campaigns, but the trajectory of Nora's political life is a reminder that women, once they obtained the political power the vote gave them, could use it in many very different ways.

38

MARGARET WINTRINGHAM (1879–1955)

From schoolteacher to politician

Maggie Andrews

On 22 September 1921, the *Pall Mall Gazette* reported on the Louth by-election noting that:

> Mrs Wintringham the Liberal candidate, is the widow of the late member, sentiment in the circumstances is naturally on her side, and women's societies irrespective of party have gone to her aid. Old-fashioned farmers, on the other hand, are said to be averse to being represented by a women. The appeal to sex has proved a double-edged weapon. Mrs Wintringham has for years been an active figure in the division.

Margaret Longbottom was born in Keighley, in Yorkshire, and educated first at the Bolton Road School in Silsden, where her father was the headmaster, and then at Keighley Girls' Grammar School. She went to Bedford Training College, where student-teachers were introduced to the progressive educational ideas of Froebel, and here developed a commitment to nursery education, one of the many issues that she campaigned for in the years that followed. Margaret, often known as Maggie, worked as a teacher, becoming headmistress at a school in Grimsby; in 1903, she met and married Thomas Wintringham. Thomas was a timber merchant and a member of a prominent local family with a strong tradition of radical local politics. John Wintringham was

Margaret Wintringham.

ILLUSTRATED LONDON NEWS LTD/MARY EVANS

Mayor of Grimsby in 1864 and, in October 1877, in Grimsby John Wintringham Junior chaired a women's suffrage meeting. A women's suffrage society was not, however, formed in Grimsby until 1912 and Maggie Wintringham supported the non-militant campaigning groups, and had risen to become vice-president of the Grimsby National Union of Women's Suffrage Societies (NUWSS) in 1921, although, by then, it would technically have been called the National Union of Societies of Equal Citizenship (NUSEC).[1]

As a middle-class married woman who had no children, Maggie Wintringham became increasingly involved in a range of philanthropic and political organizations, including the National Union of Women Workers and the British Temperance Association, where she engaged with other like-minded Liberal-leaning social reformers. A hard-working, down-to-earth woman, she was quick to take on further volunteering roles during the First World War. She helped to administer the Prince of Wales Fund for the relief of industrial distress of British workers and also undertook relief work for the quarter of a million Belgian refugees who came to Britain, seeking to escape the advancing German army in the first months of the conflict. She was on the local Grimsby committee for the Belgian refugees and lodged some in her home,[2] while also helping out as a member of the local Voluntary Aid Detachment (VAD) at Louth Hospital. Her membership of the Lincolnshire County Women's War Agricultural Subcommittee led to her involvement in the newly formed Women's Institute Movement; she became the first honorary secretary of the Lincolnshire Federation and was a member of the executive of the National Federation of Women's Institutes for many years.

As the First World War ended and some women were enfranchised, Maggie Wintringham progressively took on more political roles. She was the chair of the Louth Women's Liberal Association and a member of Lindsey County Council from 1918 to 1921; in August 1920,[3] she became one of the very first women magistrates in Britain. That same year her husband Thomas Wintringham was elected Liberal MP for Louth in Lincolnshire at a by-election in June. But the following year, the death of her husband on 8 August 1921, aged only fifty-three, while at the Palace of Westminster, propelled her into national politics. The Liberal Party nominated Margaret Wintringham to succeed him. This was by no means unusual: a number of early women parliamentarians acquired their seats when their husbands vacated them – through promotion to the House of Lords, death, or even by being removed from the Commons on account of election expenses fraud.

As Maggie was still in mourning, it was agreed that she should not make public speeches during the campaign so she attended meetings where others, including her two sisters, spoke on her behalf. It seems that the party grandees felt that such an arrangement would elicit public support. Maggie did canvass voters, ably assisted by women of all political persuasions from the National Society for Equal Citizenship, including Ray Strachey, who was to write one of the first histories of the suffrage movement, *The Cause* (1928). Mrs Wintringham won the election, gaining 8,386 votes – some 42 per cent of the vote – beating the Unionist candidate Alan Hutchings, who gained 7,695 votes, while the Labour candidate gained only 3,873 votes. In 1922 and 1923, Maggie was re-elected. Maggie was the first English-born woman to become an MP, the second to take up a seat in the House of Commons.

Margaret Wintringham joined Nancy Astor, the Conservative MP for Plymouth, then the only female MP serving in Parliament, who speedily congratulated her. The two became lifelong friends, working together on a number of women's issues, including reducing the voting age for women from thirty to twenty-one, campaigning for the right of women to sit in the House of Lords, making state education scholarships available to girls as well as boys, and insisting on the need for female police officers. At the 1922 National Federation of Women's Institutes AGM, delegates were informed that: 'Lady Astor and Mrs Wintringham, who are fighting for women police in the House, are waiting to hear the opinion of all women in the country on this question.' She also helped to ensure the passage of the Criminal Law Amendment Bill, which sought to improve the legal protection for young girls; spoke against capital punishment; was on the Select Committee on Nationality (Married Women Bill); and ensured that women's work would also be considered by the local wage committees set up under the Agricultural Wages Boards Bill in 1924.

The Women's Institute movement described Margaret Wintringham as 'our MP', and her involvement ensured that she was aware of many of the problems faced by rural domestic women, particularly that of poor housing. In 1923, she spoke in the House of Commons to express her concern that the proposed Housing Bill would not ensure that houses were built in rural areas. She also criticized the austerity measures that would result in three-bedroom houses being reduced to 850 square feet with one of the children's bedrooms being only six foot by six foot and ten inches. She explained to the House of Commons:

> I visualised that room in my mind, and I compared it with the Table in front of the Treasury bench, and afterwards I was interested to go down and measure the Table. I found that the smallest bedroom would be half-a-foot less in length than the Table. I ask the Minister, how would it be possible to use such a room as a bedroom for the accommodation of two girls or two boys?[4]

Many of the inter-war women's organizations were, like Maggie Wintringham, committed to campaigning for peace; she, along with the Women's Institute movement, strongly supported the League of Nations Union. She also joined many feminists and radicals such as Margaret Bondfield, Charlotte Despard, Margaret Llewelyn Davies, Siegfried Sassoon, George Lansbury, C. R. Attlee and George

Bernard Shaw, in writing to the *Guardian* on 9 March 1922 to encourage support for a demonstration and movement called No More War. They argued:

> We trust that the movement will be supported by every organization, which desires an end of war and by all men and women of goodwill. A united expression of the desire of all peoples for no more war would have an incalculably good effect in strengthening the bonds of international friendship at this critical period.[5]

Perhaps her most significant political campaign was the championing of the Equal Guardianship of Infants, to give women legal care for their children who, at this time, tended to be seen as being the property of their fathers. Addressing this was one of the six key legal changes to improve women's lives identified by the feminist Six Points Group, founded by Lady Rhondda in 1921. It was also a priority for the National Union of Societies for Equal Citizenship. Pressure from women's organizations led to parliamentary bills being proposed in 1921 and in 1922, but they got caught in the machinations of Parliament and then its dissolution in 1922. Nancy Astor and Maggie Wintringham worked together to get the bill back onto the agenda when Parliament reconvened. Committees met, evidence was heard, but little progress was made. In 1924, with a new minority Labour government in place, Mrs Wintringham introduced a new private members' bill 'to amend the law relating to guardianship, maintenance, custody and marriage of infants'. She explained:

> I realise I am addressing men chiefly and I want them for a few minutes, in considering the position of the law as it stands at present, to take a mental somersault. I want them to view it from the standpoint of the women who passionately desires the guardianship and ownership of the child.

She was an eloquent speaker and campaigner; the MP Hugh Edwards noted that when he heard her speech he 'felt that those who had supported the extension of the franchise to women had been absolutely justified in their action'. As a Private Members' Bill, Mrs Wintringham's proposals were again unlikely to get through Parliament and, following meetings between the government and the proponents of the bill, a draft government bill was produced, which owed much to Margaret Wintringham's original proposals. The Conservative government that came into power at the end of 1924 took over the bill, which passed into law in March 1925.[6] By this time, Maggie Wintringham had lost her seat, a victim of the dire electoral performance of the Liberal Party, which lost 118 of its 158 parliamentary seats in the 1924 general election. This did not end Margaret Wintringham's involvement in politics; she unsuccessfully contested the Louth seat again in 1929 and undertook a similarly futile attempt to become the MP for Aylesbury in 1935. She continued to play an active role in the Women's Liberal Association, both locally in Louth and nationally. In 1927, she was one of two women elected to the national executive of the Liberal Federation and, in 1929, travelled to Northern Ireland to set up the Women's Liberal Association there. She became a county councillor in Lindsey in 1933 and in the Second World War worked with the Women's Land Army.

Margaret Wintringham's life and political commitment provide ample evidence that the women's movement was very active in the post-suffrage era. Some of her opportunities came because of her husband's death; as a widow with no children she had scope to take advantage of the possibilities opening up for women that many other women with multiple caring responsibilities or financial hardships did not. As an earnest, hard-working Yorkshire woman, with a strong commitment to improving women's lives, she entered the public world of politics. However, she walked a perilous path to avoid criticism, as can be gleaned from a newspaper report of her in the *Portsmouth Evening News* (10 May 1927), which praised her saying:

> Mrs Wintringham happily avoids the extremes to which so many women in public life give way … Her speeches are delivered in quiet musical tones, such as any man might be glad to hear at his own fireside, and we have no sign either of the shrieking sisterhood.

Women, even if they had been MPs, continued to be seen in terms of their domestic roles. In the 1950s, she continued to live in her cottage Tealby in the West Lindsey area of Lincolnshire and to take an active role in local affairs. When she died in a London nursing home in 1955, leaving an estate of £10,263, it was noted in many newspapers but only briefly. Her funeral was quiet but attended by her political friend, Nancy Astor. She was then, and remains, one of the hidden heroines of both the suffrage and the post-suffrage campaigns to improve women's lives.

39

MARY MACARTHUR (1880–1921)

Trade union leader and adult suffragist

Anna Muggeridge

In February 1918, when other suffrage supporters were celebrating the passage of the Representation of the People Act, Mary Macarthur was speaking at Kingsway Hall, to demand adult suffrage – votes for all men and all women.[1] The 1918 Act had only given the vote to some women, and for Mary, the partial enfranchisement of women was only a partial victory.

Mary was born into a comfortably middle-class household in Glasgow on 13 August 1880. Her father, John, owned a drapery business, and her mother, Annie, kept house. Annie had been deeply saddened by the death of her first three children in infancy, but Mary survived and thrived. Soon after, two more girls were born, and the family lived happily in Glasgow – so happily that when Mary was sent to school in Germany for a year (having previously attended Glasgow High School) she was horribly homesick. On her return to England, she persuaded her father to employ her as his book-keeper. Interested in politics from an early age, she also joined him in the local branch of the Primrose League. Through the branch, she was

asked to attend a talk by a leading trade unionist and write an article for a Conservative newspaper scoffing at and pouring scorn on everything she heard about the movement. But instead of doing so, Mary found the experience revelatory. Later in life, she described how this was the moment that changed her life in a 'very singular way'.[2]

Mary witnessed the terrible conditions in which women worked in factories and shops and this, combined with the talk from the trade unionist, persuaded her to switch her political allegiances (her biographer notes that, despite their political differences, her parents were enormously

Mary Macarthur.

proud of their daughter and the work she would go on to do). She joined the Shop Assistants Union and was chair of the local branch while still in her early twenties. Through her involvement in trades unionism, Mary met many leading figures in the Labour movement, including her future husband, Will Anderson, one of the Labour Party's first MPs. She became good friends with Margaret Bondfield, who was also particularly concerned with women's working conditions. Just before her twenty-third birthday, Mary moved to London to take up a post as secretary of the Women's Trade Union League (WTUL). The WTUL had been founded in 1874; its aim was to unite several smaller unions into one organization that could fight collectively for better pay and conditions for women workers. Margaret Bondfield had recommended her for the position of secretary because, she said, Mary not only had excellent organizational abilities, but was a rousing speaker, with a gift for inspiring those who heard her. In the years before the First World War, she was to travel the length and breadth of the country, speaking to women workers in various professions. An oft-repeated rallying cry was her 'bundle of sticks' speech. One stick, she said, could be easily snapped in two and broken, but a bundle of sticks together was much harder to break. The same was true of a union: one woman worker on her own could be easily broken by an employer, but a group of workers together in a union was much stronger and much harder to break.

Through the WTUL, Mary met many women who were active in the women's suffrage movement – but she did not always agree with their arguments. She was a strong supporter of giving women the right to vote, but adamant that she would not work for a limited suffrage bill that only enfranchised certain groups of women (who would undoubtedly have been wealthy and middle-class). Universal male suffrage was not guaranteed until 1918; before then, men had to meet a property requirement to register to vote, which effectively excluded the poorest working-class men. Mary wanted women to have the vote – but she did not want working-class women and men to be excluded at the expense of middle-class women. Several smaller suffrage organizations campaigned on this message, including the Adult Suffrage Society (formed in 1904 and led by her old friend Margaret Bondfield), which was later re-launched as the People's Suffrage Federation, from which the WTUL leased rooms. Mary went so far as to warn against joining the suffragettes (by which she meant the Pankhursts' WSPU) when they indicated that they would not support universal suffrage and were happy to work towards a women's enfranchisement bill that had property qualifications. This was sometimes misinterpreted. When visiting WTUL branches in America, she was invited by Ava Belmont, a prominent US suffragette, to speak to a meeting, but Belmont cancelled the talk because she thought that Mary's statement meant that she was against giving women the vote. In response, Mary pointed out that she actually 'went further' than the suffragettes dared to do, because she 'believed that every man and every woman should have one vote each'. Mary never stopped supporting universal suffrage, but she recognized that 'for many trades women, suffrage is not a burning question' in part because they 'have other things to think of and not much time'.[3]

For this reason, Mary concentrated most of her energy on the trade union movement. In 1906, she formed the National Federation of Women Workers (NFWW) and the Anti-Sweating League. This worked to eradicate the 'sweated' trades, where workers were paid very low wages for very long hours, often in dangerous conditions. Women and young children were disproportionately employed in the sweated trades, because they often involved doing 'piecework' (manufacturing small items, like matchboxes or buttons) in the home. They were paid per 'piece' they produced and charged for materials and equipment from their already meagre wages. One of the worst wages for piecework in the country was in Cradley Heath, where women earned as little as five shillings per week making small chains in their backyards. Because women worked alone in their homes, rather than in a factory, it was hard for them to collectively organize. However, one of the reasons Mary was such a significant figure in the trade union movement was because of her ability to persuade those who had not previously been able to join a union to join the NFWW. In 1910, she led a strike of the chain-makers of Cradley Heath. Her celebrity helped draw attention to their plight, which became the focus of national and even international attention. Thousands gave money to the workers during their lock-out and, after ten weeks, employers were forced to give in to their demand for better pay. Legislation was enacted to guarantee the women the equivalent of eleven shillings per week for their work. Although this was still very low, it became the first government mandated minimum wage in Britain. For her efforts, Mary became affectionately known as 'Our Mary' to the women of Cradley Heath.[4]

After the victory, Mary returned to London to carry on her work with the NFWW and to marry Will Anderson. The wedding took place in 1911, by which time Will was a rising star in the Labour Party (he was elected to Parliament in 1914). He was a supportive husband to Mary, rating her abilities greater than his own, and, according to her biographer, put her career first. She continued her work with the NFWW after marrying, although, in 1913, she took some time off following a breakdown in the middle of a speech shortly after the death of her infant son (a girl, Nancy, was born in 1915).[5] After some months, she felt able to resume her work, which was about to increase enormously, because of the First World War. An avowed pacifist, Mary was totally opposed to the war. Along with many other leading Labour Party members, she protested strongly against Britain's involvement in the conflict, but their opposition was ignored. Mary spent the duration of the war campaigning for rights for women workers. She worked for the Ministry of Labour's Committee on Women's Employment, arguing for women's rights from within the government, but keeping up her NFWW role. Membership of the NFWW greatly increased during the war. A shortage of men meant jobs on the land, in public transport, in the civil service, the police and the Post Office were now opened up to women. Many more women took up positions in factories producing munitions, but few were welcome in existing all-male trade unions.

Practices of dilution and substitution meant that women rarely directly replaced men who had left for the Front. This allowed employers to justify paying women workers only a small part of the full wage a man would earn. Factory work could be particularly dangerous because of the handing of explosive materials, and ten- or twelve-hour days were common. The NFWW supported women's strikes for better pay and conditions throughout the war, and Mary was vocal in her support of the women workers. She kept up this support right to the end. In November 1918, she led a demonstration of 5,000 munitions workers through London, protesting their unfair dismissal and low rates of unemployment pay.

Three days after the Armistice, a general election was called – the first in which some women would be able to vote and to stand for Parliament. Mary was one of only seventeen women nationwide to stand, and the first woman to be selected: Stourbridge Labour Party had actually selected her before the law was changed to allow women candidates. However, like all but one (Constance Markievicz), she failed to win. This was partially due to her strongly pacifist stance, which was not popular with those who wanted to see the Germans punished for the war. What may well have lost her more votes, however, was the local electoral officials' demand that she be on the ballot papers under her married name, not her maiden name. She was well-known in the area – Cradley Heath being part of the constituency – but under her professional name, Mary Macarthur, not as Mrs William Anderson. Technically, the decision was illegal as there was nothing in the new law that demanded women use their married names if they did not wish to. But although she challenged the decision, there was no time to do so before election day, and this probably contributed to her loss.

After the war, Mary continued to work for women's rights. She was instrumental in forming the women's section of the Trades Union Congress (TUC), and she also continued to push for universal suffrage for women. Sadly, she did not live long enough to see this, as she died of cancer on 1 January 1921. Her husband predeceased her, dying of influenza in early 1919. It was not until July 1928 that the Equal Franchise Act was passed, which removed all property qualifications for voting and gave women the right to vote on equal terms with men – as Mary had originally held out for. However, in recent years, her legacy has been resurrected in Cradley Heath. The Black Country Living Museum has an exhibit about the chain-makers' strike, and a monument to the chain-makers was erected at Mary Macarthur Park, in Cradley Heath. Finally, Stourbridge, the constituency in which she stood, has elected a woman MP at every general election since 1997.

The Next Generation

40

VERA 'JACK' HOLME (1881–~~1962~~) /969)
The suffragette chauffeur

Janis Lomas

Vera 'Jack' Holmes was arrested in November 1911 while stone throwing and served five days' imprisonment in Holloway. She was also one of the Actresses' Franchise League singers who sang to prisoners in Holloway to keep up their spirits.

Vera Louise Holme (1881–1969) was born in Lancashire in 1881, the daughter of Richard Holme, a timber merchant, and his wife Mary Louisa Crowe. She was sent away from home as a young girl to be educated at a convent school in Belgium. However, in her early twenties Vera decided on a career as an actress and singer, a very unconventional career for a middle-class woman of the time. She was by no means a conformist: she smoked, and supported herself by working as a music hall singer and male impersonator, with a small, spasmodic allowance from her father. She lived a free and somewhat bohemian life, played the violin, and had even sung with the D'Oyly Carte opera company. As a renowned horsewoman and a chauffeur, she wore male clothing whenever she could. She liked to be known by her nickname 'Jack' or 'Jacko', and had several romantic liaisons with women, most notably with Evelina 'Eve' Haverfield.

Vera joined the Actresses' Franchise League in 1908 and by 1909 was also an active militant in the Women's Social and Political Union (WSPU).[1] Her first act of defiance appears to have taken place at a Liberal Party election rally in Bristol in May 1909. The organizers, fearing disruption by suffragettes, had banned all women from attending, but Elsie Howey

THE WOMEN'S LIBRARY COLLECTION, LSE LIBRARY

Vera as a chauffeur.

179

and Vera Holme rented a house opposite the Colston Hall, where the meeting was due to be held; from this house, WSPU members used a megaphone to interrupt the meeting. Elsie and Vera had a more daring plan and sneaked into the hall during the afternoon, ensconcing themselves behind the organ pipes for three hours until the meeting was underway. Despite a police search of the building, they avoided discovery and shouted 'Votes for Women' through the organ pipes as soon as Augustine Birrell, the Liberal MP began to speak. With Vera and Elsie's voices magnified through the organ pipes and the women in the house opposite the hall using their megaphones, there must have quite a cacophony! When the stewards finally found them, they went quietly, but took great satisfaction from knowing that the stewards had taken a full seven minutes to discover their hiding place. Elsie Howey said later: 'The stewards ran all about, but it never entered their heads that women could climb ladders.'[2]

This was just the first of Vera's adventurous activities. In June 1909, Vera was the advanced guard for the deputation from Caxton Hall to try to enter Parliament and speak to Prime Minister Asquith. On a horse and wearing a riding habit and a tricolour sash, Vera came cantering from Caxton Hall with hundreds of yelling young men trying to disrupt her progress by running after her horse. She hoped to deliver a message to Asquith to tell him that the deputation was on its way, but was stopped at St Stephen's church and forced to hand her letter to the mounted police inspector, who dropped it and told her to leave. In August 1909, Vera got a new job as a driver for Emmeline Pankhurst and Emmeline Pethick-Lawrence, and a new Austin motor car was purchased in the suffragette colours of white, purple and green. Vera later noted: 'Mrs Pankhurst thought I was very giddy and she wasn't at all for having me because I used to act the galoot in the office'.[3] Mrs Pankhurst's qualms seem to have been overcome after Vera drove her to Scotland with no misfortunes. Vera wore a long chauffeur's overcoat and a smart peaked cap with her RAC proficiency badge pinned to it. With her very short bobbed hair she was taken for a male driver by a butler when driving Christabel Pankhurst to a smart dinner, and was told to go around to the back door; the butler was shocked when she refused and was invited in to join the party for dinner. Her driving prowess was praised in 1911 when she was named as the first female chauffeur in Britain by *The Chauffeur* magazine. In the National Archives there is a letter from the police requesting a new police motor cycle to try to keep up with the suffragettes' car as it was impossible for the police to keep up with the speed at which the suffragettes were travelling when engaged in their militant activities.[4]

Vera appears to have been arrested only once and from 1911 lived in Devon with Evelina Haverfield. On the outbreak of war she became a major in the Women's Volunteer Reserve (WVR), established by Evelina. The group enrolled motorists, motorcyclists and aviators and learned skills such as signalling, first aid and field cooking. There was some reticence about them due to their somewhat military demeanour, the women drilling, marching and wearing khaki uniform, which members had to purchase at a cost of £2. The membership came from more affluent women and developed to undertake a range of voluntary work, including cooking and running canteens. They also played a role as interpreters, as well as caring for mothers and babies, collecting and distributing clothes, and helping with transportation. In 1915, Vera and Eve went to Serbia as part of the transport wing of the Scottish Women's Hospital (SWH), with Vera driving an ambulance in what were often very difficult circumstances. Her letters home speak of sleeping out under the stars, and she seems to have relished the freedom and overcoming the difficulties she faced. At the end of 1915, she was taken prisoner by the advancing German army. Although she could have been repatriated before they arrived, they had remained with a handful of other women to care for the seriously ill soldiers in the hospital. Their release was eventually secured by the American Red Cross in February 1916. After a horrendously difficult journey home, Jack then worked for the SWH in both Russia and Romania as a driver and horsewomen. Stationed very near the front line, ambulance drivers like Vera frequently risked death to bring wounded soldiers to the hospital. In October 1917, Vera and another colleague were entrusted by Dr Elsie Inglis, the founder of the SWH, to deliver a report on the situation of the Serbian troops on the Romanian front line to Lord Cecil, at the Foreign Office, and Lord Derby, the Secretary of State for War. This she accomplished. She then spent the rest of the war giving lectures to raise funds for the SWH. She seems to have somewhat cooled her romantic relationship with Eve; although they remained close friends, she had various liaisons with an artistic set of friends based around Kirkcudbright, Scotland, including living with the artist, Dorothy Johnstone. However, she seems to have missed Serbia and longed to return there so, in 1919, when Eve set up a charity providing comforts for soldiers and also a home for war orphans, Vera returned to work there and administer the charity.

In 1920, Eve, weakened by hard work and deprivation, died of pneumonia, leaving Vera devastated. Eve left her an annuity of fifty pounds a year in her will after changing her previous will in which she had left Vera considerably more. Vera's great-nephew later described Eve's death 'as a loss from which she never recovered'.[5] After this tragedy, Vera returned to Scotland and shared a home with two colleagues from Serbia, Margaret Ker and Margaret Greenlees, for the rest of their lives. She continued to have many friends from the theatre and artistic fields, including Ellen Terry's daughter, Edith Craig and her two partners. She also joined her local Women's Institute and supported her local cathedral. But Serbia remained close to her heart and she raised funds and corresponded with friends there until her death in 1969, aged eighty-eight.

41

ANNA MUNRO (1881–1962)

Scottish orator and Women's Freedom League campaigner

Rose Miller

At a meeting of the National Council of Women at Church House, Westminster, in 1926, Anna Munro moved a resolution calling for the enfranchisement of women of the same age and on the same terms as men. She said that a girl came of age morally at sixteen, industrially at eighteen, and legally at twenty-one.[1]

Anna Munro was born in Glasgow and moved with her schoolmaster father, Evan Macdonald Munro, to Dunfermline after her mother's death in 1892. Anna's experience of the social and economic conditions of working-class families, gained while undertaking social work among the working classes in London, fuelled her determination to help those made vulnerable by poverty. She deplored the fact that in a country governed by male politicians such families were without national protection, explaining that:

> She had worked for a long time in the East End of London, where there was no chivalry. In the slums of their big cities the little children have got to do what they can in the simpler parts of the work to bring in money to pay the landlord on Monday morning, and to provide food. No woman could keep a house and feed children on five, six, or even seven shillings a week, as some tried to do.[2]

The women's movement was strong in Scotland by the early 1900s, with many branches affiliated to the non-militant National Union of Women's Suffrage Societies (NUWSS) and to the militant Women's Social and Political Union (WSPU), for which Anna Munro founded the Dunfermline branch in 1906. She became the political theorist Teresa Billington-Greig's private secretary and, with her, joined the Women's Freedom League (WFL) and became the organizing secretary of the Scottish Council of the WFL in 1907.

Committed to the cause, in January 1908, Anna was convicted by Westminster Court for protesting, and imprisoned in Holloway for a period of six weeks.

Her uncle, Pastor Jacob Primmer, a suffragist, wrote to the Home Secretary objecting that for the same offence 'the sentence at Marylebone Police Court was 40s or twenty-one days imprisonment, and 40s, or one month'. Requesting her immediate transference to the infirmary, he provided details of the precariousness of Anna's health.[3] A

Anna Munro (left at the top) with the Scottish Women's Freedom League.

second letter reminded the Home Secretary that in Dunfermline his niece had been directly advised by Prime Minister Asquith that suffrage methods should include 'agitating and holding meetings and pestering people as much as they can'.[4] Militancy and a prison record did nothing to sway Anna's popularity; she was 'the speaker of the evening' at the Aberdeen branch of the Women's Freedom League in September 1908. Her speeches often took the form of responding to objections from Parliament concerning the granting of the franchise to women. She achieved an entertaining balance of humour and seriousness as she articulated and exposed the ridiculous reasons expounded by the politicians of the time:

> One of these objections was that women's suffrage was against the Bible (laughter). This objection was used by one of the northern members of Parliament in a debate on the subject, but, another member said, neither was there anything in the Bible about the three-mile limit and the Moray Firth (laughter and applause).[5]

Another objection was that women did not go to war, to which she replied that those who made the decisions for others to go to war did not go themselves. Furthermore, women had to pay for the war quite as much as the men. If women got the vote, then she believed that a more civilized method of settling disputes, other than cutting each other's throats, might be achieved. To the objection that women were not intelligent enough, she countered that if the qualification for a vote in this country relied on intelligence then 'a good many would be cleared off the roll at once,' a brisk dismissal that the audience loved. Her conclusion, however, was logical and serious: 'There could be only one-sided legislation as long as half the community were left out'. On what she considered to be the most important obstacle to women receiving the vote, that 'woman's sphere was in her home', Anna retorted that man's sphere was the factory or workshop, but there was no objection that he could not do his work well if he took an interest in anything else.

> The woman was in the industrial market today as a force to be reckoned with, and should have a say in the making of laws which affected her.[6]

Despite her oratory skills, her presence was not always enthusiastically received and, in 1909, she was pelted with snowballs by a group of children as she stood on a box to speak outside a factory in Edinburgh.[7] Anna also facilitated protests against participating in the 1911 census, also believing that without representation through the vote, women should not pay tax. Despite her uncle's concerns about her delicate health, Anna joined a protest march from Edinburgh to London in 1912, and completed the whole route over five weeks, cheered on by more than 10,000 spectators.[8] Determined to take the cause to rural areas, she travelled in a horse-drawn caravan, impressing crowds with her eloquence and lack of notes.[9] She met Sidney Ashman on a suffrage tour and the couple were married in Wandsworth, London, in April 1913. Although now legally Munro-Ashman, she still used her maiden name in public life. Attempting to address a meeting on Sunday in Hyde Park, in May of that year, she was arrested and taken to Crawford Place police station, along with Nina Boyle. Refusing to pay the twenty shilling fine, they were sentenced to fourteen days' imprisonment in Holloway, with members of the Women's Freedom League protesting outside.

The war and women's enfranchisement did not deter Anna's interest in politics; in 1919, she acted as a London County Council election agent for Mrs Yates, who won North Lambeth by a majority of three to one.[10] Anna and Sidney lived in the Reading area, where they had two children, a son and daughter, before moving to Aldermaston. A dedicated Socialist, she considered standing for Parliament but rejected becoming an MP to protect her husband's business. She remained involved in the community, serving on committees and assisting with local elections. She enjoyed travelling and, according to her son, rather 'erratic' driving, even when taking working-class voters to the polls in her Daimler car.[11] Her intention to become a magistrate was opposed by a leading local landowner, who had stated that it would happen over his dead body. Sure enough, she was appointed magistrate after his demise in 1935. As president of the National British Total Abstinence Movement, she was known for creating admirable non-alcoholic cocktails at parties.[12] Anna remained a campaigner for women's rights for the rest of her life until she died at home in Padworth, Berkshire, in 1962.

42

MARY GAWTHORPE (1881–1973)

Teacher, WSPU organizer and Labour campaigner

Janis Lomas

On 23 October 1906, Mary Gawthorpe was among a large number of suffragettes who went to the House of Commons; only thirty women were allowed to enter the lobby to attempt to get MPs to listen to their arguments. Mary Gawthorpe, a brand new member of the WSPU, was the first to try to speak. A tiny figure weighing little more than seven stones, she stood on a velvet settee next to Lord Northcote's statue, surrounded by the suffragettes. With Emmeline Pankhurst holding her on one side and Emmeline Pethick-Lawrence on the other, she began to make a speech, only to be forcibly pulled down by the police as the two Emmelines held her tightly. One by one different suffragettes replaced her and attempted to speak and one by one they were forcibly ejected in scuffles with the police. For this 'offence' she was one of the ten women sentenced to two months in Holloway prison.[1]

Mary Eleanor Gawthorpe was born in Leeds to a working-class family. She had four siblings, two of whom died in infancy. Her father worked in a tannery. Aged thirteen, she was apprenticed as a pupil-teacher. Studying in the evenings and teaching all day, she attained the Government Teacher's Certificate with a First Class grade. At the age of twenty, she won a schol-arship to study singing at Leeds School of Music, passing her examinations with honours. She joined the Independent Labour Party (ILP) and by 1906 was vice-president of the Leeds branch and active in many Labour and Trades Union organizations, most notably as secretary of the Leeds Women's Labour League (LWLL). She was a member of the non-militant Leeds Suffrage Society, writing to local newspapers in support of women's suffrage. When Christabel Pankhurst and Annie Kenney were arrested at the Manchester Free Trade Hall,

Mary Gawthorpe.

185

she wrote to Christabel in Strangeways Prison, telling her that she too was willing to go to prison in order to secure the vote for women. She resigned her teaching post and, as secretary of the LWLL, travelled to London to take part in suffrage meetings and attended an 'At Home' at the home of Margaret MacDonald, wife of Ramsey MacDonald and president of the LWLL. She also undertook voluntary work for the Women's Social and Political Union (WSPU).

By summer 1906, she was campaigning with Emmeline Pankhurst and in autumn became a WSPU paid organizer. She took part in the House of Commons disruption in October and was arrested alongside nine others. She refused the offer to be bound over to keep the peace or pay a £10 fine, and was sentenced to two months' imprisonment, although released unexpectedly after five weeks in Holloway Prison. The two working-class suffragette prisoners, Mary Gawthorpe and Annie Kenney, were proficient knitters, and came out of Holloway with earnings of thirteen shillings and four pence (68p) for knitting men's socks while in prison,[2] although Mary said that they would both have preferred to knit women's stockings.[3] Mary and Annie Kenney followed their welcome home reception at Caxton Hall by travelling to Huddersfield to address audiences in a by-election where large crowds cheered them. In December 1906, Millicent Fawcett, leader of the NUWSS, hosted a banquet for released prisoners at the Savoy Hotel, London. Among the 250 people attending, Mary was one of the guests of honour.[4]

For the next four years, Mary Gawthorpe, as a member of the national committee of the WSPU, lived a nomadic life with a punishing schedule, addressing meetings, organizing meetings, and travelling across the country. The hard work took its toll on her health and she suffered from stomach problems, often coughing blood. Asking questions at political meetings was a particularly dangerous activity, requiring a great deal of courage. In February 1907, Mary was one of three suffragettes assaulted at a Liberal rally where Winston Churchill was speaking. The *Manchester Courier* reporter corroborated the women's account of the meeting, in an unusually sympathetic article under the heading: 'Liberal Brutality, Bruised Suffragettes, Ladies Tell Their Stories'. Mary Gawthorpe related how:

> When I rose to speak, Mr Churchill and others invited me on to the platform, and I was assisted onto the end of the press table. They were putting out their arms to lift me on to the platform when some stewards made a rush to pull me down. Several press men fought valiantly for me, but eventually I was pulled down and pushed among the crowd, where I was badly knocked about. But for the assistance of half a dozen men I don't know how I should have fared.[5]

The newspaper reported that Adela Pankhurst was also injured, punched in the face, thrown or had fallen down a flight of stairs, and then been kicked and trampled on the ground. On another occasion during the Rutland by-election, in the summer of

1907, Mary was hit with a china 'pot egg' on the head and knocked unconscious.[6] Such violent episodes were interspersed with the mundane: Mary reported that the Hull branch was holding a jumble sale while Leeds were doing a 'roaring trade' in peppermint creams.[7] In the summer of 1910, Mary Gawthorpe's health broke down entirely; she attempted to try to continue her work as WSPU North-West regional organizer from her sick-bed, but bedridden for months, was unable to carry on. As a working woman, reliant on her salary from which she supported her mother, she was in a parlous financial state,[8] but by autumn 1911 had to resign, writing that she was 'utterly crushed at my failure to keep going, my inability to rally'.[9]

When Mary's friend and fellow activist, Dora Marsden, who had been the WSPU organizer for Southport, offered her a position as co-editor of a new journal, *The Freewoman*, work that she could undertake from home, she had little choice but to accept. She was somewhat embarrassed when editorials appeared in the journal attacking the WSPU and after six months she resigned.[10] Although still very weak, in 1912 she took part in one last unlawful action, breaking government windows to draw attention to the case of William Ball. He had been imprisoned for protesting against forcible feeding, after going on hunger strike, he had been himself been force-fed and then, allegedly, given electric shocks, which had caused him to lose his mind and be committed to an asylum. Despite her frailty, after arrest Mary risked her life by going on hunger and thirst strike while on remand in Holloway, but thankfully was released after thirty-six hours. No longer part of the WSPU and concerned that the escalation of militant actions was counter-productive, she continued her own protests: she organized a large petition in support of Mary Leigh and Gladys Evans, who had been imprisoned for five years for setting fire to a Dublin theatre, and, in a final defiant act, Mary attempted to organize a national hunger strike of all women in October 1912.[11]

In 1916, Mary Gawthorpe moved to America with her mother, ostensibly to visit her sister who lived there. Immediately, she began working for suffrage, becoming chief organizer of the New York branch of the National Women's Suffrage Party and, later, State Press chairman for the same party[12] while also working for the Cook County Labor Party and the Delaware Consumers' League. After American women won the vote in 1920, she worked for the trades union movement as an organizer for the Amalgamated Clothing Workers' Union and, in 1920, as executive secretary of the League for Mutual Aid.[13] In 1921, she married John Sanders and became an American citizen, although she retained her maiden name. She was very annoyed to discover that Sylvia Pankhurst, in writing *The Suffragette Movement* (1931), dismissed her work in America in a footnote as 'emigrated to America, [taken] up journalism and married'. She felt it was almost equal to saying 'was crucified, died and buried'.[14] She only returned to England once, in 1933, but remained in touch with many of her friends from her suffrage days by letter. She died at her home in Long Island in March 1973.

43

HELENA NORMANTON (1882–1957)

Pioneering barrister

Holly Fletcher

In 1908, in a provocative statement from a woman who would become the first female barrister in the High Court, Helena Normanton wrote to students at Edge Hill teacher training college to encourage them into suffragette militancy: 'To all Edge Hill suffragists I give this advice – it takes no moral courage whatever to walk in a procession.'[1]

Helena Normanton was born in London on 14 December 1882. Her father, William Normanton, was a pianoforte manufacturer, who was found dead in a railway tunnel when Helena was aged four. Her mother, Jane, decided to move Helena and her younger sister, Ethel, to Brighton, where her family lived, and there was able to run, first, a grocery store and, then, a boarding house. In 1896, Helena won a scholarship to York Place Science School, the forerunner of Varndean School for Girls, and progressed to become a pupil-teacher. Helena later recalled that her interest in law came when, aged twelve, she accompanied her mother to the solicitor and listened eagerly as her mother struggled to understand the advice given. At one point, the solicitor remarked: 'I am sure your little girl quite understands what I have told you, from the look on her face…. Quite a little lawyer!'[2]

In 1903, Helena began studying at the Edge Hill Teachers' Training College in Liverpool, an all-girls, non-denominational college, with links to the suffrage movement. Whether Helena chose the college because of its suffrage links is hard to tell. After

Helena Normanton as a barrister.

THE WOMEN'S LIBRARY COLLECTION, LSE LIBRARY

completing her course, she embarked on a teaching career at the Anfield Road Higher Grade School in Liverpool, accompanying her teaching career with suffrage politics and feminist writing. Further studying and qualifications followed including a Scottish Secondary Teachers' Diploma, a First Class history degree from the University of London, and a diploma in French language, literature and history from Dijon University. Helena joined the Women's Social and Political Union (WSPU), undertaking administrative and publicity activities in addition to speaking in support of the suffrage campaigns. She later recalled:

> I longed to go to prison with the rest of my comrades in the fight but I knew this could never be because if I had a prison sentence I would never have been able to open the profession of the law to women, which I regarded as my job in life.[3]

There is no record of whether the increasingly militant tactics of the WSPU in time made the organization uncomfortable for Helena, with her heart set on a legal career, but by 1914 she was a member of the Women's Freedom League (WFL) and, like others in the organization, opposed the First World War. In 1915, she published an essay on 'Magna Carta and Women' in the periodical, *The Englishwoman*, arguing that the disenfranchisement of women contravened Magna Carta's clauses 39 and 40:

> It is expressly contrary to Magna Carta to refuse, deny, or *delay*, right or justice. The right of the franchise is still unconstitutionally withheld from women, but the spirit of Magna Carta sounds a trumpet-call to them to struggle ever more valiantly to realise its noble ideal.[4]

Helena was a guest speaker when the WFL celebrated the 700th anniversary of the Magna Carta, later that year. By this time, her political engagement was widening to include support for the Indian National Congress,[5] and for equal pay, including writing a pamphlet in 1914 asking 'Should women be paid according to their sex or their work?'[6] Aged thirty-five, she began her legal career, but her application to join the Middle Temple and train as a barrister was rejected in 1918. However, within forty-eight hours of the Sex Disqualification (Removal) Act becoming law in 1919, she had lodged a further application and was accepted on Christmas Eve that year.[7] On passing her Bar Finals in 1921, she began her pupillage under Wells Thatcher, whose chambers specialized in divorce and criminal law.[8]

On 26 October 1921, Helena married Gavin Bowan Watson Clark. Helena's niece recalled: 'They had no children, and it was a marriage in which sparks could fly, for both had quick tempers, but I think it was basically a happy one'.[9] In 1924, she became the first married British woman to be issued a passport in her maiden name.[10] She made the decision to retain her maiden name before she began to practise law, recalling: 'My husband was a most charming man but his name was Clarke. There are hundreds of Clarkes.' It may well have been a name that lacked distinction for a professional woman, but Helena also disliked the obliteration of a woman's identity implied by taking her husband's surname. However, she also explained: 'I like the prefix of "Mrs" because it is more dignified. If people do not wish to address me as "Mrs", they can call me Helena Normanton.'[11]

Helena's ground-breaking legal career lasted many years: she was the first woman to obtain a divorce for a woman (1922); the first female counsel in a case at the Old Bailey (1924); the first woman to conduct a case in the United States of America (1925); and the first woman to lead a prosecution in a murder trial (1948). Little wonder that *Girl's Own* featured her in an article, 'Famous Women of Today', intended to inspire teenage girls of 1939 to aspire to a range of careers. It, however, landed her in trouble with her peers, as some thought that it transgressed the bar code forbidding advertising.[12] Nevertheless, her earnings from legal work was so low that she had to supplement her income by renting rooms in her house, and she also wrote two books on criminal cases: *The Trial of Norman Thorne* (1929) and *The Trial of Alfred Arthur Rouse* (1931).

Her politics remained consistent with the feminist and pacifist principles of the Women's Freedom League and were often controversial. In 1938, she was a founder member of the Married Women's Association, which was set up to give mothers and children a legal right to a share in the family home, secure equal guardianship rights for both parents, and give women equal National Insurance provision. In 1952, when she had been president of the Married Women's Association for six months, there was a falling out with other officials over a report she prepared for the Royal Commission on Marriage and Divorce. She also supported the Campaign for Nuclear Disarmament (CND) when it was formed.

In 1949, she and Miss Rose Heilbron became the first two women to take silk, i.e. to became King's, then Queen's Counsel. In 1962, Rose Heilbron was appointed the first female County Court judge. However, by this time Helena had died in a London nursing home aged seventy-four. In her will, she left money to what was to become the University of Sussex, in gratitude for the education she had received as a child in Brighton.

44

ELSIE HOWEY (1884–1963)

Joan of Arc and suffragette warrior

Mollie Sheehy

On Monday 19 April 1909, the *Gloucestershire Echo* reported that 'Five brass bands, and Miss Elsie Howey as Joan of Arc in silver armour on a white horse, were the chief attractions of a Suffragette procession from Hyde Park to the Aldwych Theatre on Saturday'. Elsie, who described her pastimes as 'riding, driving and hockey',[1] played the role of Joan of Arc in a number of WSPU pageants and processions, including the occasion of the funeral of suffragette martyr Emily Wilding Davison in 1913, when Elsie rode alongside the coffin.

Elsie Howey was born in 1884 in Nottinghamshire, where her father, Thomas Howey, was the local parish rector. Her mother, Emily Gertrude, moved her family to Malvern in Worcestershire when she was widowed in 1897. Between 1902

and 1904, Howey attended St Andrews University, which had devised a scheme entitled the 'L.L.A. examination' (Lady Literate in Arts) to enable women to gain a diploma from the university. After university, she travelled to Germany. She later noted, when writing for the suffragette magazine, *Votes for Women,* that it was during this short time spent in Germany that she realized the inequality that women were experiencing. Upon moving back to the United Kingdom, she became an activist for the Women's Social and Political Union (WSPU). It was her first public appearance with the group in February 1908, outside the Houses of Common, that led to her first arrest.

Elsie Howey dressed as Joan of Arc
for the Suffragette Procession.

Elsie's significant contribution to women's suffrage and the WSPU was to drum up support for the movement outside London, in areas where the campaign was slow to ignite the imagination of the public. In May 1908, Elsie teamed up with fellow suffragettes Mary Blathwayt and Annie Kenney to campaign during the Newport Shropshire by-election. It was reported by Blathwayt that Howey demonstrated great passion during the campaign, visiting different towns with the group. As her mother lived in Malvern, she next visited Worcester and Malvern with Gladice Keevil to promote the WSPU's Hyde Park meeting on 21 June. Dedicated trains took supporters from Worcester station (at a cost of six shillings return)[2] to London where they were able to see Elsie Howey speaking on platform 6 in Hyde Park.[3]

Later that month, Howey was arrested for a second time, along with Florence Haig, Maud Joachim and Vera Wentworth, for taking part in a demonstration outside the home of Herbert Asquith. Her protest involved chanting at the gates of his home. Elsie wrote about this in her edition of *Suffrage Annual* and *Women's Who's Who*, saying that, although she was charged with obstructing the police, she felt that the police were obstructing her. This incident resulted in a three-month prison sentence.[4] In true suffragette spirit, the women were supported throughout their time in prison, and their friends and fellow members of the WSPU continued to work at their campaign. When the four women were released on 16 September 1908, they were met at the gates of Holloway Prison and conducted to a celebratory breakfast in a carriage decorated with purple and white flowers.

> Fifty suffragettes, in full uniform, harnessed themselves to the traces … the women drew the carriage, preceded by a band playing the 'Marseillaise'. At the breakfast they were greeted with applause. Pocket handkerchiefs and napkins were waved and 'For She's a jolly good fellow' sung again and again.[5]

Sylvia Pankhurst also sent an illuminated scroll she had designed to honour Howey's bravery during her time in prison.

Elsie Howey stayed with Annie Kenney in Bristol, when she worked as unpaid WSPU organizer in the West Country. Kenney was the most high-profile working-class figure in an organization often attacked for only representing the demands of the middle and upper classes. She was also welcomed into Eagle House at Batheaston, near Bath, which was a refuge house for suffragettes and allowed them to recover from the effects of the force-feeding. Elsie spent time there, recovering from her imprisonment.

In 1909, Elsie Howey and Vera Wentworth demonstrated at a meeting held in Exeter by Lord Carrington. This resulted in her arrest and drastic action during her imprisonment. According to the local paper in court, Elsie threatened:

> We wish to say we don't think we are the guilty parties. We did obstruct the

police, but we were only performing our duty. The Liberal Government is directly responsible for this. We have tried again and again to get Mr Asquith to see a deputation and explain what we want but he will not see our deputation, Therefore we must go to work differently. We have warned him that other things may happen if he will not listen to us.[6]

Sentenced to seven days in prison, Elsie and Vera Wentworth went on hunger strike for 144 hours, demanding that they should be given political prisoner status. After recuperating by again staying with the Blathwayts, Elsie was given a reception by the WSPU in Torquay at which she was presented with a travelling clock. She was, however, arrested again on 5 September, and sent to Holloway Prison. The following year, Elsie was arrested again, this time for campaigning with Constance Lytton in Liverpool, and sentenced to six weeks' hard labour. By 1911, Elsie was less active and had stopped writing for *Votes for Women*. The effects of going on hunger strike had begun to take a toll on Elsie physically, and she was sent into the care of a nursing home in Liverpool.

Suffrage campaigning was very much a family affair and made possible by the financial security of Elsie, her mother and sister, Mary. They all joined the WSPU and Mary also worked as an unpaid WSPU organizer in Penzance, but was back in Worcestershire at the time of the 1911 census. Mary did not avoid the census, but used her form to make a political point, writing 'VOTES FOR WOMEN' across it. Elsie Howey returned to militancy in 1912 and was again sent to Holloway Prison, this time for setting off a fire alarm. During this period in prison, she went on hunger strike and was forcibly fed by prison officers; the injuries from this destroyed her beautiful voice. This was just one of the sacrifices Elsie made in her battle for women's rights. Her gritty allegiance to the suffragette movement won Elsie much admiration; she never undertook paid employment and all of her focus was in campaigning and working as an unpaid organizer. After the exhausting battle for the vote, she vanished from public life, no doubt still suffering from the long-lasting illnesses that she carried with her for the rest of her life.

Elsie became a Theosophist in 1923. She never fully recovered from the traumas of the suffrage campaigns, but grew old in Malvern, dying on 13 March 1963 from chronic pyloric stenosis, possible precipitated by her injuries from forcible feedings. She left most of her estate to the English Theosophy Trust. This society prides itself on being a 'brotherhood' promoting unity. Fitting to the work Elsie carried out, the society works on the mantra that 'life, and all its diverse forms, human and non-human, is indivisibly One.'[7]

45

ANNIE BARNES (1887–1982)

Stepney councillor

Maggie Andrews

For Annie, as she later recalled, participation in the East End Federation of Suffragettes was limited by her obligation to her family:

> I couldn't attend meetings regularly. I went now and again when I could slip out without my father noticing. The children didn't know, and goodness knows what the old man would have said if he'd ever found out what I was up to. I seem to have been very lucky to get away with it. There was always a risk but I just had to accept that.[1]

Annie Barnes was born Annie Cappuccio. Her father had a fruiterer's and confectioner's shop in Stepney, and she was the eldest of twelve children, although six of her siblings did not survive into adulthood. As owners of a shop and house, the family was wealthier than many of their East End neighbours. Annie recalled that her mother had help in the house and a washerwoman used to come in to assist with the weekly wash on Mondays.[2] She attended Ben Jonson School and rather than leave at the age of thirteen, like many of her fellow schoolmates, Annie began the process of apprenticeship to become a teacher herself. All this changed before she had reached her sixteenth birthday, when her mother became ill and Annie was needed to nurse her mother during the last years of her life.

As the Mrs Pankhurst's Women's Social and Political Union (WSPU) began the process of moving the centre of their activities from Manchester to London, the organization also began to explore potential support in the East End. Dora Montefiore introduced one of the WSPU's earliest working-class stalwarts, Annie Kenney, to women of the East End who had supported the Unemployed Workmen's Bill 1909. Annie Kenney and Sylvia Pankhurst, then studying at the Royal College of Art, in London, arranged for 300 East End women to march to Caxton Hall to take part in a large meeting described as the 'Women's Parliament'.[3] Annie

Cappuccio became increasingly aware of the suffragette presence in the East End, seeing meetings, protests and the women who spoke on street corners despite being heckled by men and who gathered up names and addresses of potential supporters. Annie was one of those who gave in their name, but the death of her mother in 1910 meant that militancy was out of the question. As she explained later: 'I had commitments at home looking after all my brothers and sisters. I couldn't chance imprisonment. But I did volunteer for other things that were less risky.'

Annie's involvement with the movement really began when Sylvia Pankhurst made the East End the focus of her campaigning activities. The WSPU rented a shop in Bow Road in 1912, but the organization in the East End split from the WSPU in 1914, forming the East London Federation of Suffragettes (ELFS). Sylvia and the ELFS were committed to Socialism and worked with the Labour Party, just as the WSPU were distancing themselves from their Labour Party roots. For East End women like Annie, surrounded by poverty, deprivation, poor housing and some of the worst maternal and infant mortality rates in the country, the vote for all women was only one of many reforms they wanted.

Annie's memories play down the significance of her role in the suffrage campaigns; in this she echoes so many histories of the movement. But the activities of women like Annie were vital to drum up and maintain support for women's enfranchisement. Her first 'mission' was to climb the 311 steps to the viewing platform of the monument to the Fire of London and throw leaflets saying 'VOTES FOR WOMEN' from it. Managing to dodge the police, she returned home. She later recalled the excitement that the ELFS brought to the area, with its meetings and political activities.[4] They worked with the Independent Labour Party (ILP) and Dockers Union to organize a rent strike. In March 1914, the ELFS launched its own newspaper, *The Women's Dreadnought*, which gained a readership of 8,000.[5] When her siblings were in bed and her father preoccupied, Annie slipped out of her house in the evenings and delivered the paper around the neighbourhood. In April 1914, the ELFS rented new premises, 400 Old Ford Road, which included a hall that could seat 300 and a library. It was large enough for the ELFS to hold a choir, lectures, concerts and a junior suffragettes' club there.[6] Wartime shifted the ELFS focus further

Demonstration at Monument, London.

THE WOMEN'S LIBRARY COLLECTION, LSE LIBRARY

onto welfare work: they helped women cope with the hardship caused by the war including rising food prices and delayed separation allowances.[7] For Annie, the war brought injury to her brother but also her marriage to Albert Barnes, who shared her desire not to have children and accepted that she wanted her siblings to live with them. Albert was a skilled craftsman who had travelled the world with a music hall troupe and had enough money to enable them to purchase a house with a garden.

Annie's politics were shaped by her time in the ELFS. She joined the Independent Labour Party (ILP) in 1919, and in the inter-war years became very involved in local politics, social welfare and promoting the Women's Co-op Guild. She was part of the successful team of campaigners who helped the future Prime Minister, Clement Attlee, become the MP for Limehouse, Stepney. She attended the Labour Party Women's Conferences at Central Hall, Westminster, in 1930. Labour gained control of twenty-four of twenty-eight London boroughs in the local elections of 1934, as many struggled with unemployment and poverty. Annie became a councillor and much of her work was geared towards helping women. She lost her council seat in 1937, but returned from 1941 to 1949 and later recalled:

> I was on lots of different committees at different times, sometimes as many as five at a time, I always tried to be on Housing or Public Health every year, but I was also at various times on the committees for markets, General Purposes, Libraries and Museums and Sick and Accident Pay. I was vice-chairman of the Public Health Committee three times.[8]

She also became a member of the Charity Organization Society in 1938, arguing determinedly with the titled ladies when she thought they were in the wrong, most importantly over the society's name. She contended that the stigma of charity should be removed and recalled saying to them: 'It's time that the people aren't made to feel that they're nothing. It's time they are no longer humiliated. They are fighting for their country.'[9]

Annie and Albert had a happy if slightly unconventional home life; they remained friends with Sylvia Pankhurst for years, and took in a succession of Italian refugees escaping from Mussolini and the Fascists in Italy. Their home was flattened when the East End was bombed during the Second World War, but they lived together until Albert's death in 1958. When, in her nineties, Annie was interviewed about her life, she still had a strong sense of herself as a suffragette. Her participation in the suffrage campaigns had helped to change history. It had also changed her, giving Annie a sense of confidence and an identity so that she continued to be politically active even after the vote had been won.

46

DORA THEWLIS (1891–1976)

Baby suffragette

Janis Lomas

This newspaper photo of Dora Thewlis – a small, slight, young girl, her skirt placket open, her hair in disarray – being arrested by two burly policemen was seen around the world. When the *Daily Mirror* christened her 'baby suffragette' and her court appearances were widely reported, she became something of an overnight sensation, and the photograph was even turned into a postcard, much to the dismay of many suffrage campaigners in her home town.

Dora Thewlis was one of seven children and, with most of her family, worked as a weaver in a Huddersfield woollen mill. Like most working-class girls at that time, Dora would have started work at the age of twelve.

Sixteen-year-old Dora Thewlis of Honley being arrested in London in March 1907.

Therefore, at the time of her arrest she had already been working for four years. Her family were members of the Independent Labour Party (ILP). Dora and her mother, Eliza, were both founder members of the Huddersfield branch of the WSPU when it was formed in December 1906, and Eliza was elected to the branch organizing committee. In March 1907, the WSPU planned a march on Parliament, starting at Caxton Hall with the idea of setting up a 'Woman's Parliament'. Delegates were invited from all over the country. Ten women from Huddersfield volunteered, including Dora Thewlis, all of them knowing that there was a chance they would be arrested. Dora's mother, Eliza, was unable to attend, but accompanied the delegation as far as Manchester and saw Dora onto the London train with more than 100 of the Lancashire 'clog and shawl brigade'.[1] Five hundred police had been drafted in to defend Parliament from the marchers. By ten that evening, seventy-five women had been arrested, but the main picture in the newspapers the following day was of Dora Thewlis. The photograph caught the public imagination, but views were mixed: either indignation at a young girl taking part in the demonstration, or sympathy for her rough treatment and arrest. The arrested women were all brought to Westminster Police Court in front of the magistrate, Horace Smith, who was impatient and unsympathetic; he even told one of the women to 'stop jabbering'. When Dora Thewlis, whom he thought was seventeen, appeared before him he was shocked at her youth, saying, 'You are only a child. You don't know what you're doing'. This made Dora laugh. The magistrate went on to ask her where she had come from and, on hearing that she had come from Huddersfield, went on:

> The child cannot be a delegate or anything else. She doesn't know what she's doing … Here is a young girl of 17 enticed from her home in Yorkshire and let loose in the London streets to come into collision with the police. It is disgraceful for everybody concerned.
>
> To which Dora replied: 'But I come for my Mother and sister, not [just] for myself.[2]

After more haranguing of the girl, he remanded her in custody and wrote to her parents. The court exchanges between Dora and Horace Smith were widely reported, while Dora was imprisoned in Holloway for the next six days. The magistrate was probably surprised by the indignant response he received:

> We find ourselves in agreement with his Honour when he says that girls of sixteen ought to be in school. But we respectfully remind his Honour that girls of Dora's age in her station of life … are compelled in their thousands to spend ten hours a day in health-destroying factories … Dora journeyed to London with our consent and approval, her mother accompanied her as far as Manchester, leaving her there in the hands of friends in whom she had every confidence. In these circumstances it is not our intention to bring discredit on our daughter's action by accepting the advice tendered in your communication …[3]

Horace Smith's words demonstrate how out of touch he was with the lives of working-class girls and women. As Jill Liddington writes, his use of the words 'enticed', 'young girls' and 'London streets' to describe her journey carried connotations of moral looseness and semi-prostitution. 'Dora had been "enticed" down onto London streets, in her turn to "entice" young men.'[4]

Dora was totally segregated from all other prisoners, perhaps because she was on remand or due to her age. Locked in a cell, unable to communicate with anyone, Dora's bravado deserted her and she became extremely upset. Her mother apparently wrote to her saying, 'I am very proud of the way you have acted, so keep your spirits up and be cheerful.' A local reporter who visited Dora at this time claimed that she had told him: 'Oh, I'm so glad to see you, I feel so lonely here. I want to go back home. I have had enough of prison ... Everybody has forgotten me.' She was brought back to court, where the magistrate appointed a prison wardress to accompany her and said that her fare home would be paid from the poor-box.[5]

Dora's imprisonment was far from forgotten: her mother, who newspapers described as being the founder of the Huddersfield branch of the WSPU, was outspoken about her daughter's treatment and the magistrate's comments but particularly indignant about her daughter's train fare having been paid out of the poor fund, as she explained to reporters that her daughter earned 20s (£1) a week as a weaver and so had her own money. The taint of pauperism was not one Dora's mother, Eliza, wanted associated with her family. The short time spent in Holloway turned Dora into a minor celebrity; newspaper reporters were waiting at the station when she returned to Huddersfield, although no members of the WSPU were there to greet her. For the next few days Dora's modest house was besieged and it was suggested she had collapsed in a serious condition; if so, she soon recovered and when interviewed said: 'Don't call me the "Baby Suffragette". I am not a baby really. In May next year I shall be eighteen years of age. Surely for a girl that is a good age?'[6]

Most of the members of the Huddersfield branch of the WSPU were workers at the woollen mills in and around Huddersfield and the Colne Valley, and nine had been imprisoned alongside Dora. These women suffered fourteen days' imprisonment but had attracted scant attention from the newspapers. The average age of the members of the Huddersfield branch was twenty-seven; many had young children; and there may have been some resentment at the newspapers focus on Dora. The newspapers implied that Dora was a victim, an innocent young girl whose life had been endangered when lured away by the rabble-rousing suffragettes and who had now learned her lesson the hard way. The Huddersfield WSPU was aghast at the negative publicity Dora's case had generated, and when a commercial firm produced and widely distributed a postcard of Dora's arrest, this was perhaps the last straw. Eliza was asked to work agreeably or to resign from the branch. Both Eliza's and Dora's involvement with the WSPU ceased and Dora emigrated to Australia with her elder sister and about twenty other girls from Huddersfield shortly before the First World War. There she worked as a blanket weaver, settling near Melbourne, where she married an Australian called Jack Dow, had two children. She never returned to England before her death in 1976.[7]

47

ELLEN WILKINSON (1891–1947)

Communist and cabinet minister

Paula Bartley

Ellen Wilkinson.

In January 1913 the *Manchester Courier* reported that: 'a suffrage shop has been opened in St Anne's Square, in the very heart of the fashionable shopping centre'. The newspaper went on to report that the shop would organize meetings twice a day and 'an army of enthusiastic ladies ... will give information to all who are interested.' One of the speakers at the very first meeting was Ellen Wilkinson.[1]

Ellen Wilkinson was born on 8 October 1891, in a tiny two-bedroomed terraced house with no bathroom or inside lavatory, at 41 Coral Street, Ardwick, a grimy overcrowded district of industrial Manchester. Despite her background, this 4ft 11in red-head became one of the most famous female politicians in the first half of the twentieth century, ending her life as the first female Minister of Education.[2] Ellen was clever. In 1910 she won a scholarship to Manchester University to study history. At university, Ellen helped found the Socialist Federation and later became vice-chair,[3] persuading well-known figures such as the radical trade unionist and feminist Mary McArthur to speak at meetings. In 1912 she joined the Manchester Society of Women Suffrage (MSWS), and ran the local branch of the Fabian Society; in 1913 she joined the Tyldesley branch of the Women's Labour League. She had already joined the Independent Labour Party. When she graduated Ellen worked for the Manchester National Society for Women's Suffrage (MNSWS).[4] Part of Ellen's job involved speaking at open-air meetings where she learned to capture the attention of often hostile audiences who sometimes threw stones and other objects at the young suffragist. She also organized the heckling of MPs opposed to votes for women and distributed bucket-loads of leaflets. Ellen was a minor figure in the MSWS but she was learning fast: she read the suffragist newspaper, *The Common Cause*, listened to suffrage speakers, discussed suffragist aims and strategy, gained experience in

MARY EVANS PICTURE LIBRARY

200

public speaking and developed organizational skills.

On 4 August 1914, Britain declared war on Germany. Almost immediately, the MSWS stopped suffrage activity, which meant that Ellen was without a job. At first she organized volunteers for the war effort and later worked for the Women's Emergency Corps. In July 1915, now aged twenty-three, Ellen Wilkinson found another post as national organizer for what later became the National Union of Allied and Distributed Workers (NUDAW). At the end of the war, women over the age of 30 gained the vote and women over twenty-one the right to become MPs. Ellen Wilkinson wanted to be in Parliament. In 1924, sponsored by her union, she was elected MP for Middlesbrough East, an iron, steel and ship-building town situated on the River Tees in north-east England. She was the only woman on the opposition benches and one of only four women in the grey masculine House of Commons. She was lonely. However, what is striking is the way in which Ellen Wilkinson, and indeed women MPs in general, worked together. For example, Ellen Wilkinson and the Conservative MP Nancy Astor cared passionately about the rights of women and established links that cut across party lines. They campaigned for equal pay, for an end to unjust laws against prostitutes, for the reform of the Aliens Act, for fairer pensions for women and the vote on the same terms as men. It was a double-act, which regularly exasperated male MPs on both sides of the House. Ellen, a former suffragist activist, was implacably committed to extending the franchise to women over the age of twenty-one. On 20 February 1925 when she had only been an MP a few months, Ellen seconded a private members' bill to give women suffrage equality. The Bill failed but Ellen and her colleagues kept up the pressure. Eventually on 29 March 1928, Ellen witnessed a great Parliamentary triumph when the Bill to enfranchise women on the same terms as men was passed by 387 votes to 10.

In 1931 Ellen Wilkinson lost her seat. She needed to earn a living so she resumed full-time work for NUDAW, she lectured and she developed her reputation as a writer. She published a number of books including *The Division Bell Mystery*, a crime novel set in the House of Commons, as well as co-authoring political treatises such as the *The Terror in Germany*, *Why Fascism?*, *Why War?* and the *Condition of India*. She had previously written a Workers' History of the Great Strike, *Clash* and *Peeps at Politicians* and would go on to write *The Town that was Murdered* and *Plan for Peace* as well as several Labour Party documents. In the 1930s Ellen's political interests switched to fighting the far right in Europe. She joined communist-led organizations that campaigned against Nazism in Germany and fascism in Spain. More worryingly for British security, Ellen became friends with some Russian spies, notably Willi Munzenberg and Otto Katz. Munzenberg was in charge of the Soviet Union's propaganda operations in the West[5] and a number of well-known individuals – Ernest Hemingway, Bertolt Brecht, Dorothy Parker, Kim Philby, Guy Burgess, Anthony Blunt … and Ellen Wilkinson – came under his influence. Ellen also became very friendly with Otto Katz, a Czechoslovakian who was employed by the OGPU, the Soviet Secret Intelligence Service. He was a handsome man who was very attractive to women, and a man willing to use his looks and natural magnetism to further his political cause. He certainly charmed Ellen. The British Government, quite rightly, was very wary of Otto Katz and tried to prevent him visiting Britain. Each time, Ellen intervened and the ban was overturned.[6] Katz encouraged his acolyte to help in his campaigns and asked her to introduce him to a number of high-ranking figures such as Lloyd George, Lady Rhondda and the Duchess of Athol. Otto Katz organized at least three of Ellen's visits to Spain during the Spanish Civil War. He was, in effect, her controller: she was his inadvertent spy and probably his lover.

The Security Services were naturally worried by this and tailed Otto Katz. One report spoke of how Katz 'spent the next day meeting various people until the evening when he returned in a motor car owned by Ellen who was at the wheel.... The two then drove back to Ellen's Wilkinson's home' where Special Branch noted that he stayed the night.[7] Evidently, Ellen Wilkinson enjoyed the subterfuge. Once, when her car was trailed by detectives, Ellen did her best to outmanoeuvre them. It was an intrigue straight out of a Le Carré novel. However, it was no spy fiction as Katz's activities were those associated 'with a very highly placed Comintern agent ... We therefore think it feasible to put forward the theory that he is one of the principal means by which Moscow carries out its policy in western Europe and America, and that he is either the head, or the chief mouthpiece of a Comintern-type organization.'[8] He was, in effect, a dangerous man.

The Labour Party disliked Ellen Wilkinson's sympathy with communism. Herbert Morrison knew that the Communist Party sought to influence Labour politics by creating 'a whole solar system of organizations and smaller committees around the Communist Party'.[9] The inventor of this system, Morrison argued, was none other than Willi Munzenberg, seen as the 'versatile author and producer of every piece. He chooses the titles. He is the unseen prompter, stage manager and sceneshifter'.[10] In October 1934 at the Labour Party conference, Herbert Morrison who had a visceral dislike of communism, accused Ellen of belonging to an allegedly communist organization: the Relief Committee for the victims of German and Austrian Fascism.[11] Rather than be expelled, Ellen resigned from the Relief Committee, but she continued to work closely with communists.

In 1935 Ellen returned to Parliament. Once again she was the only woman on the opposition benches. Ellen Wilkinson was now Labour MP for Jarrow, a town with one of the worst unemployment records in England: only 100 out of 8,000 skilled manual workers had work. In October 1936 she led 200 unemployed men to London to ask for work: it was the Jarrow Crusade, a march that has become symbolic of the Hungry Thirties. Ellen Wilkinson's best-selling book with that evocative and provocative title *The Town that was Murdered* made Jarrow famous.

On September 1939 Britain declared war on Germany. By now Ellen had grown to dislike the Communist Party, largely because of the Soviet-Nazi pact. When Herbert Morrison banned the Communist Party's newspaper, the *Daily Worker*, Ellen defended the ban and accused the *Daily Worker* of undermining the war effort. During the war she became closer to Herbert Morrison and many assumed they were lovers. In October 1940 Churchill appointed Ellen Parliamentary Private Secretary to Morrison who was now Home Secretary. The two faced colossal challenges as the British civilian population came under attack. In London, a series of heavy bombings – the Blitz – began on Saturday 7 September 1940 and continued until May 1941, leaving 20,000 dead and approximately 70,000 wounded. In some other cities the bombardment was equally horrific. At first Ellen was responsible for air raid shelters and the care of the homeless; later she was asked to re-structure the fire services and establish compulsory fire-watching. Ellen Wilkinson was now part of the political Establishment and she began to reap the rewards. In January 1945 Ellen became Chair of the Labour Party; in the same month she was made Privy Councillor in the New Year's Honours List. She was now the Right Honourable Ellen Wilkinson MA.

On 30 April 1945 Hitler committed suicide. A few days later Germany surrendered and the war officially ended in Europe. Ellen collapsed in a relief-fuelled exhaustion. Ellen Wilkinson was now the most important woman in the Labour Party, helping to set out its socialist principles and co-authoring the manifesto, *Let Us Face the Future* in preparation for the post-war election. The Labour Party won a sweeping victory; twenty-one women Labour MPs were elected. The new Prime Minister, Clement Attlee, appointed Ellen as Minister of Education. She was the first woman to hold this post, the second woman in Britain to become a Cabinet Minister and the only woman in a Cabinet of twenty. Ellen's main task was to implement the 1944 Education Act. This set out a contentious tripartite system of grammar schools for the most intellectually gifted, modern schools for the majority and technical schools for those with a technical or scientific aptitude. To assess which pupils should attend which schools all pupils who wished to attend a state school took an exam when they were eleven years old, known as the 11+. Those who passed went to the grammar school whereas those who failed went to secondary moderns. Less controversially, Ellen raised the school leaving age from fourteen to fifteen, persuaded Parliament to pass the 1946 School Milk Act that gave free milk to British school children, reduced the number of direct grant schools and instituted University Scholarships to help towards the cost of higher education for those who could not afford to pay. She may have been part of the establishment but she was still in contact with Otto Katz, still helping him gain entry to Britain, still introducing him to important figures.

By now Ellen's health was deteriorating fast. All her life she had suffered from asthma, bronchitis, influenza and lung infections, all aggravated by heavy smoking.

During the war she had been admitted to hospital at least seven times. Exhausted by the war effort her health was undermined further by the demands of her new post. She caught pneumonia and a few weeks later, on 6 February 1947, she died in a private ward at St Mary's Hospital Paddington.

48

LILIAN LENTON (1891–1972)

Militant, hunger striker and escape artist

Janis Lomas

Lilian Lenton, while on the run in Edinburgh and with a warrant out for her arrest, stopped to ask a policeman the way to a house where she hoped to dump the bombs she was carrying in a small attaché case. The policeman offered to show her and kindly carried the case of bombs to her tram stop and saw her safely on board.

Lilian was born in 1891 in Leicester, the eldest of five children. Her father was a carpenter and she grew up in a comfortable working-class home. When she left school she trained as a dancer but, after hearing Emmeline Pankhurst speak, became determined that once she was 21 years old she would take up militant activities. From 1912 fighting for the vote soon took up all her energies; a few weeks after her twenty-first birthday she was arrested and sentenced to two months' imprisonment for breaking a window. When released she told WSPU headquarters that her aim was to burn down two buildings a week so long as 'it didn't endanger human life other than our own',[1] until the vote was given to women. She joined up with another young suffragette, Olive Wharry,[2] and embarked on serious arson attacks. In February 1913 they burned the Kew Gardens Tea Pavilion to the ground, and when placed on remand immediately went on hunger strike. After two days the prison authorities decided to forcibly feed Lilian. The tube was accidently passed into her left lung instead of into her stomach, causing septic pneumonia. She collapsed and was in a critical condition for several hours. The prison authorities then ordered her immediate release as they didn't want her to die in prison. She was indefatigable though and related later: 'When I got out, I sent a postcard to my parents: "Out, double pneumonia and pleurisy, but quite all right!"'[3] Accompanied by a prison doctor, she was sent by taxi to a friend's house. The intention was to re-arrest her as soon as she recovered, but she managed to evade capture. Her case became something of a *cause célèbre* when a leading medical doctor, Sir Victor Horsley, spoke out about the risks of forcibly feeding a resisting person and the Home Secretary, Reginald McKenna, faced hostile questions in the House of

THE MARCH OF THE WOMEN COLLECTION/MARY EVANS

Newspaper coverage of Lilian Lenton's arrest

Commons; in correspondence he admitted that she had been in imminent danger of dying. Perhaps as a result of Lilian's case, the Cat and Mouse Act was quickly passed through parliament and received the Royal Assent on 25 April. Militants were outraged by this act and escalated their lawbreaking.

In June 1913 Lilian, accompanied by male supporter and newspaper reporter, Harry Johnson, set fire to an empty building in Doncaster. When arrested she gave her name as May Dennis; she was remanded in custody and sent to Armley Prison in Leeds while the police attempted to prove that she was the Lilian Lenton wanted for the arson attack on the Kew Pavilion. She immediately went on hunger strike and after seven days, on 17 June, was released in a very weak state. She would be re-arrested three days later under the Cat and Mouse Act, but once again managed to evade the police by escaping in a delivery van, dressed as a boy delivering groceries, munching an apple and reading a comic book. In a carefully worked-out plan, friends organized a boat to the continent where she could recover her strength fully. Lilian refused to stay away for long and in the following months was arrested, starved, released and absconded several times, earning the title 'the tiny, wily, elusive Pimpernel'.[4] However in May 1914 Lilian was discovered in Liverpool and taken to Leeds, tried for the Doncaster arson and sentenced to twelve months' imprisonment. She immediately went on hunger and thirst strike and was released after two days to recover her strength. Again she escaped re-arrest, dressed as a boy, by climbing up the coal chute, over a neighbouring back garden wall while the police stood guard over the front of the house she was in. At the outbreak of World War I, when an amnesty was granted to suffrage prisoners, police had still not tracked her down.

During the war, alongside several other suffragettes, Lilian joined the Scottish Women's Hospital Unit in Serbia and was awarded a medal for her work there by the French Red Cross. After the Russian Revolution she travelled to Russia with Nina Boyle of the Women's Freedom League (WFL) and later worked for the British Embassy in Stockholm. In 1918, when women were finally allowed to vote Lilian was too young to vote; in fact she had to wait another ten years before she could vote as even when she reached thirty years of age she had neither furniture nor a husband. She became a speaker for the Save the Children Fund and worked as a speaker, organizer and editor of the WFL's journal until 1933. The last twenty years of her working life were spent as financial secretary of the National Union of Teachers. A memorial in Christchurch Gardens, London, dedicated to all the women who fought for the vote was unveiled by Lilian Lenton in 1970, two years before her death.

Notes

Acknowledgements

1. Crawford, E., *The women's suffrage movement: A reference guide 1866–1928* (Routledge, 2003); John, A. V., *Our Mothers' Land: Chapters in Welsh Women's History, 1830–1939* (University of Wales Press, 2011); Leneman, L., *The Scottish Suffragettes* (National Museums of Scotland, 2000); Liddington, J., *Vanishing for the Vote: Suffrage, Citizenship and the Battle for the Census* (Oxford University Press, 2014); Purvis, J., *Emmeline Pankhurst: a biography* (Routledge, 2003).

Introduction

1. *Leeds Mercury*, 16 December 1918.
2. http://www.historyisaweapon.com/defcon1/pankhurstincitetorebel.html (accessed 5 April 2018).
3. https://www.parliament.uk/about/living-heritage/transformingsociety/electionsvoting/womenvote/parliamentary-collections/1866-suffrage-petition/collecting-the-signatures/ (accessed 5 April 2018).
4. *Edinburgh Evening News,* 1 July 1875.
5. Crawford, E., *The women's suffrage movement in Britain and Ireland: a regional survey* (Routledge, 2013).
6. *The Northern Whig,* 20 November 1883.
7. https://www.parliament.uk/business/committees/committees-a-z/commons-select/petitions-committee/petition-of-the-month/the-1896-womens-suffrage-petition-/ (accessed 5 April 2018).
8. Pugh, M., *Women and the women's movement in Britain: 1914–1959* (Macmillan 1992).
9. Liddington, J., *Vanishing for the Vote: Suffrage, Citizenship and the Battle for the Census* (Oxford University Press, 2014).
10. Frances, H., '"Pay the Piper, Call the Tune!"': the Women's Tax Resistance League', in Joannou, M. and Purvis, J. (eds), *The Women's Suffrage Movement: New Feminist Perspectives* (Manchester University Press, 1998).
11. https://inews.co.uk/inews-lifestyle/women/millicent-fawcett-statue-women-men-supported-suffrage-added-plinth/ (accessed 5 April 2018).
12. https://womanandhersphere.com/2016/04/07/suffrage-stories-hidden-from-history-susan-cunnington/ (accessed 5 April 2018).
13. Pedersen, S., *The Scottish Suffragettes and the Press* (Springer, 2017).
14. http://www.theosociety.org/pasadena/gdpmanu/ryan-wh/wit-hp.htm (accessed 5 April 2018).

1 Barbara Leigh Smith Bodichon

1. Letter from Barbara Leigh Smith to Dorothy Longden, 1857, in the Bonham-Carter family papers, Hampshire Record Office, Winchester, cited in Hirsch 1998.
2. Hirsch, P., *Barbara Leigh Smith Bodichon, Feminist, Artist and Rebel* (Chatto and Windus, 1998).
3. Letter from Barbara Leigh Smith Bodichon to Helen Taylor, August 1869, Mill-Taylor Collection, London School of Economics, cited in Hirsch 1998.
4. Hirsch, P., *Barbara Leigh Smith Bodichon, Feminist, Artist and Rebel* (Chatto and Windus, 1998).
5. Hirsch, P., *Barbara Leigh Smith Bodichon, Feminist, Artist and Rebel* (Chatto and Windus, 1998).
6. Crawford, E., *The women's suffrage movement: A reference guide 1866–1928* (Routledge, 2003).
7. Strachey, R., *Women's Suffrage and Women's Service: The History of the London and National Society for Women's Service* (London and National Society for Women's Service, 1927).
8. Hirsch, P., *Barbara Leigh Smith Bodichon, Feminist, Artist and Rebel* (Chatto and Windus, 1998).
9. Burton, H., *Barbara Bodichon, 1827–1891* (John Murray, 1949).
10. Hirsch, P., *Barbara Leigh Smith Bodichon, Feminist, Artist and Rebel* (Chatto and Windus, 1998).
11. *Hastings and St Leonard's Observer*, 13 June 1891.

2 Rose Crawshay

1. *Cardiff and Merthyr Guardian*, 11 June 1870, quoted in Wallace, R., *Organise, Organise: A study of Reform Agitation in Wales 1840–1886* (Cardiff, 1991).

2. John, A. V., 'Beyond paternalism: the ironmaster's wife in the industrial community', in John, A. V., *Our Mothers' Land: Chapters in Welsh Women's History 1830-1939* (University of Wales Press, 1991).
3. John, A. V., 'Beyond paternalism: the ironmaster's wife in the industrial community', in John, A. V., *Our Mothers' Land: Chapters in Welsh Women's History 1830-1939* (University of Wales Press, 1991).
4. Crawford, E., *The women's suffrage movement in Britain and Ireland: a regional survey* (Routledge, 2013).
5. Masson, U., *For Women, For Wales and For Liberalism: Women in Liberal Politics in Wales 1880–1914* (University of Wales Press, 2010).
6. Wallace, R., *The Women's Suffrage Movement in Wales, 1866–1928* (University of Wales Press, 2009).
7. *The Examiner,* 2 May 1874.
8. *Western Mail,* 7 June 1873.
9. *Gloucester Citizen,* 21 January 1885.
10. http://www.cremation.org.uk/history-of-cremation-in-the-united-kingdom (accessed 5 April 2018).
11. John, A. V. 'Beyond paternalism: the ironmaster's wife in the industrial community', in John, A. V., *Our Mothers' Land: Chapters in Welsh Women's History 1830–1939* (University of Wales Press, 2011).

3   Harriet McIlquham

1. Walker, L., 'McIlquham, Harriet (1837–1910)', in *Oxford Dictionary of National Biography* (Oxford University Press, 2004).
2. Slack, J., 'Harriet McIlquham: A True Pioneer', *Tewkesbury Historical Society Bulletin,* Issue 15, 2006, pp. 18–21.
3. Slack, J., 'Harriet McIlquham: A True Pioneer', *Tewkesbury Historical Society Bulletin,* Issue 15, 2006, pp. 18–21.
4. *Tewkesbury Weekly Record and General Advertiser,* 17 November 1894.
5. Benson, D., 'Women's Suffrage Activities in Tewkesbury', *Tewkesbury Historical Society Bulletin,* Issue 24, 2015, pp. 43–48.
6. Hollis, P., 'Women in Council: Separate Spheres, Public Space', in Rendall, J. (ed.), *Equal Politics 1800–1914* (Blackwell, 1987), pp. 192–213.
7. Crawford, E., *The Woman's Suffrage Movement in Britain and Ireland: A Regional Survey* (Routledge, 2013).
8. Broad, J., *The Philosophy of Mary Astell: An Early Modern Theory of Virtue* (Oxford University Press, 2015).
9. Benson, D., 'Women's Suffrage Activities in Tewkesbury', *Tewkesbury Historical Society Bulletin*, Issue 24, 2015.
10. *Cheltenham Chronicle and Gloucestershire Graphic*, 29 January 1910.

4   Charlotte Carmichael Stopes

1. Stopes, C. C., *British Freewomen: Their Historical Privilege* (Cambridge University Press, 2010).
2. Green, S., *The Public Lives of Charlotte and Marie Stopes* (Routledge, 2015).
3. Green, S., *The Public Lives of Charlotte and Marie Stopes* (Routledge, 2015).
4. My thanks to Josephine Adams and Josie Wall, archivists currently cataloguing the Stopes family papers, for this point and other nuances.
5. Hall, R., *Marie Stopes: a Biography* (Quality Book Club, 1978).
6. Green, S., *The Public Lives of Charlotte and Marie Stopes* (Routledge, 2015).
7. *Western Daily Press*, 19 September 1889.
8. *Chard and Ilminster News*, 23 June 1894.
9. Mayhall, L. E. N., 'Defining Militancy: Radical Protest, the Constitutional Idiom, and Women's Suffrage in Britain, 1908–1909,' *Journal of British Studies*, 39.3 (2000), pp. 340–371.
10. Green, S., *The Public Lives of Charlotte and Marie Stopes* (Routledge, 2015).

5   Elizabeth Amy Dillwyn

1. Painting, D., *Amy Dillwyn* (University of Wales Press, 2013).
2. Painting, D., *Amy Dillwyn* (University of Wales Press, 2013).
3. Bohata, K., '*Introduction', Jill by Amy Dillwyn* (Honno, 2013); also see
4. http://www.swansea.ac.uk/riah/research-projects/thelifeandfictionofamydillwyn/ (accessed 5 April 2018).
5. http://www.swansea.ac.uk/riah/research-projects/thelifeandfictionofamydillwyn/
6. Painting, D., *Amy Dillwyn* (University of Wales Press, 2013).
7. Painting, D., *Amy Dillwyn* (University of Wales Press, 2013).
8. Crawford, E., *The women's suffrage movement in Britain and Ireland: a regional survey* (Routledge, 2013).

6   Lady Henry Somerset

1. *Hereford Journal*, 24 June 1893.
2. Niessen, O. C., *Aristocracy, temperance and social reform: the life of Lady Henry Somerset*, Vol. 1 (IB Tauris & Company, 2007).
3. Liggins, E., 'Not an Ordinary Ladies' Paper: Work, Motherhood, and Temperance Rhetoric in the Woman's Signal, 1894–1899,' *Victorian*

Periodicals Review 47.4 (2014), pp. 613–30.
4. Worcester Journal, 30 April 1892.
5. Liggins, E., 'Not an Ordinary Ladies' Paper: Work, Motherhood, and Temperance Rhetoric in the Woman's Signal, 1894–1899,' Victorian Periodicals Review 47.4 (2014), pp. 613–30.
6. Shields Daily News, 4 May 1892.
7. The Cornish Telegraph, 1 February 1894.
8. Glasgow Herald, 21 October 1893.
9. Paisana, J., 'How the Other Half Lives: Under the Arch with Lady Henry Somerset,' Open Cultural Studies 1.1 (2017), pp. 161–71.
10. http://www.herefordshirelife.co.uk/out-about/lady-henry-somerset-of-eastnor-castle-1-1640638 (accessed 5 April 2018).

7 Dame Ethel Smyth

1. Smyth, E., The Memoirs of Ethel Smyth (Faber & Faber, 2008).
2. Purvis, J., Emmeline Pankhurst: a Biography (Routledge, 2002).
3. Daily Herald, 31 December 1912.
4. Smyth, E., The Memoirs of Ethel Smyth (Faber & Faber, 2008).
5. The voice of Ethel Smyth describing the incident to Vera Brittain (first recorded in 1937) can be heard via http://www.bbc.co.uk/archive/suffragettes/8314.shtml (accessed 9 December 2017).
6. St John, C., Ethel Smyth: A Biography (Longmans, 1959).
7. Crawford, E., The women's suffrage movement: A reference guide 1866–1928 (Routledge, 2003).
8. Hawksley, L., March, Women, March (Andre Deutsch, London, 2013), p.207, quoting 'Suffragette Vandalism' by the Women's Library at www.londonmet.ac.uk.
9. Crawford, E., The women's suffrage movement: A reference guide 1866–1928 (Routledge, 2003). However, Ethel Smyth's memoirs recount a different anecdote about Ethel trying to raise a Testimonial Fund for Emmeline to which Emmeline objected.
10. Smyth, E., The Memoirs of Ethel Smyth (Faber & Faber, 2008).
11. Crawford, E., The women's suffrage movement: A reference guide 1866–1928 (Routledge, 2003).
12. The Stage, 11 May 1944.

8 Margaret Llewelyn Davies

1. Cambridge Independent Press, 22 October 1909.
2. Leeds Mercury, 1 July 1889.
3. Scott, G., 'The Women's Co-operative Guild and Suffrage,' Suffrage Outside Suffragism (Palgrave Macmillan, 2007), pp. 132–56.
4. London Daily News, 10 November 1910.
5. Scott, G., 'The Women's Co-operative Guild

and Suffrage,' Suffrage Outside Suffragism (Palgrave Macmillan, 2007), pp. 132–56.
6. The Scotsman, 29 May 1911.
7. The Daily News, 16 October 1908.
8. Cambridge Independent Press, 22 October 1909.
9. Falkirk Herald, 9 August 1911.
10. Sheffield Daily Telegraph, 11 July 1915.
11. Oldfield, S., Women Humanitarians: A Biographical Dictionary of British Women Active Between 1900 and 1950:'doers of the Word' (Continuum International Publishing Group, 2001).
12. Sheffield Independent, 13 April 1931.

9 Mary Hayden

1. How women won the vote. The Irish Times ebooks 2016
2. Hayden, M., 'The Voice of Irish Womanhood: The Demand Stated and a Warning Uttered', Irish Citizen, 8 June 1912.
3. Dictionary of Irish Biography (Cambridge University Press, 2015) http://dib.cambridge.org (accessed 5 April 2018).
4. Ryan, L., 'Traditions and double moral standards: the Irish suffragists' critique of nationalism', Women's History Review 4.4 (1995).
5. Hearne, D., 'Concepts of nation in Irish feminist thought,' Canadian Woman Studies 17.3 (1997), p. 31.
6. Ryan, L., 'Traditions and double moral standards: the Irish suffragists' critique of nationalism,' Women's History Review 4.4 (1995).
7. Murphy, C., The women's suffrage movement and Irish society in the early twentieth century (Temple University Press, 1989).
8. Murphy, C., 'The religious context of the women's suffrage campaign in Ireland,' Women's History Review 6.4 (1997).
9. Daily Express, 15 March 1917.
10. Hearne, D., 'Concepts of nation in Irish feminist thought,' Canadian Woman Studies 17.3 (1997).
11. The Standard, 11 March 1938.

10 Clemence Annie Housman

1. Liddington, J., Vanishing for the Vote: Suffrage, Citizenship and the Battle for the Census (Oxford University Press, 2014), p. 149.
2. https://www.ed.ac.uk/literatures-languages-cultures/chb/events/seminars/invisible-hands-of-clemence-housman (accessed 5 April 2018).
3. Allen, G., 'Plain Words on the Woman Question,' Fortnightly Review 46, October 188, pp. 448–58.
4. Purdue, M., 'Clemence Housman's The Were-Wolf: A Cautionary Tale for the Progressive New Woman,' Revenant Issue 2 (2016); for the article, see http://www.revenantjournal.com/wp-

content/uploads/2016/12/Article-3.pdf (accessed 5 April 2018).

5. Liddington, J., *Vanishing for the Vote: Suffrage, Citizenship and the Battle for the Census* (Oxford University Press, 2014).

6. Crawford, E., *The women's suffrage movement: A reference guide 1866–1928* (Routledge, 2003).

7. Crawford, E., *The women's suffrage movement: A reference guide 1866–1928* (Routledge, 2003).

8. Housman, L., *The Unexpected Year* (Jonathan Cape, 1937).

9. *The Whitstable Times and Herne Bay Herald,* 7 October 1911.

10. Liddington, J., *Vanishing for the Vote: Suffrage, Citizenship and the Battle for the Census* (Oxford University Press, 2014).

11 Millicent 'Hetty' MacKenzie

1. *South Wales Daily News,* 4 October 1909; see also the Institutional Archives held at the University of Cardiff online at http://blogs.cardiff.ac.uk/cuarm/millicent-mackenzie/ (accessed 5 April 2018).

2. *Leeds Mercury,* 4 August 1906.

3. Matthews-Jones, L., http://www.walesonline.co.uk/lifestyle/nostalgia/how-women-classes-came-together-12596684 (accessed 5 April 2018) and http://www.walesonline.co.uk/lifestyle/nostalgia/how-women-classes-came-together-12596684

4. John, A. V., *Our Mothers' Land: Chapters in Welsh Women's History 1830–1939* (University of Wales Press, 2011).

5. https://scolarcardiff.wordpress.com/2016/03/ 08/cardiff-banner-comes-home/ (accessed 5 April 2018).

6. *Birmingham Daily Post,* 17 August 1915.

7. *Nottingham Journal,* 23 December, 1918.

8. *Western Mail,* 6 April 1943.

9. *Western Daily Press,* 12 December 1942.

12 Lady Isabel Margesson

1. *Manchester Courier and Lancashire General Advertiser,* 24 July 1914.

2. *Dundee Evening Telegraph,* 4 March 1901.

3. *Leominster News* and *North West Herefordshire & Radnorshire Advertiser,* 13 April 1894.

4. *Woolwich Gazette,* 11 June 1909.

5. *Cheltenham Looker-On,* 18 December 1909.

6. Leneman, L., 'A truly national movement: the view from outside London' in Joannou, M. and Purvis, J. (eds), *The Women's Suffrage Movement: New feminist perspectives* (Manchester University Press, 1998).

7. *Aberdeen Press and Journal,* 3 December 1912.

8. *Hastings and St Leonard's Observer,* 12 November 1913.

9. *Manchester Courier and Lancashire General Advertiser,* 3 December 1912.

10. *Birmingham Gazette,* 8 December 1921.

13 Alice Hawkins

1. http://www.alicesuffragette.co.uk/aliceslife.php (accessed 5 April 2018).

2. http://www.alicesuffragette.co.uk/aliceslife.php (accessed 5 April 2018).

3. Liddington, J., *Vanishing the Vote; Suffrage, Citizenship and the Battle for the Census* (Manchester University Press, 2014).

4. http://www.alicesuffragette.co.uk/alfredslife.php (accessed 5 April 2018).

5. Crawford, E., *The women's suffrage movement: A reference guide 1866–1928* (Routledge, 2003).

6. http://www.alicesuffragette.co.uk/alicemeets lloydgeorge.php (accessed 5 April 2018).

14 Constance Antonina (Nina) Boyle

1. *The Times,* 23 July 1913.

2. 'Nina Boyle and Janet Boyd', www.http://uncoveryourancestors.org (accessed 5 April 2018).

3. Crawford, E., *The Women's Suffrage Movement: A reference guide* (UCL Press, 1999).

4. Lock, J., *The British Policewomen: Her Story* (Robert Hale, 2004).

5. *The Times,* 14 July 1914.

6. Woodeson, A., 'The First Women Police: A Force for Equality or Infringement,' *Women's History Review,* Vol. 2, No. 2 (1993).

7. Woodeson, A., 'The First Women Police: A Force for Equality or Infringement', *Women's History Review,* Vol. 2, No. 2 (1993).

8. 'A Woman Candidate', *The Times,* 4 April 1918.

9. Pedersen, S., *Eleanor Rathbone and the Politics of Conscience* (Yale University Press, 2004).

15 Jennie Baines

1. *Nottingham Evening Post,* 18 December 1906.

2. *Aberdeen People's Journal,* 22 December 1906.

3. Smart, J., 'Jennie Baines: Suffrage and an Australian Connection,' in Purvis J. and Holton, S. (eds), *Votes for Women* (Routledge, 2000).

4. Crawford, E., *The women's suffrage movement: A reference guide 1866–1928* (Routledge, 2003).

5. Smart, J., 'Jennie Baines: Suffrage and an Australian Connection,' in Purvis J. and Holton, S. (eds), *Votes for Women* (Routledge, 2000).

6. Smart, J., 'Jennie Baines: Suffrage and an Australian Connection,' in Purvis J. and Holton, S. (eds), *Votes for Women* (Routledge, 2000).

7. Smart, J., 'Jennie Baines: Suffrage and an Australian Connection,' in Purvis J. and Holton, S. (eds), *Votes for Women* (Routledge, 2000).

8. Smart, J., 'Jennie Baines: Suffrage and an Australian Connection,' in Purvis J. and Holton, S. (eds), *Votes for Women* (Routledge, 2000).
9. http://adb.anu.edu.au/biography/baines-sarah-jane-jennie-5100 (accessed 5 April 2018).
10. Smart, J., 'Jennie Baines: Suffrage and an Australian Connection,' in Purvis, J. and Holton, S. (eds), *Votes for Women* (Routledge, 2000).

16 Emma Sproson

1. *Dundee Evening Telegraph*, 23 May 1911.
2. http://www.wolverhamptonhistory.org.uk/politics/women/emma (accessed 5 April 2018).
3. Crawford, E., *The Woman's Suffrage Movement in Britain and Ireland: A Regional Survey* (Routledge, 2013).
4. *Cheltenham Chronicle*, 11 July 1908.
5. https://nicolagauld.wordpress.com/2015/03/02/emma-sproson-the-1911-census/ (accessed 5 April 2018).
6. *Dundee Courier,* I May 1912.
7. *Daily Herald,* 8 August 1912.
8. *Express and Star,* 1 July 1914.
9. For details of this, see Nicola Gauld: https://nicolagauld.wordpress.com/2015/03/09/emma-sproson-wolverhamptons-first-female-councillor/ (accessed 5 April 2018).
10. https://nicolagauld.wordpress.com/2015/03/09/emma-sproson-wolverhamptons-first-female-councillor/ (accessed 5 April 2018).
11. *Birmingham Daily Gazette,* 24 December 1936.

17 Countess Constance Markievicz

1. *Sligo Champion*, 26 December 1896, cited in Naughton, L., *Markievicz: A Most Outrageous Rebel* (Merrion Press, 2016).
2. Haverty, A., *Constance Markievicz: an independent life* (New York University Press, 1988).
3. Arrington, L., *Revolutionary Lives: Constance and Casimir Markievicz* (Princeton University Press, 2015).
4. Arrington, L., *Revolutionary Lives: Constance and Casimir Markievicz* (Princeton University Press, 2015).
5. *Newcastle Journal*, 9 May 1916.
6. *The Daily Express,* 8 May 1916.
7. *Liverpool Echo,* 8 May 1916.

18 Ada Neild Chew

1. *The Western Daily Press,* 9 June 1912.
2. *Crewe Chronicle*, 23 June 1894, cited in Chew, A. N., *The Life and Writings of a Working Woman* (Virago, 1982).
3. Chew, A. N., *The Life and Writings of a Working Woman* (Virago, 1982).
4. Mitchell, H., *The Hard Way Up: the Autobiography of Hannah Mitchell* (Faber & Faber, 1968).
5. *Leeds Mercury*, 20 November 1900.
6. *The Clarion,* December 1904, cited in Chew, A. N., *The life and Writings of a Working Woman* (Virago, 1982).

19 Kitty Marion

1. 'Miss Kitty Marion Released,' *Votes for Women*, 19 November 1909.
2. Marion, K., unpublished autobiography held at The Women's Library at the University of London, LSE, cited in Woodworth, C., 'When Audiences Attack: The Manhandling of Actress and Activist Kitty Marion', *Theatre Symposium*, Vol. 20 (2012).
3. Marion, K., unpublished autobiography held at The Women's Library at the University of London, LSE.
4. Parkins, W., *Fashioning the Body Politic: Dress, Gender, Citizenship* (Berg, 2002).
5. Marion, K., unpublished autobiography held at The Women's Library at the University of London, LSE.

20 Ada Croft Baker

1. *The Grimsby News,* 5 April 1935.
2. Crawford, E., *The Women's Suffrage Movement in Britain and Ireland: A Regional Survey* (Routledge, 2006).
3. Crawford, E., *The Women's Suffrage Movement in Britain and Ireland: A Regional Survey* (Routledge, 2006).
4. Crawford, E., *The Women's Suffrage Movement in Britain and Ireland: A Regional Survey* (Routledge, 2006).
5. Crawford, E., *The Women's Suffrage Movement in Britain and Ireland: A Regional Survey* (Routledge, 2006).
6. *The Grimsby News,* 5 April 1935.
7. *The Grimsby News,* 5 April 1935.
8. *The Grimsby Evening Telegraph,* 3 August 1962.
9. *The Grimsby News,* 5 April 1935.
10. *The Grimsby News,* 5 April 1935.
11. *The Grimsby News,* 5 April 1935.
12. https://h2g2.com/edited_entry/A87772882

21 Catherine Blair

1. http://www.eastlothiancourier.com/opinion/tims_tales/13561689.Tim's_Tales_Catherine_Blair_of_Hoprig_Mains_Farm/ (accessed 5 April 2018).
2. Blair, C., *Rural Journey: a history of the SWRI from cradle to majority* (Thomas Nelson and Son, 1940).
3. *The Scotsman,* 19 November 1946.

4. http://www.bbc.co.uk/ahistoryoftheworld/
    objects/7ciU-wIqSWuxtuRV34IPUA (accessed 5
    April 2018).
5. https://www.wealothianwomensforum.org.uk/
    DeadInterestingWomen/cblair.html (accessed 5
    April 2018).
6. *The Scotsman*, 13 October 1941.

22 Edith Rigby

1. *Preston Herald*, 19 July 1913.
2. Dugden, P., *Village Voices* (Collins, 1989).
3. Cowman, K., *Women of the Right Spirit: Paid
    Organisers of the Women's Social and Political
    Union (WSPU) 1904–1918* (Manchester
    University Press, 2007).
4. https://uclanthroughtheages.org/2016/11/11/
    edith-rigby-apreston-legend/ (accessed 14
    December 2017)
5. Dugden, P., *Village Voices* (Collins, 1989).
6. Leneman, L., 'The awakened instinct:
    vegetarianism and the women's suffrage
    movement in Britain,' *Women's History Review*
    6.2 (1997).
7. Hesketh, P., *My Aunt Edith* (Lancashire County
    Books, 1992).

23 Hannah Mitchell

1. Mitchell, H., *The Hard Way Up: The
    Autobiography of Hannah Mitchell: Suffragette
    and Rebel* (Faber & Faber, 1968).
2. Mitchell, H., *The Hard Way Up: The
    Autobiography of Hannah Mitchell: Suffragette
    and Rebel* (Faber & Faber, 1968).
3. Mitchell, H., *The Hard Way Up: The
    Autobiography of Hannah Mitchell: Suffragette
    and Rebel* (Faber & Faber, 1968).
4. Mitchell, H., *The Hard Way Up: The
    Autobiography of Hannah Mitchell: Suffragette
    and Rebel* (Faber & Faber, 1968).
5. Mitchell, H., *The Hard Way Up: The
    Autobiography of Hannah Mitchell: Suffragette
    and Rebel* (Faber & Faber, 1968).
6. Cowman, K., *Women of the Right Spirit*
    (Manchester University Press, 2007).
7. Mitchell, H., *The Hard Way Up: The
    Autobiography of Hannah Mitchell: Suffragette
    and Rebel* (Faber & Faber, 1968).
8. Cowman, K., *Women of the Right Spirit*
    (Manchester University Press, 2007).
9. *Sheffield Daily Telegraph*, 22 March 1907.
10. Mitchell, H., *The Hard Way Up: The
    Autobiography of Hannah Mitchell: Suffragette
    and Rebel* (Faber & Faber, 1968).
11. Crawford, E., *The women's suffrage movement: A
    reference guide 1866–1928* (Routledge, 2003).
12. Hannah H., *The Hard Way Up: The*

*Autobiography of Hannah Mitchell: Suffragette
and Rebel* (Faber & Faber, 1968).

24 Chrystal Macmillan

1. *Aberdeen Press and Journal*, 11 November 1908.
2. Leneman, L., *The Scottish Suffragettes* (National
    Museums of Scotland, 2000).
3. Crawford, E., *The women's suffrage movement: A
    reference guide 1866–1928* (Routledge, 2003).
4. *The Scotsman*, 11 January 1909.
5. *Dundee Courier,* 16 August 1913.
6. Oldfield, S., *Women Humanitarians: A
    Biographical Dictionary of British Women Active
    Between 1900 and 1950:'doers of the Word'*
    (Continuum International Publishing Group,
    2001).
7. *Daily Echo and Shipping Gazette,* 22 September
    1937.
8. *Daily Herald*, 2 March 1918.
9. *Birmingham Daily Gazette*, 21 June 1918.
10. Law, C., *Suffrage and Power: The Women's
    Movement 1918–1928* (IB Tauris, 1997).
11. *Hendon & Finchley Times*, 9 March 1923.
12. *The Scotsman,* 25 September 1937.

25 Margaret Bondfield

1. Bondfield, M., *A Life's Work* (Hutchinson, 1948).
2. Herbert, T. (ed.), *The British Labour Party: its
    history, growth, policy and leaders*, Vol. 3 (Caxton
    Publishing Company, 1948).
3. Bondfield, M., *A Life's Work* (Hutchinson, 1948).
4. Bondfield, M., *A Life's Work* (Hutchinson, 1948).
5. *Western Daily Press,* 25 May 1905.
6. Bondfield, M., *A Life's Work* (Hutchinson, 1948).
7. Susan Lawrence and Dorothy Jewson were the
    other two.
8. *Western Times*, 25 January 1924.
9. Bondfield, M., *A Life's Work* (Hutchinson, 1948).
10. Snowden, P., *An Autobiography*, Vol. II, 1919–
    1934 (Ivor Nicolson and Watson, 1934).
11. Bondfield, M., 1 December 1930, Parliamentary
    Debate (Hansard), vol. 245, cc1827–1952.
12. Clynes, J. R., 'The Years 1929–31,' cited in
    Herbert, T., *The British Labour Party: its history,
    growth, policy and leaders*, Vol. 3 (Caxton
    Publishing Company, 1948).
13. Cabinet Papers, 23/67/21, 23 August 1931.
14. Margaret Bondfield to Ramsay MacDonald, 24
    August 1931, MacDonald papers NA 30/69
    1314, cited in *Dictionary of Labour Biography*,
    Vol. XI (Palgrave Macmillan, 2003).
15. Ramsay MacDonald to Margaret Bondfield, 25
    August 1931, cited in Marquand, D., *Ramsay
    MacDonald* (Anchor Press, 1977).
16. *Gloucester Citizen*, 30 September 1931.
17. Bondfield, M., *A Life's Work* (Hutchinson, 1948).

26 Adeline Redfern-Wilde

1. *Votes for Women*, 23 February 1912.
2. *Votes for Women*, 15 March 1912.
3. Reeve, H., Plender, O. and Chambers, E., 'Sylvia Pankhurst: The Suffragette as a Militant Artist' (2013). For details of this installation, see http://hester-reeve.squarespace.com/emily-davidson-lodge/ (accessed 5 April 2018).
4. Jarrett, G., interview for 'The People's Century: Age of Hope' Episode 1. BBC, 13 September 1995.
5. Crawford, E., *The Women's Suffrage Movement: a reference guide 1866–1928* (Routledge, 2001).
6. Flood, A., 'Suffragette autograph album illuminates movement's struggles', *Guardian,* 6 December 2012.
7. *Auckland Star*, Vol. XXXIX, Issue 76, 28 March 1908.
8. *Birmingham Gazette and Express*, 12 February 1908.
9. *Daily Mail,* 12 February 1908.

27 Alice Clark

1. *Shepton Mallet Journal,* 8 March 1907.
2. Holton, S. S., *Suffrage days: stories from the women's suffrage movement* (Psychology Press, 1996).
3. Berg, M., *The First Women Economic Historians: the LSE Connections,* The Warwick Economics Research Papers No. 328 (University of Warwick, 1989).
4. *Gloucester Journal*, 10 October 1908.
5. Holton, S. S., *Suffrage days: stories from the women's suffrage movement* (Psychology Press, 1996).
6. Holton, S. S., 'Feminism, History and Movements of the Soul: Christian Science in the Life of Alice Clark (1874–1934),' *Australian Feminist Studies*, Vol. 13, Issue 28 (October 1998).

28 Mrs Arthur Webb

1. https://womanandhersphere.com/tag/suffrage-banners (accessed 5 April 2018).
2. *The Standard,* 6 May 1907.
3. https://www.theguardian.com/lifeandstyle/2011/apr/01/suffragettes-census-1911-boycott (accessed 5 April 2018).
4. *Radio Times,* 17 December 1935.
5. For more about Mrs Webb, see Andrews, M., 'The Indefatigable Mrs. Webb: Food, Radio, and Rural Women – a Legacy of World War I; Ambrose, L., and Jensen, J. (eds) *Recipes for Rural Life: Food History and Women Professionals, 1880–1965* (University of Iowa Press. 2017), pp. 139–55.

29 Grace Hadow

1. http://www.st-annes.ox.ac.uk/about/history/principals/grace-hadow-1929-40 (accessed 5 April 2018).
2. Crawford, E., *The Women's Suffrage Movement in Britain and Ireland: a regional survey* (Routledge, 2013).
3. Maguire, G., *A History of Women and the Conservative Party, 1874–1997* (Palgrave Macmillan, 1998).
4. *Cheltenham Chronicle and Gloucestershire Graphic,* 1 June 1912.
5. *Gloucester Journal*, 19 July 1913.
6. Deneke, H., *Grace Hadow* (Oxford University Press, 1946).
7. Deneke, H., *Grace Hadow* (Oxford University Press, 1946).
8. Deneke, H., *Grace Hadow* (Oxford University Press, 1946).
9. https://www.thewi.org.uk/faqs/why-was-jerusalem-chosen-as-the-wis-anthem (accessed 5 April 2018).
10. Deneke, H., *Grace Hadow* (Oxford University Press, 1946).
11. Deneke, H., *Grace Hadow* (Oxford University Press, 1946).
12. *Derby Evening Telegraph,* 6 July 1939.

30 Rosa May Billinghurst

1. Rosa May Billinghurst, quoted in http://spartacus-educational.com/Wbillinghurst.htm (accessed 5 April 2018).
2. Abrams, F., *Freedom's Cause: Lives of the Suffragettes* (Profile Books, 2003).
3. Lenton, L., *Women's Bulletin*, 11 September 1953, cited in Abrams, F., *Freedom's Cause: Lives of the Suffragettes* (Profile Books, 2003).
4. *Manchester Courier*, 10 January 1913.

31 Mrs Aubrey Dowson

1. Advertisement for *The Women's Suffrage Cookery Book* in *Common Cause*, 'The Organ of the Women's Movement for Reform', 18 November 1909.
2. *London Evening Standard*, 26 July 1897.
3. Birmingham Moseley Rugby Club website, 'A. O. Dowson', nd [2017], available at URL http://www.moseleyrugby.co.uk/report_display12.php?menitem=252 (accessed 15 Jan 2018)
4. Kirwan, C., 'The Rectors and Fellows of Exeter College, Oxford 1901–2005', nd [2005], available at URL: https://www.exeter.ox.ac.uk/wp-content/uploads/2017/03/rectors-and-fellows-of-exeter-college.pdf (accessed 1 February 2018)
5. 1901 census return for Frimley, Surrey.

6. Crawford, E., 'Osler [née Taylor], Catherine Courtauld (1854–1924)', *Oxford Dictionary of National Biography* 2017, available online at https://doi.org/10.1093/ref:odnb/101357 (accessed 5 April 2018).

7. Crawford, E., *The Women's Suffrage Movement: A reference guide 1866–1928* (Routledge, 1999).

8. Crawford, E., *The Women's Suffrage Movement in Britain and Ireland: A Regional Survey* (Routledge, 2006).

9. Schlossberg, L., 'Consuming Images: Women, Hunger, and the Vote,' in Heller, T. and Moran, P. (eds), *Scenes of the Apple: Food and the Female Body in Nineteenth- and Twentieth-Century Women's Writing* (State University of New York Press, 2003).

10. *Warwick & Warwickshire Advertiser,* 7 September 1912.

11. *Warwick & Warwickshire Advertiser,* 20 April 1912.

12. A report from the Solihull branch of the NUWSS notes that Mrs Dowson is about to leave Lapworth (*Warwick & Warwickshire Advertiser,* 7 September 1912). On his British Army WWI Medal Rolls Index Card, 1914–1920, Aubrey Osler's address is given as Upper Fulbrook, Stratford upon Avon.

13. A.O. Dowson's obituary, *Birmingham Daily Post,* 12 October 1940.

32 Princess Sophia Duleep Singh

1. Crawford, E., *The Women's Suffrage Movement: A reference guide 1866–1928* (Routledge, 2003).

2. Suffragette index of names of persons arrested 1906–1914, TNA HO45/24665, cited in Anand, A., *Sophia Princess, Suffragette, Revolutionary* (Bloomsbury, 2015).

3. WC Note to the Commissioner of Police for observations, TNA HO/1106/200451, cited in Anand, A., *Sophia Princess, Suffragette, Revolutionary* (Bloomsbury, 2015).

4. Census of England and Wales 1911, Public Record Office (PRO). *Daily Mail,* 30 December 1913.

5. *Daily Mail,* 30 December 1913.

6. *Daily Mail,* 30 December 1913.

7. Women's Social and Political Union (WSPU), 7th Annual Report 1913, cited in Anand, A., *Sophia: Princess, Suffragette, Revolutionary* (Bloomsbury, 2015).

8. Anand A., *Sophia: Princess, Suffragette, Revolutionary* (Bloomsbury, 2015).

33 Muriel Matters

1. Newinson, M., *Life's Fitful Fever: A Volume of Memories* (A&C Black, 1926). pp. 214–215, cited in Liddington, J., *Vanishing for the Vote: Suffrage, Citizenship and the Battle for the Census* (Manchester University Press, 2014).

2. Hansard, House of Commons, 28 October 1908.

3. *Miss Muriel Matters: The Fearless Suffragist who fought for Equality* (Allan and Unwin, 2017).

34 Mabel Lida Ramsay

1. *Western Morning News,* 13 September 1910.

2. Crawford, E., *The women's suffrage movement: A reference guide 1866–1928* (Routledge, 2003).

3. https://www.revolvy.com/main/index.php?s=Mabel%20L.%20Ramsay (accessed 7 April 2018).

4. *Western Daily Mercury,* 12 January 1912.

5. *West Briton and Cornwall Advertiser,* 13 November 1912.

6. *Western Times,* 8 February 1913.

7. Leneman, L., 'Medical women at war, 1914–1918,' *Medical History* 38.2 (1994).

8. http://www.scarletfinders.co.uk/165.html (accessed 7 April 2018).

9. *British Medical Journal,* 5 June 1915.

35 Margaret Cousins

1. Cousins, J. and Cousins, M., *We Two Together* (Ganesh and Co., 1950), cited in Watkins, S.-B., *Ireland's Suffragettes: the Women who Fought for the Vote* (History Press, 2014).

2. Moriarty, T., 'How Women Won the Vote' (*Irish Times,* 2016).

3. Candy, C., 'Relating feminisms, nationalisms and imperialisms: Ireland, India and Margaret Cousins's sexual politics,' *Women's History Review* 3.4 (1994).

4. Owens, R. C., *Smashing Times: A history of the Irish women's suffrage movement, 1889–1922* (Irish Books & Media, 1984).

5. Cousins, J., and Cousins, M., *We Two Together* (Ganesh and Co., 1950), cited in Watkins, S.-B., *Ireland's Suffragettes: the Women who Fought for the Vote* (History Press, 2014).

6. https://womanandhersphere.com/tag/margaret-cousins/ (accessed 7 April 2018).

7. Cousins, J., and Cousins, M., *We Two Together* (Ganesh and Co., 1950), cited in Watkins, S.-B., *Ireland's Suffragettes: the Women who Fought for the Vote* (History Press, 2014).

8. Candy, C., 'Relating feminisms, nationalisms and imperialisms: Ireland, India and Margaret Cousins's sexual politics,' *Women's History Review* 3.4 (1994), pp. 581–94.

36 Kate Parry Frye

1. Crawford, E. (ed.), *Campaigning for the Vote: Kate Parry Frye's Suffrage Diary* (Francis Bootle, 2013).

2. Crawford, E. (ed.), *Campaigning for the Vote: Kate Parry Frye's Suffrage Diary* (Francis Bootle, 2013).

3. Crawford, E. (ed.), *Campaigning for the Vote: Kate Parry Frye's Suffrage Diary* (Francis Bootle, 2013).

4. Crawford, E. (ed.), *Campaigning for the Vote: Kate Parry Frye's Suffrage Diary* (Francis Bootle, 2013).

5. Crawford, E. (ed.), *Campaigning for the Vote: Kate Parry Frye's Suffrage Diary* (Francis Bootle, 2013).

6. Crawford, E. (ed.), *Campaigning for the Vote: Kate Parry Frye's Suffrage Diary* (Francis Bootle, 2013).

7. Crawford, E. (ed.), *Campaigning for the Vote: Kate Parry Frye's Suffrage Diary* (Francis Bootle, 2013).

37 Nora Dacre Fox

1. McPherson, S. and McPherson, A., *Mosley's Old Suffragette: A biography of Norah Dacre Fox* (lulu.com, 2010).

2. McPherson, S. and McPherson, A., *Mosley's Old Suffragette: A biography of Norah Dacre Fox* (lulu.com, 2010).

3. Kean, H., 'Some problems of constructing and reconstructing a suffragette's life: Mary Richardson, suffragette, socialist and fascist,' *Women's History Review* 7.4 (1998).

4. Gottlieb, J. V., *Feminine Fascism: Women in Britain's Fascist Movement 1923–45* (IB Tauris, 2003).

5. Durham, M., *Women and Fascism* (Psychology Press, 1998).

38 Margaret Wintringham

1. Crawford, E., *The Women's Suffrage Movement in Britain and Ireland* (Routledge, 2006).

2. Storr, K., *Excluded from the Record: Women, Refugees and Relief 1914–1929* (Verlag Peter Lang, 2009).

3. *Boston Guardian,* 14 August 1920.

4. http://hansard.millbanksystems.com/commons/1923/may/02/housing-etc-no-2-money (accessed 7 April 2018).

5. https://www.theguardian.com/theguardian/2010/jun/23/archive-letter-no-more-war (accessed 7 April 2018).

6. For a more extensive exploration of the passage of this bill, see Takayanagi, M., *Parliament and Women c1900–1945,* Kings College London, unpublished Phd thesis 2012, which I have drawn upon here.

39 Mary Macarthur

1. *Daily Herald,* 10 February 1918.

2. Hamilton, M. A., *Mary Macarthur: A Biographical Sketch,* 1926 (reprinted by Hyperion Press, 1976).

3. Hunt, C., *The National Federation of Women Workers, 1906–1921* (Palgrave, 2014).

4. http://www.striking-women.org/main-module-page/women-and-work (accessed 7 April 2018).

5. Hamilton, M. A., *Mary Macarthur: A Biographical Sketch,* 1926 (reprinted by Hyperion Press, 1976).

40 Vera 'Jack' Holme

1. Crawford, E., *The women's suffrage movement: A reference guide 1866–1928* (Routledge, 2003).

2. Raeburn, A., *The militant suffragettes* (Michael Joseph, 1973).

3. Raeburn, A., *The militant suffragettes* (Michael Joseph, 1973).

4. Iglikowski, V., 'Motoring towards Liberation', 11 August 1914. Letter showing the Metropolitan Police requesting a motorbike to keep up with the WSPU drivers (MEPO 2/1566).

5. Kisby's interview with John Holme in London (2007), cited in Kisby, A., 'Vera "Jack" Holme: cross-dressing actress, suffragette and chauffeur', *Women's History Review* Vol. 23, issue 1. pp. 120–136 (2014).

41 Anna Munro

1. *Citizen,* 21 October 1926.

2. *Montrose, Arbroath and Brechin Review,* 25 December 1908.

3. *Dundee Courier,* 5 February 1908.

4. *The Courier and Argus,* 13 February 1908.

5. *Dundee Courier,* 26 November 1910.

6. *Montrose, Arbroath and Brechin Review,* 25 December 1908.

7. *The Evening Telegraph and Post,* 3 March 1909.

8. *The Scotsman,* 14 December 2006.

9. Russell, V., *Oxford Dictionary of National Biography* Munro [married name Munro-Ashman], Anna Gillies Macdonald (1881–1962); also available online at http://www.oxforddnb.com/view/10.1093/ref:odnb/9780198614128.001.0001/odnb-9780198614128-e-63880 (accessed 7 April 2018).

10. *Evening Telegraph and Post,* 17 July 1919.

11. https://discovery.nationalarchives.gov.uk (accessed 7 April 2018). Catalogue description: Munro-Ashman, Dr Donald. Reference: 8SUF/B/052. 30 July 1975.

12. *The Scotsman,* 14 December 2006.

42 Mary Gawthorpe

1. Gawthorpe, M., *Up Hill to Holloway* (Traversity Press, 1962).
2. Raeburn, A., *Militant suffragettes* (Michael Joseph, 1973).
3. Gawthorpe, M., *Up Hill to Holloway* (Traversity Press, 1962).
4. Gawthorpe, M., *Up Hill to Holloway* (Traversity Press, 1962).
5. *Manchester Courier and Lancashire General Advertiser,* 6 February 1907.
6. Raeburn, A., *The militant suffragettes* (Michael Joseph, 1973).
7. Abrams, F., *Freedom's Cause* (Profile Books, 2003).
8. She had encouraged her mother to leave her father because of his drinking and violence, so she was dependent on Mary; Cowman, K., 'A Footnote in History? Mary Gawthorpe, Sylvia Pankhurst, *The Suffragette Movement* and the Writing of Suffragette History,' *Women's History Review,* Vol. 14, Nos 3–4 (2005).
9. Liddington, J., *Rebel Girls, Their Fight for the Vote* (Virago, 2006).
10. Cowman, K., 'A Footnote in History? Mary Gawthorpe, Sylvia Pankhurst, *The Suffragette Movement* and the Writing of Suffragette History,' *Women's History Review,* Vol. 14, Nos 3–4 (2005).
11. Cowman, K., 'A Footnote in History? Mary Gawthorpe, Sylvia Pankhurst, *The Suffragette Movement* and the Writing of Suffragette History,' *Women's History Review,* Vol. 14, Nos 3–4 (2005).
12. https://localsuffragettes.wikispaces.com/Mary+Gawthorpe (accessed 7 April 2018).
13. Crawford, E., *The women's suffrage movement: A reference guide 1866–1928* (Routledge, 2003).
14. Cowman, K., 'A Footnote in History? Mary Gawthorpe, Sylvia Pankhurst, *The Suffragette Movement* and the Writing of Suffragette History,' *Women's History Review,* Vol. 14, Nos 3–4 (2005).

43 Helena Normanton

1. *Edge Hill Magazine* (1908), cited in Bourne, J., *Helena Normanton and the Opening of the Bar to Women* (Waterside Press, 2016).
2. Bourne, J., *Helena Normanton and the Opening of the Bar to Women* (Waterside Press, 2016).
3. Speech to the Suffragette Fellowship (6 February 1950), quoted in Bourne, J., *Helena Normanton and the Opening of the Bar to Women* (Waterside Press, 2016).
4. Normanton, H. F., *The Englishwoman,* vol. XXVI, no. 77 (May 1915).
5. First 100 years, Helena Normanton, October 2014 https://first100years.org.uk/helena-normanton/
6. Dangerous Women Project: Women at the English Bar: http://spartacus-educational.blogspot.co.uk/2010/02/helena-normanton.html (accessed 7 April 2018).
7. Dangerous Women Project: Women at the English Bar: http://dangerouswomenproject.org/2016/04/15/gender-inequality-legal-profession/ (accessed 7 April 2018).
8. Bourne, J., *Helena Normanton and the Opening of the Bar to Women.* (Waterside Press, 2016).
9. Bourne, J., *Helena Normanton and the Opening of the Bar to Women* (Waterside Press, 2016).
10. Archive details of papers of Helena Normanton, held by The National Archives: http://discovery.nationalarchives.gov.uk/details/r/559abc4e-d914-4c9b-a365-e0604ec1d91d (accessed on 7 April 2018).
11. *Yorkshire Post and Leeds Intelligencer,* 26 March 1954.
12. Bourne, J., *Helena Normanton and the Opening of the Bar to Women* (Waterside Press, 2016).

44 Elsie Howey

1. Kay, J., 'No Time for Recreations till the Vote is Won'? Suffrage Activists and Leisure in Edwardian Britain,' *Women's History Review* 16.4 (2007), pp. 535–53.
2. Boyce, L., The Worcester Suffragettes: www.lucienneboyce.com
3. Crawford, E., *The women's suffrage movement: A reference guide 1866–1928* (Routledge, 2003).
4. Crawford, E., *The women's suffrage movement: A reference guide 1866–1928* (Routledge, 2003).
5. Purvis, J., *Emmeline Pankhurst: a biography* (Routledge, 2003).
6. *Torquay Times and South Devon Advertiser,* 6 August 1909.
7. http://theosophicalsociety.org.uk/ (accessed 7 April 2018).

45 Annie Barnes

1. Annie Barnes in conversation with Kate Harding and Caroline Gibbs, *Tough Annie* (Stepney Book Publications, 1980).
2. Annie Barnes in conversation with Kate Harding and Caroline Gibbs, *Tough Annie* (Stepney Book Publications, 1980).
3. Winslow, B., *Sylvia Pankhurst: Sexual politics and political activism* (Routledge, 2013).
4. Annie Barnes in conversation with Kate Harding and Caroline Gibbs, *Tough Annie* (Stepney Book Publications, 1980).
5. Crawford, E., *The women's suffrage movement: A*

reference guide 1866–1928 (Routledge, 2003).

6. Winslow, B., *Sylvia Pankhurst: Sexual politics and political activism* (Routledge, 2013).

7. Pankhurst, E. S., *The home front: a mirror to life in England during the World War* (Hutchinson, 1932).

8. Annie Barnes in conversation with Kate Harding and Caroline Gibbs, *Tough Annie* (Stepney Book Publications, 1980).

9. Annie Barnes in conversation with Kate Harding and Caroline Gibbs, *Tough Annie* (Stepney Book Publications, 1980).

46 Dora Thewlis

1. Liddington, J., *Rebel Girls: their fight for the vote* (Virago, 2006).

2. Liddington, J., *Rebel Girls: their fight for the vote* (Virago, 2006).

3. Liddington, J., *Rebel Girls: their fight for the vote* (Virago, 2006).

4. Liddington, J., *Rebel Girls: their fight for the vote* (Virago, 2006).

5. Liddington, J., *Rebel Girls: their fight for the vote* (Virago, 2006).

6. Liddington, J., *Rebel Girls: their fight for the vote* (Virago, 2006).

7. Liddington, J., *Rebel Girls: their fight for the vote* (Virago, 2006).

47 Ellen Wilkinson

1. *Manchester Courier*, 21 January 1913.

2. Much of the material in this chapter is based on Bartley, P., *Ellen Wilkinson: From Red Suffragist to Government Minister* (Pluto Press, 2014).

3. *The New Dawn*, April 1923.

4. Minutes of the MSWS Executive Committee, 2 September 1913.

5. See Koch, S., *Stalin, Willi Munzenberg and the Seduction of the Intellectuals* (Harper Collins, 1995).

6. KV2/1384, 20 May 1938.

7. Special Branch report: KV2 1382/ (24 July 1933).

8. Memo to Miss Bagot: KV2/1384 (25 August 1948).

9. Morrison, H., *The Communist Solar System* (Labour Publications, 1933).

10. Morrison, H., *The Communist Solar System* (Labour Publications, 1933).

11. *Daily Express*, 2 October 1934.

48 Lilian Lenton

1. Liddington, J., *Rebel Girls: the Fight for the Vote* (Virago, 2006).

2. Crawford, E., *The women's suffrage movement: A reference guide 1866–1928*. (Routledge, 2003). Olive Wharry was arrested with Lilian Lenton for the arson attack on the Kew Pavilion. She also went on hunger strike and was only released after 32 days of starvation during which she lost 2st 2lb in weight. By passing her food to other prisoners unnoticed by the prison authorities she had avoided force-feeding.

3. Raeburn, A., *The Militant Suffragettes* (Michael Joseph, 1973).

4. Lilian Lenton's obituary, *The Times*, 4 November 1972.

INDEX